D0805586

Diary of a Witness, 1940–1943

RAYMOND-RAOUL LAMBERT

Diary of a Witness
1940–1943

Translated from the French by Isabel Best

Edited with an Introduction by Richard I. Cohen

Ivan R. Dee Chicago

PUBLISHED IN ASSOCIATION WITH THE UNITED STATES HOLOCAUST MEMORIAL MUSEUM

 For information, address: Ivan R. Dee, Publisher, 1332 North Halsted Street, Chicago 60622. Manufactured in the United States of America and printed on acid-free paper.

www.ivanrdee.com

Published in association with the United States Holocaust Memorial Museum, 100 Raoul Wallenberg Place, S.W., Washington, D.C. 20024

The assertions, arguments, and conclusions herein are those of the author. They do not necessarily reflect the opinions of the United States Holocaust Memorial Council or of the United States Holocaust Memorial Museum.

Library of Congress Cataloging-in-Publication Data:
Lambert, Raymond-Raoul, 1894–1943.
[Carnet d'un témoin. English]
Diary of a witness : 1940–1943 / Raymond-Raoul Lambert ; translated from the French by Isabel Best ; edited with an introduction by Richard I. Cohen.
p. cm.
"Published in association with the United States Holocaust Memorial Museum."
Includes index.
ISBN-13: 978-1-56663-740-4 (cloth : alk. paper)
ISBN-10: 1-56663-740-6 (cloth : alk. paper)
1. Holocaust, Jewish (1939–1945)—France—Personal narratives. 2. Jews—Persecutions—France. 3. Union générale des israélites de France. 4. Lambert, Raymond-Raoul, 1894–1943—Diaries. 5. France—Ethnic relations. I. Cohen, Richard I. II. United States Holocaust Memorial Council. III. Title.
DS135.F83L3413 2007
940.53'18092—dc22 2007030266

Contents

Raymond-Raoul Lambert in his military uniform, probably from World War I. (Courtesy of the Lambert Family)

Lambert, left, with a fellow worker, Gaston Kahn, in 1941. (Courtesy of the Lambert Family)

Preface

IN 1985 the wartime diary of Raymond-Raoul Lambert, a leading figure in French Jewry during World War II, was published in Paris. It covers three years of the war, terminating on the day before Lambert's arrest on August 21, 1943, and his deportation to Drancy. The diary had been in the possession of Lambert's cousin, Maurice Brener, who in 1977 allowed me to photocopy it. Brener was close to Lambert during the war and also preserved four letters Lambert sent him from Drancy. Brener shared with me his intimate contact with Lambert and helped me decipher some of the code language in the letters. Members of Lambert's family, Gilles Lambert (a nephew) and Erik Lambert (Gilles's son), granted permission to publish the diary. Brener's untimely death in 1978 has left the whereabouts of the original manuscript unknown. The diary is published here in its entirety together with the letters Lambert sent to Brener, the last from November 5, 1943.

Lambert's diary provides an intimate encounter with one of French Jewry's important leaders from the 1930s through the war years. From the end of 1941 until his arrest, Lambert served as general director of the Union Générale des Israélites de France (UGIF) in the "free zone." UGIF was a compulsory organization established by Vichy in November 1941. Lambert and his family of four children were deported from Drancy to Auschwitz on December 7, 1943, and were gassed three days later.

Lambert kept a diary from 1916, meticulously preserved it, encased the notebooks in a special binding, and gave the diary the title *Carnet d'un témoin* (Diary of a Witness), *1916–1940*. After the war these notebooks remained in the possession of Lambert's brother Jacques, whose son Gilles donated them to the Centre de Documentation Juive Contemporaine (CDJC) in Paris, in either 1973 or 1974. Unfortunately these diaries, which cover an important period in Lambert's life and social involvement, have never been seen since, and all efforts to find them have proved futile. The interwar years were central to Lambert's growth as a public figure, as a dynamic member of the organized Jewish community, as an intellectual, and as a family man, and his diaries could certainly have helped merge these elements to create a more composite picture of his development.

Fortunately the family preserved an earlier notebook, covering the period from September 17, 1917, to June 5, 1918, and only recently presented the original manuscript to the CDJC. This notebook provides a direct link to the wartime diary as it shows how Lambert fastidiously copied his text to the notebooks in a handsome, tight, cursive script with no emendations, and how the diary served his personal needs. It enabled him to record at regular intervals his meetings, reflections on literature, innermost thoughts and deliberations, poetry or prose, and memorable quotations from books that were especially important to him. The prewar diaries are the best evidence that the wartime diary did not emerge as a result of the political events in France or the trauma of the war, as was common with many diarists of the period, but was a natural continuation of Lambert's self-reflections and personal deliberations. In this sense his diary differs even from those of remarkable diarists of Jewish origin such as Victor Klemperer and Mihail Sebastian, who began their diaries before the war but in the thick of the transformation of their lives, the former in 1933 in Germany, the latter in Romania in 1935. With the absence of Lambert's first notebook, it is difficult to determine what prompted Lambert to begin his diary in 1916, whether it was related to events in World War I or to issues of a personal nature.

The diaries available also leave open a larger, literary concern—the question of literary influences on Lambert. It would appear that his diary did not emerge from a Jewish tradition of diary writing but may have been associated with a contemporary European practice of using the diary as a form of "self-realization" and moral exercise. The essence of my Introduction and notes are devoted to the historical context in which Lambert figured prominently, not to the diary's literary genre.

Written by a man who from his youth was actively engaged in the affairs of his country and the destiny of his co-religionists, the diary has no humor or levity, maintaining throughout a rhythm of seriousness and intensity. It transmits Lambert's internal conflict and struggle to understand how his vision of France could withstand the ideological revolution of Vichy, and evokes his pain and revulsion at efforts to turn the Jews into pariahs of the society he so cherished. The diary also captures Lambert's inability to accept this new status as it reveals his deep attachment to French literature and traditions, to the writings of Stendhal, Romain Rolland, André Gide, Maurice Barrès, and so many others. Indeed, his world of associations and cultural habits was shaped almost exclusively by French writers and thinkers and only minimally by Jewish sources. Yet he felt a continuing sense of loyalty to and identification with both worlds and failed to see any point of conflict between them. Suddenly confronted with the French about-face, Lambert was left reeling and searching for answers. Thus the relatively minor role the Nazis play in his diary. For him the shattered universe he confronts is that of the historic relationship between France and French Jewry, nurtured over generations and sealed in endless forms of dedication to the common cause. *Diary of a Witness* is riveted with these preoccupations, making it a seminal document for the study of French Jewry in modern times in general and during the Holocaust in particular.

UGIF and Lambert's activity in its southern council have been the source of a mixed historical appraisal. Openly condemned as "collaborators" with Vichy, maligned for showing little sympathy to the plight of foreign-born Jews (especially those from Eastern Europe), and castigated for remaining overly deferent to legalistic and official policies, UGIF and Lambert were seen as typical examples of Jewish councils and leaders across Europe, who turned into agents of their own destruction. This harsh portrayal has been challenged in some circles by other historians who see the councils' activity as a staunch and valiant attempt to preserve the relief agencies and bring some form of succor to the community at large. Attempting to avoid hindsight, they have rejected categorical judgment in favor of a more nuanced approach to both UGIF and Lambert.

The wartime diary permits a microcosmic look at the dilemmas Lambert faced and how he responded. These dilemmas were similar to those that Jewish leaders across Europe confronted during the Holocaust. Like many of these leaders, Lambert assumed a position of authority in the hope that his official status would help alleviate the trials and tribulations of the Jews in France. Clearly he trusted in his experience as a French public servant in the interwar years. He thought he knew the ropes, trusted the sensibilities and goodwill of his French colleagues in the Vichy administration, and was convinced that his French credentials made him no less of a Frenchman than they.

The wartime diary is by no means a personal apology—it contains many controversial decisions taken by Lambert in times of stress and conflict, chronicles his untiring effort to assist all elements of the community, and documents his wavering trust and confidence in France. Although the diary leaves open the interpretation of his actions, it offers an intimate encounter with the complexities of the individual who guided UGIF-south during two harrowing years and sharpens our historical understanding of the period. Yet, even with the publication of the diary, certain questions remain unanswered about the nature of Lambert's activity, in particular his attitude to or involvement in illegal and resistance activity. Necessarily silent on such matters, the diary does provide some indications that from February 1943 he embarked on a path that suggests he supported other forms of activity alongside his legal initiatives.

Raymond-Raoul Lambert has left behind a candid, humane document of a man who firmly believed in a vision of service to his country and his co-religionists. A man of letters and action, his diary illuminates the destiny of a French Jew who struggled to make sense of a dramatically changing world while he held firm to the legacy of 150 years of emancipation.

* * *

The publication of the Lambert diary in English, more than twenty years after its original appearance in Paris, is due to the efforts of Benton Arnovitz, Director of Academic Publications of the United States Holocaust Memorial Museum. Taking the lead from Raul Hilberg, the doyen of Holocaust historians, who encouraged the project, Benton energetically pulled the pieces together and guided the publication with an eagle eye, as did Ivan Dee, the publisher. I am grateful to both of them for their dedication and to Professor Hilberg for his support. Karen Ackermann handled the production of the book ably and attentively.

Working under great time constraints and constant second thoughts of the editor, Isabel Best brought her considerable talent to the translation of the diary and has made the text readable, accurate, and as close as possible to Lambert's literary style.

Rachel Wygoda served as an indispensable research assistant throughout this project. Vicki Caron encouraged the English-language edition of the diary and contributed to it by dint of her important scholarship on the interwar years in France. Amos Goldberg of the Hebrew University generously shared his ideas and knowledge.

I gratefully acknowledge the support of the Paulette and Claude Kelman Chair in French Jewry Studies at the Hebrew University.

My sincere thanks, once again, to Gilles Lambert for helping to make possible the English-language edition.

R. I. C.

Jerusalem, 2007

A Note on the Translation

THROUGHOUT HIS DIARY Lambert refers to dozens of books he has read. In this edition the name of the book is generally given in its original French with an English translation. In such cases the name of the book is a translation by the translator. Many books to which Lambert refers have never been translated; where an English edition has been found, its title appears without the original French. Although we have attempted to find all the translated works, we acknowledge that some may have eluded us. First names of authors, years, publishers, and places of publication have been omitted, as they were in the original diary.

As in the original publication, words and passages that had become illegible in the original manuscript have been indicated by an ellipsis (. . .). Brief editorial comments appear in the text of the diary within brackets [ ].

The terms *Juifs* (literally Jews) and *Israélites* (literally Israelites) used by the author have been invariably translated as "Jews," even if this blurs somewhat the difference between them. The original French terms *Statut*, to refer to the law on the Jews from October 1940, and *Commissariat*, to refer to the institution set up by Vichy in 1941 to deal with Jewish affairs, have been preferred.

Abbreviations used in the notes:

CDJC	Centre de Documentation Juive Contemporaine, Paris
JTS	Jewish Theological Seminary of America, New York
YIVO	YIVO Archive, Center for Jewish History, New York
YVA	Yad Vashem Archives, Jerusalem

Introduction

BY RICHARD I. COHEN

FROM THE Dreyfus Affair at the turn of the twentieth century to the nightmare of the Vichy years, France and French Jewry lived amidst continuing turbulence. Years of hope and security mingled with years of despair and fear. One could seek balm in the writings of Zola, Péguy, the Barrès of *Les diverses familles spirituelles de la France*, and Anatole France, bask proudly in the presence of the circle of Montparnasse artists, or wallow in despair when reading the litany of anti-Semitic writings of a Drumont, Bernanos, Giraudoux, Blanchot, or Brasillach. These were years when the French liberal tradition asserted itself and struggled to curb the power of Catholic influence, culminating in the separation of church and state (1905), and when French Jews faced intermittently the penetration of anti-Semitic thought and activity.

The French saw their country ravaged and debilitated during World War I, and though France emerged victorious, it lost almost 1.5 million men and desperately needed manpower. In response to the Great War, the country opened its doors to several million immigrants, including tens of thousands of Jewish refugees from Eastern and Central Europe, and sought to assimilate competing memories, traditions, and challenges. France gave rise to a variety of manifestations—creativity, nationalist expression, the trauma of war, and compelling social and economic needs, some occasioned by the return of its northeastern region of Alsace-Lorraine from Germany. Throughout this period it was the positive side of French life that confirmed for most native French Jews their ardent belief in their *Patrie* and their road of integration into French society.

Even if the "politics of assimilation" was not always its mode of existence, French Jewry had inculcated the norms and *esprit* of French society. Neither its filial connection to France nor its loyalty to the formative principles of the Third Republic was mere lip-service. Indeed, nothing could be more telling of French Jewish involvement in and support for the Republic than the impressive number of Jews in the French civil service and the army (prefects, subprefects, justices, and high-ranking officers), not to mention their unparalleled (in comparison to other countries) representation in French politics as ministers, deputies, and senators. Léon Blum's election as prime minister in 1936 brought to an apex the rise of Jewish participation in the state apparatus.

On the whole, Jewish devotion to France and its republican institutions replaced involvement and identification with the Jewish community, yet a residue of ethnicity and belonging prevailed even among those who occupied the highest echelons of the French state.[1] What one astute observer of the Jewish scene rightfully remarked at the time of the Dreyfus Affair—that from the time of Napoleon, the Jews had been tied to the state and avoided any actions that might damage their cherished status—persisted long after the separation of church and state. But this did not erase certain personal affiliations and practices.[2] The attachment

1. Pierre Birnbaum, *The Jews of the Republic: A Political History of State Jews in France from Gambetta to Vichy*, trans. Jane Marie Todd (Stanford, 1996).

2. Hippolyte Prague, "Sur le budget des cultes," *Archives israélites*, December 19, 1901, pp. 401–403.

to the state also held serious ramifications for Jewish organizations, especially for its most representative body, the Central Consistory, which from the days of Napoleon saw its mission as leading the community to total allegiance to the state while maintaining institutions to preserve Judaism. *Patrie* and *Religion* were its banners.

The Interwar Years

The years between the world wars transformed the nature of the French Jewish community and saw an upsurge in anti-Semitism that challenged the idyllic vision of a Jewish symbiosis with France. Native French Jews also had to contend with large immigrations of East European Jews, whose numbers swelled following the Russian Revolution of 1905 and again after the Bolshevik Revolution of 1917. On the eve of World War II, East European Jews numbered almost 200,000 in France, about two-thirds of all Jews in the country. Migration did not end there. After Hitler's rise to power in 1933, some 30,000 Jewish refugees from Germany and Austria found asylum in France. These in-migrations supplanted the monolithic nature of French Jewry and the particular French-Jewish symbiosis.

A wide network of East European Jewish culture flourished and found resonance among the French lower classes and petty bourgeoisie, particularly among artisans and workers in Paris. The new sensibility expressed itself in a fashion alien to most native-born French Jews: radical politics, workmen's circles and labor organizations, Yiddish culture, and organized secular institutions. Few parallels existed among the long-established French Jews. Culture shock was apparent even in the area of religious affiliation. East European Jews brought with them a more distinct approach to religion—either antagonism to any religious framework or a more orthodox tradition—and had little attraction to French Jewry's form of religious attachment. In all, the mosaic of this cultural boom transfused new expressions of Judaism into the tired veins of French Jewry but at the same time generated tense and antagonistic responses by its leadership. Measures to assimilate the foreign Jews *à la française* often backfired and instead solidified the separateness of the two groups. Underlying tensions between them proved to be stronger than their common origin, as witnessed in the 1930s when French liberal principles were challenged by the rise of anti-Semitism in France. The divided community could find no mutual basis to overcome its differences; rather, the various bodies further entrenched themselves in their contrasting appraisals of the situation and their responses, exacerbating relations between them.

The influx of Jewish refugees from Germany and Austria taxed the French-Jewish symbiosis in a different manner. A series of dilemmas presented themselves: How to accommodate the new refugees, fleeing from anti-Semitism? How to confront the French government as its attitudes and policies toward the immigrants hardened—obedience or challenge? How to consider the plight of the refugees in the face of France's growing economic problems and the rise of French anti-Semitism? As native French Jews and immigrant East European Jews were divided on these questions, a wide spectrum of reactions emerged. One figure who was outspoken on these problems and on the nature of the French-Jewish relationship in this time of crisis was Raymond-Raoul Lambert.

Lambert's life offers a microcosmic look into the internal world of native French Jews from the time of the Dreyfus Affair through Vichy. His career illustrates the irresistible hold of France on native Jews and portrays poignantly and tragically their inner sense of belonging to French culture and traditions. His dialectic was more than typical: his frames of reference, cultural associations, literary pursuits, metaphors, manners and way of life, dreams, nostalgia, and recollections were thoroughly French—yet he was a conscious and engaged Jew. He nimbly balanced between the two worlds, finding succor in both.

Born in 1894 in Montmorency, a northern suburb of Paris, Lambert was the third son of a middle-class family that had come from Metz and was well integrated into French society. Lambert, whose father, Michel, died when Raymond-Raoul was still a small boy, was reared in a French atmosphere both at home and at school, and like most native French Jews of his day received a minimal Jewish education. In his youth he attended the prestigious Parisian lycée Collège Rollin, where he developed an interest in the arts. His sense of satisfaction with his education overflows in the odes he and a fellow classmate wrote in honor of their lycée.[3] The humanistic education had a formative role in shaping Lambert's outlook and character; at Rollin he began his intimate acquaintance with French literature and developed an interest in German culture. Although the traditional animosity between France and Germany, intensified by the collective memory of the Franco-Prussian War (1870–1871) and the loss of the eastern provinces of Alsace-Lorraine, was still acute in French society, Lambert followed a trend among his fellow students in supporting a détente between France and Germany and called for a rapprochement between the two peoples. After graduation he tutored at the Court of Saxony-Meiningen and taught French at Godesberg and Paris. But while Lambert was nurturing his cultural mélange, France and Germany again found themselves on opposite sides with the outbreak of war in 1914.[4]

French society entered the war under the banner of a sacred union (*union sacrée*) of patriotism among all its citizens, a call that resonated deeply with Lambert and the French Jewish community, natives and immigrants. Its leaders were convinced that the moment was ripe to cleanse the past of the bad memories of the Dreyfus Affair and to emphasize again the everlasting link between France and French Jewry. Thousands of Jews were drafted

3. R. R. Lambert and André Legrand, *Charlemagne à Paris* (Paris, 1912); Lambert and Legrand, *Adieu au Collège* (Paris, 1913). Both booklets were in the possession of Frédéric Empaytaz.

4. See also Michel Laffitte, *Un engrenage fatal: L'UGIF face aux réalités de la Shoah 1941–1944* (Paris, 2003), pp. 39–48; idem, *Juif dans la France allemande: Institutions, dirigeants et communautés au temps de la Shoah* (Paris, 2006), pp. 26–36.

into the military, and a great number of immigrant Jews volunteered to fight within the ranks of the French Foreign Legion. French Jews welcomed Barrès's *Les diverses familles spirituelles de la France* (1917), in which he regarded them as one of the nation's spiritual families and presented as a unique example the act of fraternity of Rabbi Abraham Bloch, the chaplain who was killed as he handed a crucifix to a wounded Catholic soldier.[5] Barrès's book took on mythic proportions and remained a sacred text for Lambert and other native Jewish leaders in the succeeding generation. (None other than the chief rabbi of France, Isaïe Schwartz, would recall it, nostalgically and emphatically, in his protest to Pétain against the *Statut des juifs* of October 1940.)

Lambert was very much part of this ambience. He was called to active duty and fought in the celebrated battles of Champagne and Chemin des Dames, and for his bravery in the latter was awarded the Croix de Guerre. He was appointed to the Legion of Honor and felt extremely proud of his service and birthright, often invoking with much pathos the solidifying nature of the war experience and France's deep commitment to those who fought together for her freedom: "In the cemeteries on the front the graves of all of our brothers are piously close, without distinction of origin, religion or blood, showing our children the indivisibility of our nation. Between the spirit of France and all her spiritual families a wedding of love has been sealed for eternity."[6]

Lambert's memories of the war sustained him at times of despair a generation later. But the impact of World War I went far beyond that and left a marked impression on his life. He encountered war's havoc and ruthlessness, and saw its terrible consequences for the families of the fallen soldiers, the hundreds of

5. This story was widely disseminated among French Jews. It may have been the Central Consistory that was responsible for printing a special postcard *Pour La Patrie* (For the Fatherland) in which Bloch is seen handing over the crucifix as he is fatally struck by a shell. See Eli Barnavi, *A Historical Atlas of the Jewish People: From the Time of the Patriarchs to the Present* (London, 1992), p. 210.

6. R. R. Lambert, "La méditation du 11 novembre," *L'Univers israélite*, November 15, 1935, p. 114.

thousands of homeless, and the devastation of France. But he continued to believe in a rapprochement between French and Germans and in a more unified Europe.[7] He joined the French civil service and spent four years in Bonn (1920–1924) as a representative to the Allies' Rhineland High Commission. There he acted as an appeasing negotiator among the various separatist and local factions after the French and Belgian occupation of the Ruhr (1923), gaining the respect and admiration of Germans and French alike. In 1924 he was appointed as a deputy to Edouard Herriot in his first, short-lived tenure as prime minister of France. The appointment was understandable. Herriot, a leader of the Radical party, had broken with French policy and was instrumental in evacuating the French from the Ruhr in 1925. He knew of Lambert's efforts there, and both men opposed the more militant French attitudes to the Weimar government in Germany. Lambert wrote eloquently of Herriot's actions to restore peace to the Ruhr, sharply criticized former Prime Minister Poincaré's policies that had led to the occupation, and expressed his own belief in the need for greater understanding of and respect for the local population so as to contribute to a renewed and unified Europe.[8] Like Herriot, Lambert was enamored of the Pan-European movement initiated by Richard von Coudenhove-Kalergi in 1923, believing that it promised an end to anachronistic wars and to the miseries of humankind.[9]

In the 1920s Lambert emerged as a staunch supporter of pan-Europeanism and repeatedly censured writers who favored a nationalistic culture at the expense of opening themselves to cultural creativity, even of the former enemy. He wrote on various

7. R. R. Lambert, *Prologue pour la soirée organisée le 25 mars 1922 à Bonn au profit du berceau français et des veuves de Guerre* (Bonn, 1922). This was a poem written by Lambert.

8. Lambert published regularly on the need for a new, unified Europe in the mid-twenties in the *Opinion République*, *La Volonté*, *Notre Temps*, and other journals. See Lambert, "Les Allemands et l'art français," *Comoedia*, September 11, 1922, and a later article on other aspects of these issues, "La destine rhénane," *Notre temps*, September 7, 1930, p. 487.

9. On Lambert's pacifism, see Laffitte, *Juif dans la France allemande*, pp. 35–36.

authors, especially Germans, to bring to the French public their sensitivities and appreciation of French letters. For him it was clear: "Germany and France, after having been combatants, have to collaborate or decline."[1] Europe had to find a new universal vision that gave pride of place to the liberty of spirit and creation, and recognized the singular achievements of cultural luminaries, from whatever country they might be. *Beethoven rhénan (reconnaissance à Jean-Christophe)* was Lambert's most concerted effort to bring together a cultural, pan-European union. In this work he emphasizes the eternal connections between Beethoven and Romain Rolland, whose literary creation of Jean-Christophe "can be considered as the literary reincarnation of the author of the Ninth Symphony."[2] But Lambert was concerned and engaged no less with political developments, especially in Germany, and maintained a constant vigil of the attitudes and policies of the French governments toward Weimar, encouraging greater reciprocity.[3]

Lambert's pan-Europeanism and strong identification with France did not exclude his personal involvement in matters Jewish, culturally and professionally, and may even have given him certain credentials to pursue his specific Jewish concerns. His diary from 1917–1918, composed in part while in hospitals recuperating from medical problems, in part when he returned to army duty, reveals very little of his earlier thoughts on Jews and Judaism. A fleeting diary remark on his desire to write a book about the modern Jewish spirit is left without further comment.[4] Several years later he published a collection of poems under the title

1. R. R. Lambert, "La conscience occidentale," *Opinion république* (1926?), p. 12 (I have not located the exact year of publication).

2. R. R. Lambert, *Beethoven rhénan (reconnaissance à Jean-Christophe)* (Paris, 1928), p. 45. See also his brief comments on the relations between French and Germans in Bonn during those years, ibid., pp. 70–71.

3. R. R. Lambert, "Le manifeste de 'Notre Temps' et la presse allemande," *Notre temps*, February 22, 1931, pp. 289–293. Lambert wrote on German political developments in the twenties in *Opinion République* and other newspapers.

4. Entry from March 15, 1918, in Lambert's unpublished diary, September 17, 1917–June 5, 1918.

Musiques juives (Jewish Music), apparently his first publication on Jewish themes. In these poems he evoked his sense of belonging to a Jewish historical past and to the trials and tribulations of being a Jew, his appreciation of the Zionist vision of Max Nordau and the leadership of Victor Basch ("But for us you are like a father / When you are wronged we hurt and unite"), the latter a Jew of Hungarian origin, a scholar of German language and culture, a Dreyfussard, and a long-term activist for civil rights.[5] The poems suggest that Lambert was already molding a synthesis of his political and cultural leanings and his Jewish inclinations.

The case of Victor Basch is especially interesting as Lambert refers to him under the category of *Musiques juives*, intimating that he regarded him as a kind of spiritual father who stood for the Jewish and humanistic values to which Lambert subscribed. Lambert would portray the German foreign minister Walther Rathenau ("this German thinker of the Jewish race") in a similar spirit several years later. Reviewing the publication of Rathenau's private letters, Lambert felt a clear bond with him in Rathenau's endless cultural pursuits, his dream of an alliance with France even as Germany fought her in World War I, his utopian vision of the future, his keen awareness of the "Jewish contribution" to German society and culture, and his struggle against anti-Semitism. Lambert saw in Rathenau one of the finest architects of the new Europe; he attributed his assassination in 1922 to the fact that "he was a Jew."[6]

Fragmentary as is our knowledge of Lambert's Jewish involvement in the 1920s, it is clear that he was beginning to emerge as an intellectual voice within the Jewish community, bringing together his literary and political interests. He contributed reviews of contemporary Jewish writers to various

5. The poems dedicated to Nordau and Basch appeared in *Menorah*, November 24, 1922, p. 85. Other poems, some under the general title of *Musiques juives*, appeared in *Illustration juive*, September 15, 1922; *Menorah*, November 10, 1922, December 22, 1922.

6. R. R. Lambert, "Rathenau Intime," *La revue littéraire juive*, 2 (April 1928), pp. 289–298.

Jewish periodicals, translations from German of the romantic and "Zionist" poetry of Elsa Lasker-Schüler, and from time to time a more programmatic essay that stressed his own cultural and social ideas. Lambert saw himself as a bridge between worlds: through his connection with Herriot, the former prime minister warmly greeted the founding of *Revue littéraire juive* (Jewish Literary Review) while he was minister of public education in 1927, stressing the importance to France of the "new Hebraic literature." Lambert brought Jewish writers in Germany and France to the greater attention of their citizenry and strived to bring Jewish youth (the generation of 1914) to an awareness of their common fate and the need to help build "a new notion of the universal order" that would mediate and merge East (Orient) and West (Occident). A freethinker, Lambert associated himself with the Union Universelle de la Jeunesse Juive (Universal Union of Jewish Youth), which originated in Salonika, and he served as its representative to several international bodies. Although he was pleased to see some of Zionism's successes in Palestine, he did not subscribe to an outright Zionist position, nor did he fear Judaism's extinction if it discarded its religious attachment as the sole form of belonging: "We are Jews of the twentieth century, and everything that is narrow constrains us. Our conviction itself—in whatever continent it may be—proves that Judaism can exist in the heart without nationality and without belief."[7]

Lambert strove to move Judaism out of its parochialism—in the spirit of Marc Sangier's efforts to revitalize French Catholicism through his social Catholic movement, Sillon—and advocated joint activities with Protestants and Catholics to bring the religions to greater social awareness. Yet Lambert's repeated calls for pan-Europeanism and joint cooperation between Germans and French, the Occident and the Orient, Jews and non-Jews, did not minimize his sensitivity to anti-Semitism nor his recognition of

7. R. R. Lambert, "Chronique des livres," *Chalom*, 1928, p. 16. I have been unable to determine whether Lambert visited Palestine between the wars.

the "injustice and barbarism" that continued to plague the lives of Jews in some countries.

Lambert followed closely political developments in Germany in the 1920s and their emerging anti-Semitic tendencies. Before Hitler's rise to power in 1933, he devoted several articles to anti-Semitism and to the response of the Jewish community in Germany. His insight into the nature of Nazism did not penetrate beyond the accepted wisdom of these years: Lambert did not appreciate the Nazi threat as an ideological turn in the evolution of anti-Semitism and tried to find a source for optimism in the various governmental alignments that appeared in Germany, such as Kurt von Schleicher's 1932 cabinet. Like most observers of his day, Lambert vacillated between recognizing the depths of anti-Semitism in Germany ("the dangers that threaten German Jewry will not disappear by themselves as the causes of German anti-Semitism are more profound"[8]) and rejecting the possibility that German traditions and values might foster a return to the religious confrontations of the Middle Ages. Indeed, he refused to believe that Europe was witnessing the end of an age of spiritual values and retreating to barbarism. He supported the reorganization of German Jews into a central body in order to enhance their struggle against political apathy and neutrality, and looked favorably upon the reassertion of their Jewishness.

It was only logical that Lambert, in reflecting on the implications of developments in Germany, consider the implications for France and French Jewry. He was unswerving in his belief that France was not Germany; anti-Semitism, he was sure, would find no support under French skies. He never failed to remark, whether in 1932 or 1939, that France, the stalwart of libertarian principles, had never reneged (as exemplified by the Dreyfus Affair) and never would renege on her revolutionary act of emancipating the Jews. This ultimate confidence in France expressed itself in Lambert's insistence that notwithstanding Hitler's racial

8. R. R. Lambert, "Chronique d'Allemagne. A l'est, rien de nouveau," *L'Univers israélite*, September 30, 1932, p. 18.

politics, the Western tradition of liberalism continued to have a secure place in the world. Paris was not Berlin, for France had found a *modus vivendi* between the diverse elements of its society. Writing in the wake of the Nuremberg Laws (1935), Lambert reaffirmed this trust:

> . . . In France a healthy breeze always appears at the right moment and disperses the dangerous miasmas. An indivisible nation, created by the gradual work of an incomparable history, enriched by the contribution of diverse races; embellished by the excesses even of its passions that reflect against all odds the disposition of the climate, France will preserve forever, for all its children, a maternal and luminous face.[9]

Lambert was scarcely oblivious to Hitler's success in implanting a French version of his anti-Semitism, in the likes of Brasillach and Rebatet; but he was wont to admit, like most representatives of the French-Jewish establishment, that this had inherently French roots. He grudgingly acknowledged that in his campaign against all things Jewish, Hitler had succeeded in raising the anxiety of French Jewry and "had increased the universal sensitivity to everything that relates to us."[1] Nowhere was this sensitivity to anti-Semitic currents more acutely felt than in the response of French Jewry to the immigrant question that engaged Lambert extensively in the thirties.

Jewish immigration to France in that decade was a consequence of the dramatic rise in the anti-Semitism of nationalistic regimes in Germany and East Central Europe (Poland, Hungary, and Romania). With Hitler's rise to power, the first large influx of Jews arrived, reaching more than 21,000 by the summer of 1933. France presented few obstacles to the immigrants and received them without much ado, continuing its rather liberal immigration policy begun after World War I; but voices of opposition soon began to be heard. In May 1933, Lambert responded

9. R. R. Lambert, "Foi en la France," ibid., December 13, 1935.
1. R. R. Lambert, "France d'abord," ibid., May 27, 1938.

to the first exodus of German Jews to France with an unreserved embrace: "The saddest of exoduses has begun. Whole families have arrived here. They have to be housed, fed, and their future attended to. One needs to anticipate other arrivals if the borders will be opened."[2] He expected the Jewish community to rise to the occasion and provide a welcoming hand to the unfortunate, but in his capacity as secretary-general of the nonsectarian Comité National Français de Secours aux Réfugiés Allemands, Victimes de l'Antisémitisme, he realized very soon that France's economic crisis and growing opposition to the immigrants would take their toll. He found himself embroiled in conflicting attitudes toward the refugees, yet tried to steer a more humanitarian direction and "bring about a true accommodation between the needs of the refugees and what he perceived to be the very best interests of France."[3] Thus we find Lambert intervening on the one hand with the Paris police to expel two Communist agitators from France in 1933, but on the other hand working assiduously to procure jobs for the refugees to guarantee their stay in the country.

In the face of what he regarded as the xenophobic characteristics of French society, the unwelcoming and restrictive position of leading members of French Jewry (in particular Jacques Helbronner of the Central Consistory), and the constant flow of immigrants, Lambert sensed the need at times to reassess and readjust his proposals to find creative solutions to the plight of the refugees. This was brought home to him when he faced his former employer, Edouard Herriot, who stood from 1934 at the head of the Interministerial Committee on Immigration and opposed Lambert's efforts to find work for the refugees. Herriot's position was a consequence of France's economic problems.[4] Resigned to the ramifications of the new government attitude—a crackdown on immigration—Lambert called for an immigration policy that

2. R. R. Lambert, "L'Accueil de la France," *Revue juive de Genève*, 1 (May 1933), p. 349.

3. Vicki Caron, *Uneasy Asylum: France and the Jewish Refugee Crisis, 1933–1942* (Stanford, 1999), p. 105.

4. On Herriot's commission and its more restrictive guidelines, see ibid., p. 46.

would spare France the entire wave of immigration, would disperse it within the country, and would place some restrictions on immigrant activity. Like many other officials, he strongly encouraged the immigrants to assimilate quickly to France by denying their unique attributes, by accepting the guardianship of the native community, and by maintaining a low profile until they were perfectly comfortable in the French language and environment. Lambert also called upon the leading French-Jewish organizations, the Alliance Israélite Universelle and the Central Consistory, to take the lead in this regard and not leave "the initiative for the interventions to committees of foreigners without any authority and often run by Christians. If one allows this storm to pass over simply by bowing one's head, who would be able to assure us that in several years someone wouldn't dream of remedying an even more severe economic depression, by revising those naturalizations granted after the war?"[5]

Lambert regarded this as a propitious moment for native French Jewry to show the immigrant Jews its concern and its sense of responsibility. This was not the first time that Lambert had tried to build a bridge between the established community and the immigrant Jews. In order to contend with the changing contours of the Jewish population, Lambert had called in 1932 for unity within the French Jewis community, for an organization that would represent Jewish interests at a national level. He acutely perceived that the diversity of the community, with its growing immigrant and Zionist elements, confounded by the intricate international situation, demanded greater cooperation. In 1935 his call for unity was even stronger:

> The Jews of France appear to have fallen asleep in a happy optimism, ignoring deliberately all the possibilities and consequences of Zionism and make of assimilation a narrow and absolute doctrine. The immigrants, truthfully, may have the il-

5. R. R. Lambert, "Statut des etrangers," *L'Univers israélite*, December 14, 1934, p. 210. Part of this quotation also appears in Caron, *Uneasy Asylum*, p. 112.

> lusion that they are occasionally standing in front of a wall. But the times have changed. New generations have emerged everywhere. The international conditions are no longer the same. One can no longer deny either Zionism nor the universal responsibility that the Hitlerian antisemitism has summoned. If assimilation determines completely the political situation of Jewry in the democratic countries and if nobody sees fit to challenge its necessity or legitimacy, it nevertheless should not be a synonym for a state of numbness. Far from closing itself in an ivory tower, French Jewry needs to expand this narrow notion by recognizing all the obligations offered by the present times.[6]

In urging the two established French Jewish organizations to seize the initiative, Lambert envisaged that native French Jewish leaders, who held a clear understanding of the nature of French society, could direct the activist tendencies of the immigrants into proper channels "*a goût de France.*" In essence this proposal took the Consistory to task for its ineffectiveness vis-à-vis the immigrants and the changing times; were the Union to accomplish what Lambert asked of it, the special status the Consistory enjoyed would undoubtedly have been undermined. But, alas, Lambert received no support from these bodies for a union or for a joint struggle for the refugees. They accepted Helbronner's more restrictive approach and decided to close the Comité National to avoid any claim that French Jewry was placing Jewish concerns before French exigencies.[7] Faced with this rejection but determined to continue working for the relief of the refugees, Lambert accepted in 1936 the position of secretary-general of the newly established Comité d'Assistance aux Réfugiés (CAR), a relief organization supported by the American Jewish Joint Distribution Committee (the charitable organization established in 1914 in the United States, which aided imperiled Jews throughout the

6. R. R. Lambert, "Pour une 'Union Juive de France'," *L'Univers israélite*, August 30, 1935, p. 791.

7. Caron, *Uneasy Asylum*, p. 115.

world), with representatives of East European and German refugee organizations but free of Consistory influence.

CAR came into existence as France experienced the victory of the Popular Front, under Léon Blum, and the fleeting return to a more liberal policy on refugees. Lambert figured prominently in CAR's policy decisions and, with several other figures, advocated and supported measures—such as the Serre Plan—to enable the growing number of refugees (some sixty thousand by 1938) to find a home in France. He firmly opposed the 1937 Madagascar Plan to concentrate refugees on the French island, warning of its implications for refugees in France and other countries. But the tide was clearly running in the opposite direction. In the wake of the German annexation of Austria—the Anschluss of March 1938—and the defeat of the Popular Front and the election of a member of the Radical party, Edouard Daladier, to head a new French government, Lambert noted gravely the growing xenophobic and anti-Semitic atmosphere and how certain immigrants disregarded the legitimate sensitivities of the French. In an editorial entitled *France First*, he emphasized a more considerate attitude toward the immigrants while chiding the French Jewish leadership for instilling in the immigrant community a sense of having been disowned: "If we could promise the immigrants that we will never leave in doubt the solidarity that we affirm with them, we can, in return, demand not to exercise a guardianship—the word and fact are too pretentious—but a certain restraint."[8]

Indeed these were trying times, intensified by the radicalization of anti-Jewish legislation in Germany, followed by the Kristallnacht of November 1938. In France this mood expressed itself in the anti-foreign laws of May and November 1938. Designed to close France's borders to illegal immigrants and expel—later intern—those who arrived illicitly, the laws exacerbated the plight of the refugees. Internment camps were set up in 1939, and thousands of Jewish and other refugees were sent there, necessitating new provisional solutions. CAR and Lambert were in-

8. Lambert, "France d'abord," *L'Univers israélite*, May 27, 1938.

volved in many different refugee efforts in this period, acting with others to find reasonable solutions within the parameters of French policy while advocating more liberal alternatives. In some cases these efforts brought significant success as large sums of money were expended to provide basic relief for thousands.

Lambert asserted his open opposition to the new government regulations, sharply criticizing their inhumane nature. In 1939 he repeatedly called for a relaxation of the measures and a revocation of those laws. Lambert claimed that, as a countermeasure to the declining French population, the immigrants should be freed from the internment camps and allowed to serve the nation. This expression of loyalty, he maintained, would reduce xenophobic claims against the immigrants. French legislation in July 1939 seemed to accede somewhat to this pressure. But Lambert conceded that in this situation he could no longer oppose the government's efforts to close France's borders to future immigration, and he again cautioned the immigrants about their behavior in France during this strained time. Always aware of the international implications on the situation in France, Lambert recognized that the refugee "problem" was intimately related to the deterioration of European politics. He argued in November 1938: "As long as Europe is living in a state of disquiet, as long as the international community fails to resume its normal activities and intercourse, we can expect no plan nor any discovery of new lands that might offer the solution for the great distress of those Jews still forced to wander."[9] From then until war broke out in September 1939, Lambert continued to work tirelessly to alleviate the plight of the refugees.

Thus on the eve of World War II a man of forty-five with three young children, Lambert had already formulated his trust in France and his commitment to Jewry:

> I am indebted to Jewry for providing me some nutrition, and it is to the rationality of my country that I am indebted for the possibility of profiting from it. . . . Beyond my religious

9. Quoted in Caron, *Uneasy Asylum*, p. 317.

> belonging, I do not belittle in any way my country for the gift I owe it for my reflections, social work, and, if need be, my life, while I acknowledge Jerusalem for myself and my children as an inspiration, source of emotion, capable of enriching and enhancing my internal life as a Frenchman.[1]

In this spirit, Lambert maintained repeatedly in 1938 and 1939 that Jews could stand up for war only if France itself was menaced. In his prewar articles he echoed the *union sacrée* of 1914: France and Jerusalem must achieve total unity against the forces of immorality and barbarism. Yet the turmoil of the thirties had taken its toll on him. He had encountered French policies and ideas that were anathema to him, and he had faced Jewish leaders (Jacques Helbronner in particular[2]) whom he regarded with contempt for their lack of compassion and concern. By now a well-known personality in French Jewry, he was highly regarded by the leaders of the American Jewish Joint Distribution Committee, appreciated by East European and German refugees and immigrants (though certainly not by all), and maintained a broad network of connections within the French bureaucracy. In both Jewish and French circles he was noted for his independent voice. At the close of 1939 he was mobilized, ready to serve his country and uphold the principles in which he believed.

The War Years

France's military defeat in the spring of 1940 was stunning. The strategy of a passive defense, which had prevailed in French military circles during the 1930s, proved a miserable failure. Its fore-

1. R. R. Lambert, "Nos pensées au 11 novembre," *L'Univers israélite*, November 6, 1936.

2. For a more detailed portrait of Jacques Helbronner, see Simon Schwarzfuchs, *Aux prises avec Vichy: Histoire politique des Juifs de France (1940–1944)* (Paris, 1998), pp. 96–98; Laffitte, *Juif dans la France allemande*, pp. 46–50. Schwarzfuchs makes no mention of the earlier tension between Helbronner and Lambert.

most bulwark, the Maginot Line, could scarcely contain the German blitzkrieg. Within six weeks France fell once again to the hands of its historic rival—once again to be occupied and once again to forfeit its eastern territories of Alsace and Lorraine. French leaders sought an armistice quickly in order to salvage the unoccupied regions of the country and to prevent a replay of World War I on French terrain. Only a few French were willing at this time to risk an escape to London to fight for a free France from outside the country.

French society and its parliamentary representatives chose to utilize the defeat to rechannel French energies into new and traditional paths. From the abyss of defeat a nationalist program emerged, one that promised to restore France to its pre-republican days and assert its historic identity. The New Order that came to replace the parliamentary debates of the Third Republic promised to return France to the French (*France aux français*)—the principles of *Liberté, Egalité, Fraternité* were to be replaced by *Travail, Famille, Patrie*. By early July 1940 the French government had reinstalled itself, in Vichy, responding to a lingering demand for change within French society.

For those whose existence depended on a continuation of the principles of the French Revolution, the consequences of the Vichy government would be grave. The Jewish community of France found itself in that particular predicament. In one of the last issues of *Univers israélite* in 1939, dedicated to the 150th anniversary of the Revolution, leading community figures recounted events of the Revolutionary period with pride and security in the historic pact between France and Jewry. A year later they faced a France that was beginning to reshape that bond; they found the transformation brutal and not easily understood.

Here too the inner turmoil that transpired in the life of Raymond-Raoul Lambert, one of French Jewry's leading spokespersons, provides a means to gauge the pulse of the community. His wartime diary and public activity offer a window into the experience of a native Jew in Vichy France. As France experienced a quiet revolution and French people in the hundreds of thousands made their way to the unoccupied zone, Lambert returned to his notebooks to express his innermost thoughts. His words left little room for comment: "After the past four weeks, which have seen unfold the most tragic events in our history, and for me the most terrible anxieties I have ever known, I am trying to recover my intellectual balance, to regain my awareness of the passage of time" (July 12, 1940).

Awe-struck by the havoc of defeat, Lambert, like many others, sought to unravel the causes of that defeat and to find ways to provide moral support for the French army before demobilization. He blamed the defeat in part on the soldiers' lack of enthusiasm and moral stamina, and believed that only a spiritual reformation could lift the country. He proposed holding seminars on themes from French history to show that the defeat could become a source of rejuvenation for the nation. Some of the guidelines he proposed are worthy of note: (a) in France's history, military defeat had never overwhelmed the country (for example, in 1815 and 1871); (b) France possessed a spiritual mission unencumbered by historical developments—after 1870 it had seen vast colonial expansion; (c) victory weakened nations while defeat regenerated them—as in Germany after 1918 (!); (d) illustrious French public servants (such as Thiers, Clemenceau, and Pétain) had appeared in the darkest moments of its history. This moralistic perspective and positive outlook on defeat were not unique, yet Lambert did not share the common French attitude that saw defeat as a fortuitous moment for France—an opportunity to terminate the Third Republic. He was too enamored with the Republic's libertarian principles to reject it. He reaffirmed, as in the 1930s, that his and his family's loyal devotion to France could not have been in vain. He could not imagine life on a different soil.

> French Jewry is enduring a particular kind of anguish. It accepts suffering along with everyone else but dreads the discrimination the enemy may demand. This fear makes me particularly dread the future, for myself and for my sons. But I still have confi-

dence. France cannot accept just anything, and it is not for nothing that the bones of my family have mingled with its soil for more than a century—and that I have served in two wars. For my wife, my sons, and myself, I cannot imagine life in another climate; pulling up these roots would be worse than an amputation. (July 15, 1940)

But Lambert's anxiety was more appropriate to the times than his confidence in France. In early October 1940 the Vichy government revealed another aspect of the New Order. It enacted three racial laws that seriously curtailed the rights of all French Jews, extended the prerogative of Vichy officials to intern foreign Jews in special camps, and abrogated the Crémieux Law of 1871, thus rescinding the French citizenship of forty thousand Algerian Jews.[3] These laws terminated the emancipation tradition and struck deeply at the synthesis that French Jews had seemingly created.[4] Lambert minced no words. He placed the responsibility for these anti-Semitic laws at the doorstep of Germany but did not leave Vichy inculpable.

Lambert wrestled with the causes of the discriminatory laws and gave them greater attention than their impact on his daily life might have deserved. Several months after the first onslaught of the anti-Semitic legislation, he again inquired into the causes that brought France to rupture its humanitarian tradition. German propaganda, he observed, had succeeded in penetrating the writings of French journalists and authors, and together with the anti-Semitic activity of the nationalist *Action française* movement had gradually eroded French ideals. Undoubtedly Jewish influence in politics, the arts, finance, and the press lent credence to racist arguments, but it was the unsolved immigration issue that weighed

3. On these laws, see Michael R. Marrus and Robert O. Paxton, *Vichy France and the Jews* (New York, 1981), pp. 3–21.

4. For other reactions to these laws, see Schwarzfuchs, *Aux prises avec Vichy*, pp. 88–94; Adam Rutkowski (ed.), *La lutte des Juifs en France à l'époque de l'occupation (1940–1944)* (Paris, 1975), pp. 44–46, 49–50, 52–53.

heavily upon public opinion. Here Lambert's criticism was directed at Jewish leadership for its inability to develop a clear position on immigration.[5]

In all, Lambert could reach no definitive conclusion with regard to the roots of the anti-Semitic legislation; as the months passed and the laws were intensified, he placed even more responsibility on France's leaders and seriously questioned whether the country could ever return to its previous ways. Although he continued to assign German inspiration to the laws (such as the legislation of July 22, 1941), his disappointment with France in forgoing all its commitments, including its "imperial mission," was enormous and overriding. France was rejecting its historical path as it now enacted laws that twenty years earlier had been condemned. He speculated: ". . . I am more and more fearful that there will be some settling of accounts in blood in our country" (July 28, 1941). Yet for Lambert the decay of France was only a symptom of the general eclipse of freedom throughout Europe and the bleak future of the Jewish people.[6]

Following Lambert's diary from the anti-Semitic legislation of October 1940 to the summer of 1941 allows us an intimate appreciation of the pain and suffering he felt and the many questions he and the Jews in France faced concerning their security. To the *Statut* of October he replied with stubborn persistence: he would remain French and not deny his Jewishness. Even as he condemned France, he recognized that nothing in the world was closer to him, and he resigned himself to endure. He foresaw a dark future for French Jewry, a return to medieval days, to ignominy and persecution. Although thoughts of revolt flashed through his mind without any concrete formulation, they were quickly discarded when he considered his familial and communal responsibilities. Seen from a wider perspective, Lambert's acceptance of his fate seemed to fit with the atmosphere of *attentisme* that

5. See Diary entries for February 24 and 25, 1941.
6. See Diary entries for June 4, 10, 15, 22, and July 8, 1941.

prevailed in the "free zone." On the one hand, in early 1941 few French spoke out publicly in the south against Vichy; on the other hand, Jewish organizations enjoyed a relative freedom of operation, which mitigated a radical opposition.[7] After several months without activity, CAR resumed its functions. By May 1941 it was offering some form of assistance to more than fourteen thousand individuals. Clandestine activity was thus not a serious alternative for Lambert at this point. Rather, his thoughtful deliberations and his social work took other directions, recalling those that faced German Jews in 1933: emigration, endurance, a reassertion of a Jewish sense of belonging, suicide.

In the first half of 1941 Lambert treated each of these possibilities. He rejected suicide, even though he noted several times that he would have preferred an honorable death on the battlefield to the life of a pariah.[8] Yet he was well aware that intensified anti-Semitism would lead more Jews to that end. He was again critical of the Jewish community's leaders and its wealthy members who fled France immediately after the beginning of the German occupation, leaving the community without leadership. Still, in May 1941 he too toyed with the idea of leaving France, and overtures were made on his behalf. This decision filled him with deep personal turmoil:

> So I am taking the first steps toward finding temporary asylum in New York. It pains me to do so, but do I have the right not to assure my sons a future? I shall remain French until my death, but if the French nation legally expels me from its bosom, do I have the right to decide that my sons should be pariahs? (June 4, 1941)

Whether Lambert remained in France because of difficulties in obtaining a visa or because of his own reluctance to leave is not clear from his diary or from other sources. Thus his fate, like that

7. H. R. Kedward, *Resistance in Vichy France: A Study of Ideas and Motivation in the Southern Zone 1940–1942* (Oxford, 1978).

8. See Diary entries for May 10, 15, 1941.

of many native French Jews, was to remain in Vichy France, to endure and to suffer.

All this being said, Lambert's description of the first year under Vichy rule in the south is also deceptive. It provides one dimension only—a spiritual one. We hear little of daily life in the "free zone," implying that it was bearable for him and his family. In fact life in the south was considerably less oppressive than in the north of France, especially for a native French Jew in 1940–1941. Lambert's diary rarely mentions discomfort or hardship caused by anti-Semitic legislation; Lambert seems to be able to pursue his normal French way of life without major obstacles. The dichotomy that emerges from this description is instructive and needs emphasis: on the one hand there is no limit to Lambert's sense of rejection by "France"—a source of endless spiritual pain—while on the other hand material hardships and rejection by French society seem to be remote from the experience of elements within the native community. This situation allowed native French Jewish leaders in the south to reach a jaundiced perception of reality, which at times even ignored the hovering shadow of Nazi racism. In some sense the lack of daily pressure and isolation, combined with the quasi-freedom of the south, worked against a more telling view of Vichy's Jewish policy and further distanced the reality of native French Jews from that of their immigrant brethren. At this juncture of the war, their malaise was more spiritual than material.

Even if he personally led a relatively normal life during this first period of the armistice, Lambert nevertheless lived in the constant shadow of the plight of the internees, the refugees, and the immigrants. Having resumed his social work in CAR in 1940, he was active in trying to bring relief to the Jews in the internment camps in southern France. He writes repeatedly of their plight with humanity and concern, and looks forward to cooperating with others in addressing the problem of foreigners and immigrants after the war. Constantly looking for ways to extend them assistance, Lambert assumed an important role in the

Nîmes interreligious commission for aid to deprived foreigners, but he feared that private charities would be futile in the face of the growing suffering.[9]

In the summer of 1941, Lambert resumed his negotiations and contacts with officials of the Vichy government, including the head of the Commissariat Général aux Questions Juives (the Commissariat—CGQJ), Xavier Vallat, a figure with strong right-wing and anti-Semitic views.[1] His meetings apparently persuaded Lambert that French officials were highly pessimistic about the future of France and French Jewry, especially as the German penetration into the Soviet Union was at the height of its success and Pétain was moving toward a dictatorial regime and outright collaboration with the occupying authorities. Lambert sensed a changing atmosphere among his former colleagues, who seemed to be overly cautious in their discussions, adhering closely to the New Order line.

In the midst of these negotiations, Lambert was summoned by Vallat on September 23, 1941, to discuss the establishment of a central Jewish organization. The meeting took place four days later and covered the state of the relief organizations, German pressure to establish such a central organization, and a promise to provide funds for the agencies. Lambert was clearly chosen by Vallat because he was known among French officials for his welfare activities over several years and in his capacity as secretary-general of CAR. Ten days later Vallat met with Jacques Helbronner, by now the president of the Central Consistory, and presented to him the overall scheme of the organization. Once again Lambert and Helbronner were to find themselves at opposite sides of communal deliberations—this time, on the response to Vallat's overture.

Behind Vallat's negotiations stood the policy of Reinhard Heydrich, head of the SS Sicherheitsdienst (SD, the Security

9. See Diary entries for July 6, 7, 1941.

1. For an astute analysis of his views, see Marrus and Paxton, *Vichy France and the Jews*, pp. 87–96; on the meeting between Lambert and Vallat, see Pierre-Bloch, *Jusqu'au dernier jour: Mémoires* (Paris, 1983), p. 185.

Service), to establish Jewish councils in occupied countries to coordinate communal affairs. The SD went about this actively in various countries, pursuing leading Jewish individuals who could assume such a role. In France, initial attempts to establish an organization analogous to the German *Reichsvereinigung* were not successful; even the Comité de Coordination, established in Paris in January 1941, did not meet Nazi expectations. Eventually, after much internal disagreement and strong pressure from the SD, the occupying powers turned to Vichy's Commissariat général aux questions juives on August 29 to create such an organization in the occupied zone. Several weeks later French officials decided to form such an organization in all of France to promote a sense of French sovereignty over the entire country.

Lambert has left us with a brief report of his meeting with Vallat. The plan consisted of establishing a compulsory organization of two sections, one in each zone. Vallat promised him that the welfare organizations in the "free zone" would be able to operate freely and draw their operating funds from confiscated Jewish property taken according to the law of July 22, 1941. Lambert, who went to the meeting with the consent of Albert Lévy, the president of CAR and a member of the Central Consistory, responded positively. Safeguarding the relief agencies was the priority for both men. Lambert added, with a touch of arrogance:

> . . . We cannot refuse since the important thing is for the social workers to carry on. I accept it from him since he is the legal authority. But I hope this will put me in a position, some day, to preside over the liquidation of this Commission on Jewish Questions, that it won't last any longer than the longer ministries we had in the olden days. (October 3, 1941)

Following their meeting, Lambert sent Vallat a list of six representatives, including himself, of leading Jewish organizations in the "free zone." Furthermore he requested that their conversation remain secret and its content be kept from the others.

What prompted Lambert to show immediate interest in Vallat's proposal, and why did he fear their meeting would be leaked? Meeting Vallat was not on the face of it condemnable, for he was a French official and had a saving grace: though an ardent anti-Semite, he was a patriotic Frenchman who was also known for his strong anti-German feelings. Cocky but sensitive to the growing needs of thousands of Jews, Lambert saw himself as the appropriate figure to head the central organization. Anticipating no doubt that it would create a cleavage within the Jewish community (especially since it would challenge the Consistory's standing), he asked for Vallat's discretion. Whatever the reasons for Lambert's behavior, it seems grossly anachronistic to stamp this original contact between the two men in September 1941 with a more distinctly pejorative meaning: at this stage neither Lambert nor Vallat had any sense of the outcome of their deliberations.

During the ensuing two months, the proposed organization was discussed among Vichy officials and hotly debated among Jewish relief organizations in the south.[2] The relative freedom of the southern zone allowed Jewish leaders to ponder seriously and closely every aspect of the intended organization, as if their ultimate decision would determine its contours and the proposed legislation. Two basic positions emerged: one vigorously opposed any negotiation on the law, the other saw the need to continue discussion with French officials to produce a more positive outcome. Lambert emerged as the leading proponent of the latter view, shared by some leaders of the native and immigrant community. He carried the initiative forward, undauntedly preserving his personal contact with Vallat in the face of recriminations and censure by others. This was the Lambert of the late 1930s, taking risks and criticizing those who were not willing to go the extra

2. As these deliberations have been discussed extensively in the literature they will be treated briefly here. See Richard I. Cohen, *The Burden of Conscience: French Jewish Leadership During the Holocaust* (Bloomington and Indianapolis, 1987), ch. 3; Schwarzfuchs, *Aux prises avec Vichy*, pp. 120–166; Laffitte, *Juif dans la France allemande*, pp. 371–383 offers a summary of different historiographical positions.

mile for the dire needs of thousands. Now he stood openly against the nobility of the native French Jews—the Central Consistory and the chief rabbi of France—rejecting their criticism with utter disdain. He vehemently denied their claim that he was "Vallat's man,"[3] noting that it was because of his years of experience and ministerial contacts that he had been summoned by Vallat. He maintained vigorously that what lay in the balance of the negotiations was the future of Jewish welfare work in France.

Unfortunately his diary offers little insight into his thoughts throughout this period, aside from two markedly different entries on October 12 and November 30, 1941. In the former, before a discussion on the law, Lambert again contemplates the future of France and the Jews in the wake of further German military success:

> . . . What will become of France, and of us Jews—what will happen to us in the meantime? It is clear that in this huge inferno, Jewish concerns are only one element in the general anxiety—we all have to wait. This calms me at least with regard to my sons' future, since the Poles, the Belgians, the Dutch are no more sure of tomorrow than I am. . . . As I have said to myself many times in the past year, we must have the energy to endure. I myself may perhaps not see the new world to come. Our individual lives are counted in years, but what are twelve months in the lives of peoples, and in the evolution of humankind? (October 12, 1941)

Yet on November 30, three days before the public announcement of the new law, after having been in the center of the negotiations and the source of much criticism, Lambert appears as a man of action, convinced of his capabilities and of his decision to assume a leading role in the new organization—the UGIF (Union Générale des Israélites de France). Conscious of the heavy responsibility, he dismisses his critics as "Jewish princes" and is certain that the

3. Diary entry, December 11, 1941.

Union will be established "with us, without us or against us." He entertains no qualms of having compromised with his internal values: "But I am pursuing my course with a clear conscience and the clear desire to remain both an excellent Jew and an excellent Frenchman. I am rereading Maurice Barrès and Henri Franck" (November 30, 1941).

The moral issue faced by leaders of Jewish communities throughout Europe—whether to participate in an enforced, racial organization of Jews or to resist—was at the center of French Jewry's deliberations in these months. Lambert was not oblivious to it, and though his inclination was to accept Vallat's appointment, he established moral boundaries in keeping with the principles he articulated in the 1930s: the organization would represent Jews only in social and philanthropic matters, would not tax its fellow Jews, and would refuse to utilize funds derived from the seizure of Jewish property. Lambert viewed his task in a strictly technical manner, intending to preserve the relief organizations from disintegrating and falling into the hands of incompetent and inexperienced individuals. He was relieved to note that all the Commissariat's other nominees for the UGIF council were qualified community leaders who were actively involved in relief organizations.[4]

Yet, even after the publication of the law establishing the UGIF, debates within the community barely subsided. As before, Lambert's positive attitude toward UGIF was directly opposed to the majority of the Central Consistory who rejected this nonreligious definition of French Jewry that considered all French Jews, native and immigrants alike, on equal footing. Lambert's insistence on returning to Vichy to see Vallat, at times alone, in defiance of the decisions of the Central Commission of Jewish Relief Organizations[5] and the Central Consistory, raised the ire of his opponents. In December 1941, marathon meetings within the

4. Diary, December 2, 1941.

5. This umbrella organization of Jewish aid societies was set up in October 1940 in Marseilles under the sponsorship of the chief rabbi of France.

community continued, in which the position of the Central Consistory was basically upheld, allowing participation of the nominees under certain circumstances. In the face of opposition and vacillation, Lambert became more intransigent, self-centered, and convinced of his position, feeling that his critics were out of touch with reality and somewhat jealous of his new role: "Why not admit that the Marshal did accept the law, and that he knows that Germany gives the orders, from Paris, directly to the Commissariat of Jewish Affairs, the same as to the press and the information service? Whom do they think they're fooling?" (December 11, 1941). Consequently, whenever Lambert sensed that endless deliberations would torpedo the Union, he used his personal contact with Vallat to prevent it.

The opposition nonetheless took its toll. On December 23, 1941, eight of the appointed council members, including Lambert, passed a resolution rejecting participation and submitted it to Vallat. Lambert and Joseph Millner of Oeuvre Secours des Enfants (OSE) then went to see Vallat secretly.[6] During a remakable meeting on December 30, Vallat declared that he was leaving for Paris on January 5 and that if he did not have an agreed list of leaders by that date he would appoint eight "lackeys," unassociated with the relief organizations, to head the council. This threat, of a kind so common during the period of the Holocaust, prompted Lambert to ask Vallat to stay the decision and send separate telegrams to the appointed eight council members, reiterating Vallat's earlier promises on the nature of their jurisdiction. Vallat agreed. Lambert then drafted the telegram, which was sent by Vallat on January 2.

Lambert hoped thus to make the responses individual: whoever agreed to join would do so, and whoever procrastinated further would be replaced. Lambert's singlehanded tactic, albeit with Millner's concurrence, placed their fellow appointees under intense pressure; it also offers a striking example of the divergence

6. Lambert had originally suggested his name. Millner, a designated council member, was in favor of participating in the organization.

among the Jewish leadership in "reading the moment." Lambert believed that everything must be done at this point to help Vallat obtain the best possible conditions, while others believed in biding time.

After receiving their telegrams, the nominees met for six more hours of deliberations, and again two positions emerged: those in favor of responding positively, and those preferring conditional acceptance (Marc Jarblum, William Oualid, and David Olmer).[7] Lambert was instrumental in convincing the supporters. The moment held for him deeper significance than met the eye:

> . . . I know that in Paris the Germans give the orders and Vallat can't do anything. Oualid refuses to understand and goes on talking straight nineteenth century. . . . These poor old fellows are still thinking in prewar terms and forgetting that a minister under an authoritarian regime has asked them to reply by telegram. (January 8, 1942)

Vallat rejected the conditional responses. Two hesitant nominees then turned to Lambert to salvage the affair, but his response was unrepenting:

> We shall just get along without people who dither too much and refuse to understand that in the Free Zone we have to place our bets on the sincerity of Vallat, but in the Occupied Zone he and we can do absolutely nothing. The *Union* will be founded without these folk, and the Jewish community can only benefit. (January 8, 1942)

On January 9, 1942, the names of the eighteen members of the two UGIF councils were published, the replacements in the south being individuals suggested by Lambert. In retrospect, a month later, after having been attacked again by the Central Consistory, Lambert remained convinced that French Jewry had gained by his negotiations and had sacrificed nothing: collaboration would go

7. On each of these figures, see the notes to the Diary.

forward on technical matters alone; the relief organizations were saved from liquidation and were to be headed independently by their Jewish functionaries. In the following months Lambert laid the structure for UGIF's operation in the south; only in May was its inaugural council meeting held. By then Vallat was already persona non grata and on his way out, to be replaced by a hardened anti-Semitic Pétainiste, Darquier de Pellepoix, who had gained the support of the German authorities.[8]

Lambert's diary leaves little room to doubt that he was the central figure within UGIF-south from the outset. Albert Lévy, the UGIF president, was very much under his influence. More important, the diary discloses Lambert's secret relations with Vallat in defiance of the chief rabbi of France, the Central Consistory, and other nominated members of UGIF, and raises important questions for the historian: What brought Lambert to act with such boldness and independence, defying the organizations and personalities with which he was associated? Was he ideologically inclined to the New Order? Was he personally motivated to collaboration and to authoritarian behavior?

In responding to these questions one must bear in mind the past history of the relationship between Lambert and some of the leaders of French Jewry in the 1930s and the atmosphere in Vichy France in the winter of 1941. Lambert had little faith in the competence and compassion of the leaders of the Consistory at the time, first and foremost Jacques Helbronner.[9] His difficult encounters in the 1930s with Helbronner and others continued to gnaw at Lambert and inform his opinion. He often returned to their disagreement, as he did when CAR was dissolved and merged into UGIF:

> Those who are attacking us should be applauding us instead, because it is we who are carrying on the struggle! . . . That evening I understood that the *Statut* really was diminishing us, and that

8. On Darquier, see Marrus and Paxton, *Vichy France and the Jews*, pp. 283–286; Carmen Callil, *Bad Faith: A Forgotten History of Family, Fatherland and Vichy France* (New York, 2006).

9. Lambert to Rabbi Maurice Liber, December 19, 1941 (CDJC: CCCLXVI-48).

> we are the ones who are showing courage in working under such conditions. (May 25, 1942)

Yet the nature of the individuals involved contributed its share to the clashes and mutual recriminations. Lambert and Helbronner were both blessed with inflated egos that could not easily harmonize. Lambert's political assessment was moreover born of his pessimistic appraisal of Europe's changing contours. Associated with Herriot's moderate center–left Radical party, and a liberal anti-Communist, Lambert even harbored a form of pacifism in the 1930s. By 1941 he sensed that the German occupation and the New Order in France had put a temporary end to parliamentary and republican ideals of the Third Republic, and that Jews in France would have to make the best of working with French officials. Like some members of UGIF-north, he trusted Vallat and believed that owing to his animosity to the Germans and respect for veteran French Jews, he was willing to ease somewhat the suffering of French Jewry.

Thus it was not ideological or political motivations that brought Lambert to engage with Vallat as he did. Rather it would seem that here, as in similar situations in Europe during the war (including northern France), different interpretations of the same moral dilemma existed; morality was not Manichean. Lambert, like many other Jewish leaders in occupied Europe, staked his reputation and life on participation in the council. He did so in complete rejection of his critics, with the absolute conviction that he could salvage more than was being sacrificed and that he was acting within moral boundaries.[1]

* * *

Three months after the first UGIF council meeting, Lambert found himself catapulted into the crisis concerning the mass shipment of Jews from the "free zone" to Drancy, the French internment

1. The Central Consistory's efforts to remove Lambert from his position in the UGIF continued throughout the dramatic events of the summer, 1942. See Schwarzfuchs, *Aux prises avec Vichy*, pp. 165–186.

camp north of Paris, set up by Vichy in August 1941. These deportations followed mass arrests in mid-July 1942 in Paris. Almost 13,000 Jews, mostly "foreigners," were sent to Drancy following Prime Minister Laval's acquiescence to the German authorities; even children below the age of sixteen, not originally stipulated in the German orders, were included by the French government. But the German plan was far more ambitious and projected the deportation of some 50,000 Jews from each zone. Here too the German authorities found a pliable French government that consented to the deportation of some 10,000 "foreign" Jews from the internment camps in the south. These deportations began in early August. By September 2, 1942, German calculations noted that the summer deportations had yielded 27,000 Jews, a third of them from the south.[2]

The mass arrests of July find little echo in Lambert's diary. At this critical moment in French Jewish history, all that was left for Lambert to recall were the soothing words of Barrès (1914) and to reread Péguy's moving passage on the Dreyfus Affair from *Our Youth* (1910).[3] His nostalgia for the France of another generation could not, however, mitigate the stark reality of Vichy. Even Lambert's presence at the large anti-Vichy demonstration in Marseilles on Bastille Day could not lift his spirits: "We must not emigrate, nor give up; we must submit and wait, hold on and endure" (July 21, 1942). Little did he know what was in store for him a week later.

From the moment Lambert learned on July 28 of the intended deportations, his struggle to prevent them was unrelenting. Although it would seem that he had no illusions about the possibility of reversing the German-directed decision, he acted firmly and energetically. On July 31 he and two co-workers went to Vichy and by chance encountered Prime Minister Laval. Defining his position as a legal one, Lambert refrained from presenting an

2. For a discussion of the summer deportations, see Susan Zuccotti, *The Holocaust, the French, and the Jews* (New York, 1993), pp. 118–137.

3. Diary entry, July 21, 1942.

official protest by French Jewry, considering it outside his jurisdiction. It was the role of the Consistory to intervene on behalf of French Jewry, and Lambert had no intention of usurping that position. Later in the day he attended a prearranged meeting with Laval's secretary-general, Guérard, where they submitted their "technical demand" to prevent the deportation of Jews who held American visas. This was the first "preferred category" of exemption that the UGIF was to propose to Vichy officials.

Lambert made it clear to Guérard that if Laval wished to meet the official representatives of the community, he should turn to Albert Lévy and Jacques Helbronner. Guérard reiterated the Vichy mantra that the deportations were a necessary evil and that little could be done. As for a meeting between Laval and the two Jewish presidents, he promised a reply—but paradoxically such a meeting was unacceptable to Helbronner, who insisted that if Laval wanted one, he needed only to notify him and he would go—on his own. Lambert's description of his conversation with Helbronner on August 2, in Lyon, where the latter expressed this position, portrays the Consistory leader as a thoughtless individual, unworthy of his position: "Is it possible that a leader of French Jewry would dare to have so little heart and conscience? We deserve these ordeals for having accepted such leadership."[4]

From that point, and during the ensuing weeks of deportations, Lambert and the UGIF made no further effort to achieve "peace" with the Consistory officials. In fact, no joint protest was ever made. Lambert turned his energies solely to relief activity, often in cooperation with the Consistory-supported chaplaincy, the Aumônerie Générale, headed by Rabbi René Hirschler.[5] During

4. Schwarzfuchs, who had access to the Consistory archives, brought Lambert's report of the meeting in detail without comment or a conflicting source. This leads me to accept the veracity of Lambert's description. See Schwarzfuchs, *Aux prises avec Vichy*, p. 251.

5. Hirschler often sharply disagreed with the Consistory over issues of aid and treatment of the immigrants and refugees. At one point he even submitted his resignation, but retracted. He maintained close relations with Lambert and UGIF officials throughout the war.

these weeks Lambert, with his colleagues, sought to alleviate the misery of the deportees by taking care of their individual needs as those arose, providing sanitary conditions for the deportation and caring for the abandoned children. Lambert himself was present for several days at Les Milles, a camp near Aix-en-Provence, which became the center of deportations from the Marseilles region. On these occasions he witnessed the horrible moments of deportation and demanded that children aged two to fifteen be placed in the custody of the UGIF. This demand for exemption, the second "preferred category," was partially accepted. Lambert struggled with the moral predicament involved in this request far differently from the way hindsight has treated it. It was hardly preferred selection that troubled him but rather the separation of the children from their parents. "Is this humane? Their parents will entrust them to us, so that they may escape this hell" (October 11, 1942).

Throughout these tragic events, Lambert felt deeply his impotence; he could salvage a few random Jews, but by far the majority was to be deported, with little attention paid to UGIF's special requests. Indicative of this dilemma was a moving moment he described: After having been present at several deportations in Les Milles and having successfully disguised his humiliation and frustration, his internal equilibrium finally snapped upon seeing a Jewish editor from Vienna, decorated by France, in the deportation line. Lambert burst through the queue "like a madman," shouting at the officer in charge, "You can't deport a Knight of the Legion of Honor!" and leading the man from the line. No doubt Lambert saw in front of him a reflection of his own existence: France had reached bottom if it could deport its own war heroes. His pain was profound, both as a Frenchman and a Jew: his country had totally dishonored itself and disregarded its tradition of refuge by permitting the inhuman persecution of foreign Jews; the leaders of the native Jews, the Central Consistory and its president Jacques Helbronner, remained insensitive to the plight of the foreign Jews, preferring respectability to outspoken involvement.[6]

Lambert's involvement in the deportations of August had many sides to it. He was far from the aloof bureaucrat who received reports of events and responded accordingly. He was on the scene and intervened with emotion and vigor. He recognized that he had no power to turn back the clock to a different period of French history, so he resigned himself to alleviating in some small measure the pain of the unfortunate. But beyond his humanitarian impulses lay more serious questions on the nature of the UGIF's actions during the deportations.

First among these questions is the role of the UGIF in the German-French design. Documentation on this matter points in one direction alone: UGIF was to provide various sanitary and relief assistance. This mission it fulfilled with the active assistance of various welfare organizations, French and international, that functioned in the south.

A second question concerns the functions UGIF assumed voluntarily. Other than their various protests and condemnations, UGIF officials agreed to participate in a "selection committee" with representatives of the various welfare associations. Here efforts were made by all to secure the safety of those victims who might be excluded from deportation because of extenuating circumstances. The choice of "preferred categories" was decided by the relief organizations, but they rejected outright the idea of presenting a different deportees list from that filed by the camp authorities. All who accepted this process understood that the moral imperative was to save those who could be saved, but an alternative list was regarded as morally condemnable.

6. Clearly this is Lambert's perspective. The Consistory did not remain totally inactive during the month of August as Schwarzfuchs has shown, but Helbronner's attitude remains puzzling.

A third question is the decision-making process within UGIF-south. UGIF policy during the deportations was formed by a few council members—Lambert, Lévy, Raphaël Spanien, sometimes Robert Gamzon—who were close to Marseilles, and others, such as Gaston Kahn, who were prominent in the organization. Lambert, due to his role and personality, often decided on forms of intervention on his own or with another member. Finally, due to the federative nature of UGIF-south, the various welfare organizations that were coerced into the organization acted autonomously with a wide range of independence. They were not bound by a UGIF policy, for that, in effect, did not exist. This amorphous contact with the UGIF leaders (not even "the UGIF council") allowed certain figures within the organization to navigate, as early as August 1942, a dual course—that is, to provide social assistance both legally and illegally, under the guise of UGIF, and without fear of "UGIF" intervention. At this juncture all the Jewish organizations within UGIF, native and immigrant, maintained some sort of official veneer; some began to harbor plans for illegal activity alongside their official work; none saw armed opposition as a possibility. Lambert remained tied to a legal orientation and framework, and chose to remain at his post.

* * *

Jewish communities in Nazi-occupied Europe often found themselves in a twilight zone. Between the extreme pressure of searches, roundups, and deportations, a certain lull often set in, reinstating a sense of the *status quo ante* and a return to earlier routine. These intermezzos were deceiving, but they offer a partial psychological explanation for the ability of the UGIF council to return to a normal existence. Extreme situations would become the new point of reference, and what followed would be assessed in that perspective. Those who construed the extreme as being the status quo reached a predisposition to illegal activity or resistance.

French Jewry in the southern zone underwent such a development. The deportations of summer 1942 incited public outcries of high-ranking church leaders, pushed certain organizations into illegal activity, and encouraged hiding or escape to neighboring countries. But these activities diminished in the following months as a hiatus prevailed in the south after the deportations of August and early September, and before the German occupation in early November 1942. This period provided Lambert the opportunity to help coordinate internal arrangements for the plan to send Jewish children to the United States until the end of the war. The efforts expended for this emigration scheme by various Jewish organizations and international welfare associations attested to their lingering trust in Vichy's goodwill. But the delaying tactics employed both by the head of the French national police, René Bousquet, and by Prime Minister Laval torpedoed the project and contributed significantly to a declining faith in Vichy.[7] Lambert and certain UGIF council members (especially Wladimir Schah, Spanien, and Gamzon) were also coming to a more realistic appraisal of Vichy. And with the German occupation of the south, which definitively ended the legal emigration project, each of them in his own way supported or condoned clandestine emigration or the hiding of Jewish children. Spain and the newly created Italian zone in southern France loomed as the desired destinations.[8] None of them, however, advocated the dissolution of UGIF. The twilight activity continued to exist.

Even as German soldiers were taking over Marseilles, Lambert responded with his usual sense of persistence and confidence in his direction. He felt that it was not appropriate "at this time of greatest danger" to leave the organization as "My instinct is to have absolute faith in the future, and duty compels me to be the last to leave the ship" (November 29, 1942). Lambert could not follow the course of his president, Albert Lévy, who escaped to Switzerland on the eve of 1943. Although now the father of four,

7. Marrus and Paxton, *Vichy France and the Jews*, pp. 265–269.

8. For the attitudes of Spanien and Schah, see their reports and correspondence, YIVO: RG 245.4, XII, France, B-27.

Marie-France (!) recently born, Lambert moved from frightening thoughts ("Anxiety is swelling in our circles. Will this war last long enough for all of us to be deported to Poland?" [December 18, 1942]) to dreamlike fantasies of spending his later years on the French coast. But he appears to have been at this stage so deeply invested in his hubris and direction that the growing awareness of impending disaster could not alter his determination.

In early December Lambert was informed by a leading Commissariat official, Joseph Antignac, that he must terminate the employment of his foreign workers and dissolve the Youth department of his organization, including the scout movement. The scouts had been suspected of hiding children and aiding their passage over the border. The order originated with the leading officials of the Commissariat, Darquier de Pellepoix and Antignac, both of whom actively pushed for stronger anti-Semitic measures, and with whom Lambert had tense relations. After considering resigning over their intervention in the organization's affairs, Lambert protested the decision together with his personal secretary and confidant, Maurice Brener. They succeeded in retaining two sections of the department, but the scout movement was disbanded, though it continued to function in a clandestine manner. The release of the foreign workers was to be resolved differently. Meanwhile events of greater proportion took center stage.

On January 22, 1943, German authorities initiated a major operation in Marseilles, ostensibly in reprisal for underground activity against German soldiers early in the month. The action came as part of Himmler's directive of January 18 to his representative in Paris, Karl Oberg, in which he ordered the deportation of some 100,000 persons to concentration camps in Germany and the destruction of entire areas of the city, to be carried out with the cooperation of the French police. Oberg contacted the French authorities, who succeeded in limiting the German demolition plans and reducing its human demand to 20,000. Jews were also targeted in a "cleansing" process (Operation Tiger) that began in the Old Port and gradually covered the entire city. Local Jewish organizations had no advance notice of this action, but beginning January 22 they were faced with a wave of house-to-house arrests that indiscriminately rounded up Jews, even those who had been "privileged"—native French Jews and UGIF workers.

Once again the efforts and activities of the UGIF council were coordinated by Lambert, who was stationed in the city. His consultations with Chief Rabbis Salzer and Hirschler, and Professor Olmer of the Consistory, a Marseilles resident, led to joint action. Together Lambert and the rabbis appealed to all the French bodies in the city that had a hand in the arrests, in the hope they would work for the release of the Jews who had been deported to Compiègne, a camp in the north, or were still interned in the Fréjus camp in the south. They sent telegrams to Pétain and Laval, and Lambert wired the Commissariat demanding the immediate cessation of the deportations. They also turned to Helbronner to protest to the authorities.

Their interventions had little effect. The minor French officials they met with personally were essentially powerless, and their telegrams to Laval and Pétain went unheeded. Even relief activity was limited as their freedom of movement was severely restricted by a curfew, and they were refused entry into the Fréjus camp from which Jews were deported to Drancy. A concerted effort, apparently supported by French authorities, to bring back a train of some two thousand Jews from Compiègne was also in vain, though for several weeks Lambert continued to entertain hopes for its success. All told more than two thousand Jews were arrested in this roundup and deported to Drancy before further transit to Auschwitz.[9]

Caught by surprise in the whirlwind of events, Lambert and his colleagues presented their demands to the authorities within the context of French legal procedure: because Jews were not

9. André Sauvageot, *Marseille dans la tourmente, 1939–1944* (Paris, 1949); Donna Ryan, *The Holocaust and the Jews of Marseille: The Enforcement of Anti-Semitic Policies in Vichy France* (Urbana and Chicago, 1996), pp. 179–190; Schwarzfuchs, *Aux prises avec Vichy*, pp. 275–279.

prohibited from moving freely in the south, their arrest had been illegal; the safeguarding of a public institution (UGIF) was a precondition to its continued existence, thus its employees must be protected from deportation. Their conviction that it was in the French government's power to free some of the internees and would actually strive to do so was further evidence of the French Jewish leaders' inability to grasp the dramatic change that had taken place in France. In all, little was achieved by their joint efforts, but on another level—relations between the Consistory and UGIF—a major breakthrough ensued. Although a month earlier Lambert had remarked that "peace has been fully reached with the Consistory . . . [and] justice has been rendered to the sincerity of our effort and the utility of our action,"[1] the road to a real coordination of efforts had to wait for the tragic events of Marseilles.

Unlike his behavior in August 1942, Helbronner reacted without delay to the request of the Jewish leaders, protesting to Laval and requesting the release of the interned in order to preserve France's reputation in the eyes of its allies.[2] As events in Marseilles wound down, Lambert submitted a detailed, secret report to the Consistory on his attempts to intercede at Vichy. He also sent a special note to Helbronner, who replied by thanking him for his devoted and invaluable work, and opened to him the channels to the Consistory.[3] Helbronner's letter marked a turning point in his attitude toward Lambert and signaled the beginning of a new period in relations between the two organizations. For Lambert it was a significant moral victory after having been at odds with the Consistory for more than a year, not to speak of his prolonged rivalry with Helbronner from the 1930s. Apparently Lambert needed this backing more than he was willing to admit.[4]

1. Lambert to Pierre Seligman, January 8, 1943 (CDJC: CDX-103).

2. Helbronner to Laval, January 27, 1943 (JTS: Box 13).

3. Helbronner to Lambert, February 1, 1943 (formerly in possession of Maurice Brener, Paris). See also Helbronner's presentation at the General Assembly of the Consistory on February 28, 1943 (YVA: 09/30-1) and the Consistory's unanimous resolution acknowledging the important charitable and social work undertaken by UGIF-south.

4. See his somewhat deferential letters to Helbronner in March and May, discussed by Schwarzfuchs, *Aux prises avec Vichy*, pp. 188–190.

From the events of Marseilles, the course of Lambert's diary takes a different direction. Often he laconically records events without personal commentary, leaving the reader much room to wonder what he was thinking. But other documentation of the period provides certain options for interpretation.

The UGIF council met in Nice on February 5, 1943, in the wake of the Marseilles arrests and subsequent raids on synagogues, the Consistory's central headquarters, and UGIF offices in Lyon.[5] The official minutes of the meeting that were submitted to the Commissariat contain indications of a reassessment of the situation by Lambert. The council agreed to nominate five regional directors to be in charge of the various affairs in the area; they were to be the official UGIF representatives to the French and German authorities. Events in the south were developing too rapidly for decisions to be taken at long intervals by the council. The new situation further allowed for each representative to direct UGIF in the particular area in an almost autonomous manner. More significant, however, was a rather routine announcement, at Lambert's suggestion, that Maurice Brener and Jules Jefroykin were to be appointed "social inspectors" of the organization. Both Jefroykin and Brener were important figures in the Jewish underground movement in the south, serving, among other capacities, as financial contacts between resistance groups and the American Jewish Joint Distribution Committee.[6] It would appear that the appointment was meant to provide them with the "protection" of the UGIF, to allow them free access throughout the south and even protected access to the north in order to coordinate illegal activity. In May 1943, for example, together with Robert Gamzon (also a member of UGIF-south's council), Brener and Jefroykin went on a "special mission" to the north, ostensibly to discuss the reorganization of UGIF. It is difficult to believe that the choice of these three individuals, all involved in illegal work of one form or

5. YIVO: XCII-12; YVA: 09/12-1.

6. Yehuda Bauer, *American Jewry and the Holocaust: The American Jewish Joint Distribution Committee, 1939–1945* (Detroit, 1981), pp. 241–242.

another, was incidental and for that purpose alone.[7] More conceivably, their ten-day stay in Paris was designed to further contacts between certain resistance groups in both zones; a French report on their mission, submitted to the German SD, noted that Gamzon was involved in stirring up resistance activity.[8] Behind their appointment and their mission stood Lambert. He clearly knew what each of these individuals represented, and he voluntarily extended to them the service of the legal organization in order to widen the scope of illegal activity. Lambert had tangentially placed himself in the realm of the sympathizers and supporters of illegal work, though he continued to hold steadfastly to the need for UGIF's legal framework and refused to evacuate the UGIF offices from Marseilles against the advice and criticism of Wladimir Schah, a council member.[9]

Lambert's diary includes a detailed report on a new series of arrests and deportations that began at the end of April 1943 in Marseilles and in neighboring cities (Carpentras, Avignon, Aix, Ciotat) and lasted until mid-May, once again as a seeming reprisal for attacks against SS men. The focus of Lambert's account was a Gestapo demand either to surrender a list of names with one hundred Jewish notables in Marseilles or to surrender himself with 10 percent of his staff. Lambert rejected the ultimatum. UGIF offices in Marseilles were subsequently raided by the Gestapo under SS functionary Willy Bauer. Bauer summoned Lambert to the premises and warned him that those arrested in the UGIF offices were to serve as the nucleus for the hundred notables. Furthermore he threatened Lambert that any act of resistance would immediately bring serious repercussions for all of Marseilles' Jews. Lambert,

7. CDJC: CDX-3; YIVO: RG 210, IV-4. See also minutes of the UGIF-south council meeting of May 20, 1943 (YVA: 09/12-1).

8. CDJC: XXVIII-159, May 18, 1943; Laffitte, *Juif dans la France allemande*, pp. 257–259; interviews with Brener and Jefroykin in October 1977, Paris.

9. Schah to Lambert, February 10, 1943 (YVA: 09/13-2) in which he criticized Lambert for his optimism that led to passivity in Marseilles in January 1943. He claimed that UGIF's presence in Marseilles "created a dangerous illusion of protection." See Lambert to Schah, February 20, 1943 (YVA: 09/13-2); Schah tried to involve the American Jewish organization HICEM in this disagreement.

who was accompanied in these interventions by his brother, Jacques Lambert, also employed in the UGIF, protested the German action against the relief organization and insisted that measures be taken to avoid similar raids. In the ensuing negotiations, which included the French regional intendant of police, Robert Andrieu, the SS promised to arrest those individuals trapped in the UGIF office peacefully.

These imprisonments did not bring an end to the arrests of Jews in Marseilles, which continued in smaller numbers.[1] For Lambert, the events of early May did not cause him to follow Schah's call to abandon Marseilles but rather affirmed his own strategy: he continued to intervene proudly before the Germans, and even Bauer later told him that his actions had prevented a more extensive sweep of Marseilles Jews. His relations with French officials served him in good stead as Andrieu had passed Lambert's protest to Vichy and had himself protested energetically to the German authorities the abrogation of the Franco-German agreement. Finally, Lambert succeeded in liberating several special cases.

Whether Lambert was at peace with himself over these achievements is difficult to say, but repeatedly in his last entries he expressed profound joy that he had saved another group of Jews. He maintained to the end his belief that he had chosen the right path, and that if only Laval had understood the Germans as he did, and chosen his direction, the results would have been far better. Are we to take at face value his excitement on learning, three days before his own arrest, that eighty-nine Jews were liberated thanks to his efforts, or should we challenge its authenticity?[2]

* * *

After the trials and tribulations of May 1943, Lambert returned to his daily tasks, traveling constantly through southern France to

1. Diary entry, May 18, 1943; cf. Zuccotti, *The Holocaust, the French*, p. 174; Marrus and Paxton, *Vichy France and the Jews*, p. 308.

2. Diary entry, August 18, 1943.

visit the various UGIF centers and returning now and then to Vichy. This was the pattern of the last months of "freedom" which saw UGIF under increasing pressure from the Commissariat and greater intervention by the German authorities. The Commissariat increased its objection to the diffuse nature of the southern organization and decreed (May 11, 1943) that the councils would be forced to tax their fellow Jews to increase their institutional budget. Meanwhile the German authorities tightened their web around UGIF and made their presence felt in the way they strangled the Jewish councils of Europe in their second year of existence.

Lambert's thoughts during these last months wandered along different tangents. His personal solitude seemed to grow deeper, accentuated by his heavy responsibilities, on the one hand, and his disdain for most of the other Jewish relief workers on the other. His readings continued to evoke reflective thoughts on the nature of man, France, and Judaism. Fragmentary and undeveloped as they were, they expressed a certain exasperation: ". . . I must watch myself, for in times of discouragement I can see only two parallel solutions to the Jewish problem: Zionism, or baptism in the diaspora . . . Barrès, help!" (July 2, 1943).

From every corner a new threat appeared. The tax of May 11, 1943, was followed on July 2 by the German takeover of the operation of Drancy and the institution of a much stricter regime under the direction of Eichmann's notorious henchman SS-Hauptsturmführer Alois Brunner. André Baur, head of UGIF-north, was arrested with his family in mid-July and sent to Drancy. In the wake of these ominous signs, Lambert, who by then had also assumed the role of president of UGIF, faced the intensification squarely, continuing, so I assume, the dual path he had been treading during the preceding months. He created illegal contacts with the influential Italian Jew Angelo Donati, a central figure in the Nice Jewish community,[3] and sought to redi-

3. The relations between the two remain unclear. Donati was a wealthy Italian banker, who was seemingly involved in helping children reach the Italian occupied zone.

rect the organization of welfare into clandestine channels while preserving its legal structure.[4] Toward the end of July, the time had come to play his final card—to mount a major protest to the French authorities, to Laval. This would be the first and only time that Lambert addressed himself to the political authorities in the name of the entire Jewish community.

In order to strengthen his case, Lambert turned to the vice president of the Consistory, Léon Meiss. Lambert was burdened by the waning effectiveness of UGIF, the imprisonment of Baur, and UGIF's inability to prevent the suffering of the community.[5] On his way to Vichy, he stopped off in Lyon where he attempted to convince Meiss to join him in seeing Laval. Unsuccessful, he traveled on to Vichy alone, and on August 14 he met Guérard and Laval and protested sharply against the recent developments. He left the meeting with a feeling of despair, which he related to Meiss as he solemnly reviewed his predicament:

> . . . In this struggle today, in the midst of a world in disarray or in agony, I look at my wife and my admirable children and must weigh my responsibilities in the face of an uncertain future. . . . So I find myself throwing accusations at my country. Have I deserved to be treated as a pariah? Haven't I been a loyal son, proud to breathe the air of France? I have always contributed my building block to the edifice we share, in both happy and perilous times. . . . And yet today I am one of those who can be chain-ganged and deported, at your mercy. When peace and quiet come again, if I get through this torment, I shall revise all my ideas of the morals of society. (August 17, 1943)

Three days later Lambert made his last diary entry. He saw the writing on the wall. He returned at this moment to the

4. Gaston Lévy, *Souvenirs d'un médecin d'enfants à l'OSE en France occupée et en Suisse 1940–1945* (Paris and Jerusalem, n.d.), p. 43.

5. Lambert to Meiss, August 2, 1943 (YIVO: RG 210, XCII-26); Richard I. Cohen, "French-Jewry's Dilemma on the Orientation of Its Leadership (From Polemics to Conciliation: 1942–1944)," *Yad Vashem Studies* XIV (1981), p. 189.

community discussions on the establishment of UGIF and the role of the organization as he had perceived it in 1941. His concluding paragraphs may be seen as his own, perhaps even conscious, epitaph:

> They preferred their comfort to uncertainty and the heroism of struggle. . . . It was easier to protest and to abstain than to stand fast through action. . . . It is the purpose assigned to an action that justifies one's attitude. . . . We have an awareness of Judaism itself, while they preferred and defended only the garment that covers it. We chose the heroism of uncertainty and of action, the reality of concrete effort. . . . Material aid is a means of last resort, intended for use in facing unexpected occurrences, or in situations that are beyond the resources of families or individuals. Moral support is more precious and often more effective. (August 20, 1943)

The following day, at the order of Heinz Röthke, head of the "Jewish Section" of the SD, Lambert and his family were arrested and sent to Drancy. Although some sources claim that the initiative for his arrest came from Antignac, who was furious with Lambert's protest, it would appear that it was part of the German plan to curtail the authority and freedom of the UGIF.[6] Indeed, it had a paralyzing effect upon the central administration of UGIF-south, which never fully recovered. Lambert's arrest was viewed by the Central Consistory as a severe blow to French Jewry. The man who had so severely judged Lambert in 1941–1942, Jacques Helbronner, would call Lambert's and André Baur's release imperative, "for without them there is nothing to be done."[7]

Lambert was imprisoned in Drancy from late August until December 7, 1943. From Drancy he corresponded with several individuals, including his confidant Maurice Brener. In the letters

6. Conflicting accounts exist on the arrest of the Lambert family. See Serge Klarsfeld (ed.), *Die Endlösung der Judenfrage im Frankreich* (Paris, 1977), pp. 210–213; cf. CDJC: XXVIII-187; XCVI, p. 7; CDJC: X-92.

7. See the Consistory meeting of October 6, 1943 in Cohen, "The Dilemma," p. 204.

he sent to Brener from early October to early November, Lambert revealed in code language his inner thoughts and feelings, providing a kind of continuation to his diary. He was hurt that his fellow council members had failed to resign in protest and present a united stand before the authorities. This, he thought, might have had some effect. So too, he felt deceived by the northern council members interned in Drancy, who were better treated and did not try to alleviate the Lamberts' situation. This was especially painful for him as he felt he had risked his life for them by intervening in their favor. Nevertheless, beyond his personal concerns and suffering, Lambert continued to be involved in UGIF affairs, providing Brener with instructions and suggestions to the council: to cease providing UGIF-north with a subsidy, to take special precautions with the Vichy-appointed treasurer of the UGIF (Maurice Couturier), and to make greater efforts to avoid further shipments to Drancy, like that from La Rose.

In October 1943 the Gestapo presented Gaston Kahn with an ultimatum: either notify UGIF's children's home in La Rose (Bouches-du-Rhône) to prepare for their arrest within twenty-four hours or place Marseilles Jewry in serious danger. Fearing widescale reprisals, Kahn rejected Brener's advice to disperse the children immediately, and fulfilled the Gestapo order. The children and the director of the home, Alice Salomon, were subsequently transferred to Drancy.[8] On October 26, Lambert declared his position unequivocally:

> Alice told us about the consultation before their trip. If what she told me is true, I am of the same mind as you and hope that if a crisis of this sort arises again, the action taken will be bolder and in accordance with Dr. Sabord's prescriptions. These concessions to illness will not postpone the admission to the clinic of those who are fainthearted, the most fainthearted . . ."[9]

8. This tragic development was corroborated by interviews in 1977 with Brener and Jefroykin and from a letter sent by Alice Salomon to Brener, from Drancy, formerly in the latter's possession.

9. See notes to the letter for the deciphering of code words.

The issue shocked Lambert, and he returned to it again on November 5, maintaining that had he been there he would have imposed Brener's position.

Did Lambert know what followed Drancy? Although Auschwitz was never mentioned in the diary, it is hard to believe that in November 1943 he was unaware of its existence, as he had written on October 17: "I am beginning to think we shall be spending the winter under these same conditions. We shan't complain as long as we are not referred to Dr. Kamenetz [code for Auschwitz]. In the end that's the only thing that matters." Yet in typical fashion Lambert ended his last letter to Brener on November 5 with a note of optimism, albeit somewhat diluted: "But all these troubles will pass, and quickly too, I hope. These patients will be cured by Christmas at the latest."

* * *

The portrait of Raymond-Raoul Lambert that emerges from his writings, diaries, and rather extensive archival material is many-sided. An authoritarian figure, haughty and arrogant, deeply convinced of his direction, Lambert never doubted his own capabilities and competence. A man of action, perseverance, and intellectual interests, he did not suffer critics lightly and dealt forcefully with them, disparaging their talents and attitudes. Although his public service in the interwar years provided him with essential experience for dealing with knotty human and bureaucratic issues, it scarcely prepared him for the dilemmas he encountered during World War II. Once he became the ardent supporter of UGIF-south and then its central figure, he assumed the roles with great energy and determination, provoking others with his imperious behavior. Under the constant tension of the deteriorating situation of French Jewry and the need to make decisions under duress, Lambert became more certain of his actions, belittling those who challenged him. Not surprisingly, the southern council often appears as a one-man performance with the other members far removed from center stage. Lambert never saw the need to have them all concentrated in Marseilles, as they would have only encumbered his freedom of action and decision. His raison d'être was to attend to the growing and changing social and material needs of Jews in the south. Refugees, immigrants, children, internees, and native Jews in the thousands benefited from the aid and assistance of the UGIF's organs, and found in Lambert a voice for their concerns and predicaments, one who never feared to represent them before French and German authorities. But some Jews were trapped by their continued contact with UGIF and paid a human price.

Aware of the failure to dent the deportation process, Lambert acknowledged that he was at least fulfilling a moral mission to those in need of assistance, and believed that few could fulfill it better. Yet, decisive individual that he was, he could not determine whether to join clandestine activity wholeheartedly or to remain solely within a legal course of action. He wavered and chose, so it appears, a middle road. From February 1943 until his arrest there is circumstantial evidence that Lambert was aiding and abetting clandestine forces within the community to further their agendas, yet he continued his legal presence and position, maintained open offices in Marseilles and other cities, and withstood his critics.

How are we to make sense of his actions? Was he drunk with the new power he wielded and so enamored of himself that he became oblivious to the calls to remove him from office and deaf to those who pushed for the closing of UGIF and further involvement in clandestine work? Did he believe that his position protected him from the fate of deportation? How can we understand the decision-making process of this father of four, bombarded with requests for aid, cognizant of the deteriorating fate of French Jewry and constant deportations? Certainly Lambert consulted and confided with individuals who probably offered conflicting suggestions; certainly he enjoyed his influence and felt comfortable in the company of others who possessed it, though he wanted the influence to achieve the ends he valued. Lambert had become so invested in the ways he acted in the world, and remained so determined to make them work, that he lost sight of his and his family's fate. The writing was indeed on the wall, especially after the arrest of André Baur in July; but to claim that a realistic prognosis of the future might have brought him to alter his course and override his fantasies and illusions is to minimize his power of persistence and illusory self-confidence.

Lambert's tragic end in the gas chambers of Auschwitz put an end to a controversial Jewish leader. He remained undaunted during months of torment and true to his inner calling, never relinquishing his craving for the arts and literature nor his sense of duality as a Frenchman and a Jew.

Diary of a Witness, 1940–1943

Zones of Occupied France, 1940–1944

1940

Nîmes, July 12, 1940

After the past four weeks, which have seen unfold the most tragic events in our history, and for me the most terrible anxieties I have ever known, I am trying to recover my intellectual balance, to regain my awareness of the passage of time. So naturally I thought of the notebooks, which, during the Great War, saved me from inertia and despair.

As an officer assigned to a central administrative unit, I was not directly involved in the fighting, but I have witnessed the disarray and paralysis of my country's central nervous systems. I have been most dreadfully worried about the fate of my wife and our three sons, who are my whole life and my only reasons now to go on living and struggling—for even though the real danger is gone, at least for the moment, the future will bring serious problems.

I should begin by putting down matter-of-factly, as well as I can remember clearly, the details of my odyssey from Paris to Nîmes; as I owed it to myself to be during that time, I am aware of having been lucid, energetic, and concerned to do my duty.

Until June 10: Still in the technical section of the Colonial Troops, captain for a month now (and very happy about it), stationed at the Hotel des Invalides. On May 19 I decided to have Simone and the children evacuated to Bellac, more because of the danger of air raids than the strategic situation. Left alone in Paris, I waited. Several alarms.

Monday, June 3: At 1:30 P.M., aerial bombardment of Paris, targeting the Citroën factory, which was hit; some bombs in my Auteuil neighborhood, in Coussin Street where Lionel[1] has been going to school. . . . So the evacuation is justified and I accept the separation. One official statement after another announces disaster in overly enigmatic terms.

June 10: At 11 A.M. I go with my superior, Commandant Pascot,[2] to the Eighth Department office of the ministry under which we work. . . . They are moving out, without letting us know. They were just going to forget about us. The General Headquarters staff has already left Paris, during the night. Destination: Candé, near Blois. It's up to us to find transportation: a dump truck belonging to one of my noncommissioned officers—he deals in fertilizer; the cars of two of our secretaries. The commandant goes to Ribérac this evening to kiss his wife, then catch up with us at Candé. I am to leave in the morning with the office things and the files.

By evening Paris is emptying out, its public buildings are dead. The winds of defeat are already blowing. At street corners

1. Lionel was Lambert's eldest son, born in 1929.

2. Colonel "Jep" Pascot was to succeed Jean Borotra as general education and sports commissioner on April 18, 1942. This position was created by the Vichy government in September 1940 to encourage sports and physical education. Pascot, who had first served under Borotra, wanted to organize the physical reeducation of France through an active sports policy. He was convinced that the defeat in 1940 was due to a lack of energy of French soldiers, and the only way for the French to regain their strength was to establish a policy of sports ideology. Pascot was an intimate friend of Raymond-Raoul Lambert (RRL) and is often mentioned in the diary; their relationship offers, through the prism of the diary, a microcosmic view of the relationship between Vichy and the Jews. Cf. W. D. Halls, *The Youth of Vichy France* (Oxford, 1981), pp. 198–200; see also the diary entries for December 20, 1940, and October 11, 1942.

women sit on bundles, waiting for the taxis, all of which are gone. At St. Lazare train station, floods of refugees. "They" have reached Pontoise and Nantes. I go on calmly arranging our departure. We [are to] meet at 8:30 A.M., unless there are suspicious noises during the night.

June 11: I awake to one of the most horrible sensations of my life, a feeling of being smothered, of dying all alone. The maid rouses me at 6 A.M.: gas attack! I open the window. Paris is drowning in a black, stifling fog that is plunging the sky and the streets into mourning. . . . It smells of oil and soot, but it's not a gas attack. It is oil fumes from the storage tanks that have been set on fire from Rouen to Bonnières, along with smoke with which the Boche [the Germans] are screening their crossing of the Seine. . . . It feels like being crushed by something sinister, and I truly sense that Paris will never be the same again. This deep gloom is our defeat. In the street people's faces have black spots from the soot and eyes outlined in black. The few souls still passing by are running like crazy toward the train stations.

We leave Invalides at 10:30. I requisition gasoline from the military school. We head for Candé by the Orléans highway, which I know well. . . . The spectacle there is dumbfounding, a whole people in flight. The road is hopelessly jammed: workers fleeing on bicycles, on foot, pushing wheelbarrows, cars full to bursting. . . . With my lieutenant I go ahead on foot to restore some order and make a way through, but there are no longer any police or any authority that people recognize, and of course no priority possible for the military either. Lunch is in a ditch where we are forced to wait for an hour coming out of Longjumeau. By evening we are at Étampes. My second-in-command and my men sleep in the vehicles, which I have parked off the highway on a dead-end road, since it would be dangerous to keep going at night. I take the responsibility for this; we will get there when we can, and we are more than seventy kilometers [forty-five miles] beyond the enemy's reach on the ground. For myself, in a nearby house I am able to find a free bed on which to stretch out. My experience of the previous war is serving me well; the filling station on the square in Étampes is overwhelmed but is obliged to give me gasoline to continue my journey. Senator Breton, traveling in his Bugatti, is sleeping in the open air, and there is no more bread to be found. . . . I scrape together what I can for dinner with my men.

July 15, 1940

Military ceremony held yesterday at the Monument to the Dead. Not at all imposing. No awareness among either the leaders or the audience of the ordeals we face, present and future. The Appeal to the Dead drew some tears, but only among a few of the elite. More would have been needed than a small parade, 1913 style, and a few flags at half-mast, with the civil and military authorities on display. Is it because the exuberant southern sun makes our thoughts seem out of place, or do we still have no feeling for a collective demonstration?

I have been thinking a great deal about this need for a rebirth of morale in our country, which has to come before its material rebuilding. Are our leaders thinking of this? I have sent the following memo to Pascot, who is still at the ministry and would never have received it through the normal hierarchical channels:

"Memorandum on the need for an initiative to rebuild morale among our troops before they are demobilized.

"It must be recognized that one of the reasons for our defeat was the lack of energy and enthusiasm among our troops, along with the effects of underhanded propaganda that generated a collective feeling of terror.

"According to our leaders, getting our country back on its feet needs to be part of a spiritual reformation. This reformation will be more difficult if the troops returning home do not have the will to take part in the national community's struggle for recovery.

"However, among all these soldiers who are about to be demobilized, the dominant mood in many areas reminds one of the psychosis of May 1917. The feeling of defeat, of which each one wants to declare himself individually innocent, is already being exploited by those who spread 'tall stories,' who are suggesting for example that, once again, the search for someone to blame will have consequences for no one except the rank and file. To be excessively hard on the troops, especially with measures intended to maintain order and discipline—measures that seem only to call for superficial signs of respect—goes exactly against what we are trying to achieve. Moreover, the inactivity to which our former soldiers are sometimes abandoned, and on the other hand the many work gangs that are being organized, have a dangerous influence on soldiers' morale, so that they become easy prey for agents of suspicious or foreign origin. Such distractions [. . .] as sports competitions for young recruits have no effect on those who have just been through weeks of pain; on the other hand, cinema or concert evenings are out of place at such a time, when many soldiers are worried about the fate of their families.

"What is important, for the sake of our country, is for the following to take place before demobilization:

1. to restore to every soldier, whatever role he played or errors he committed, his pride in his uniform;

2. to turn every former soldier into a factor for energy within the national community, a witness for unity among all social classes and all geographical and spiritual divisions, welded together in the face of the danger we confront.

"To accomplish this, one might suggest that in the weeks to come talks be organized in all military units, for which competent speakers easily can be found among the reserve troops still present (teachers, writers, civil servants, etc.) or officers in active service who have particular experience at the personal level (in the colonies, as explorers and geographers, on juries, etc.). Such meetings could be arranged immediately in the *depots* where isolated men gather and whose morale shows that they are in need of "recovery." But sending out reservists to countless service areas and small units would make it more practical to organize them by *arrondissement* [city district] or by canton. Single officers traveling around could quite usefully repeat the same speech several times a day.

"These talks, if they are to find interested listeners and be fruitful, should be entrusted to officers who have earned honors in the war, and should be conducted in the spirit of Marshal Lyautey's[3] teaching on the *social role* of an officer. They should be brief, lively, and accessible to all comers.

"Among the topics that could usefully be discussed, one might suggest the following—to which analogous topics could easily be added in respect of different regions, means of recruitment, where the recruits come from, or the social class, particular aptitudes, or military ranks of the contingents being educated:

1. France has never been crushed by a military defeat—Crécy, 1815–1871.

2. The spiritual mission of our country remains independent of the vicissitudes of history. After the fall of the *Ancien Régime*, spiritual expansion of human rights. After the Roman conquest, French humanism and the cathedrals. After 1870, colonial expansion.

3. Victory makes nations soft, defeat regenerates them. France under Napoleon the first; Germany in 1918; Turkey under Ataturk.

4. A nation that accepts a hierarchical structure is certain to endure. The need for accepted discipline. Freedom and scope of action. Solidarity within classes and provinces.

3. Since the publication of his article "Le rôle social de l'officier" ["The Socializing Role of an Officer"] in 1891, Marshal Hubert Lyautey had been considered a paragon of military virtue, and his ideas spread through almost the entire hierarchy of the French professional army. During the 1930s his ideas were highly popular in the right-wing Fustel Club of Coulanges. His famous article was republished in 1935 with a preface by General Maxime Weygand. Lyautey's treasured concept of the officer as educator of his troops was adopted by Georges Lamirand, who was named general secretary for youth affairs in Vichy's Ministry of Education. On Lyautey, see Guillaume de Tarde, *Lyautey, le chef en action* (Paris, 1959).

5. *The moral causes of military defeat.* Lack of preparation of young people. Desire just to enjoy life. Neglect of the idea of sacrifice. Collective cowardice. Decline of the nation's values. Neglect of spiritual discipline.

6. *Those who have been greatest in serving France have appeared during its darkest days.* Henri IV. Talleyrand. Thiers. Clemenceau. Pétain.

7. *Military occupation and peace.* Legal and economic conditions, 1814–1871. Occupation of the Rhineland (1918–1926). The armistice of today: reasons why liaison with the TC [Colonial Troops] is difficult; inevitable slowness to adapt."

After the military ceremony yesterday, I went to services at the little synagogue, which was full to bursting. In the prayer for our country, "France" was substituted for the word "Republic." I encountered friends evacuated from Paris and Lunéville. . . . French Jewry is enduring a particular kind of anguish. It accepts suffering along with everyone else but dreads the discrimination the enemy may demand. This fear makes me particularly dread the future, for myself and for my sons. But I still have confidence. France cannot accept just anything, and it is not for nothing that the bones of my family have mingled with its soil for more than a century—and that I have served in two wars. For my wife, my sons, and myself, I cannot imagine life in another climate; pulling up these roots would be worse than an amputation.

Details to be added to the scene at the square in Étampes, when we fled there on June 11: In the midst of the crowd, a car moving at walking pace: Valot, director of services for Alsace-Lorraine under the president of the Council. I haven't seen him since 1924, and he recognizes me. The authorities are powerless amidst this national migration. Things happen that prove certain propaganda persists: a Citroën car being driven along the edge of the ditch past the people walking, a man on the running board holding up a slate with a chalked notice: *Citroën Factory, evacuation orders canceled.* But no one pays any attention. On trucks passing through Antony, civilians are writing what they think is true: *TSF {French Radio} announces that Russia has declared war on Germany!* Reading this raises some people's hopes. But we soon find out that it's all wrong.

Just to whip up the crowd's anxiety to a peak, coming out of Longjumeau, a French flyer, after a rapid series of acrobatics, swoops down obliquely over the road as if he were going to strafe us. . . . Those with experience throw themselves face down in panic. A pretty bad joke.

Overall we find a certain dignity and good humor in these columns of refugees. People respect one another's impatience, and everyone waits without indulging in bad language. Around the rare filling stations the crush reaches epic levels, but with a little patience everyone's need can be met in the end—though the road is a total bottleneck for hours. There is even a special area for military convoys, and I manage to refuel my vehicles without waiting long. All I have to do is sign the requisition coupons.

July 20, 1940

Members of the military take revenge for the defeat in any way they can. . . . For the second time since I have been here in Nîmes I was working downtown today, responsible for four patrols under command of an officer whose mission is to monitor the conduct of soldiers and those frequenting the cafés. . . . It's impossible in practice to require a salute from these half-civilians, who have been demobilized or who were part of the retreating army. . . . As I was reflecting a few days ago, this way of approaching things does no good.

But the general in command of this department is a worthy descendant of the one who played billiards in 1870. With Paris under the conqueror's heel, he's here playing at being a warrant officer. The weather is torrid, and the men, wearing their helmets, are hot. . . . One of the patrols stopped for a bit in the middle of town. The general saw them resting there. The warrant officer in charge and the captain each got two days' arrest. When I was called into the department office to be informed of this, the colonel excused himself by telling me the general was "sick." But it really got on my nerves. Is this symbolic, on the eve of my discharge, to prove to me that the army in 1940 is the same as the one I thought was fine as a simple soldier in 1916? I'll talk to the colonel of my depot about it tomorrow, but I hope in any case to take my leave before being assigned to that duty again. Is it wrong of me to speak humanely to the men, and not to give my instructions to the warrant officers in a threatening tone?

It seems to me that I have been saved from being brutalized, because since Condom [in the Gers region of France] I have enough concentration to be able to read again. So I first reread *L'Aiglon* [*The Eaglet* by Edmond Rostand] (which this time was nothing but words to me; all that sort of thing strikes me as artificial these days); then I read *Uncle Tom's Cabin*; *Jean Villemeur*, a good novel about fishermen, by Roger Vercel; and finally Saurat's *Histoire des Religions* [*A History of Religions*], an excellent book, which helped to clarify my thinking. I am glad I have not adopted any religious practice. . . .

July 21, 1940

This morning I spoke to the colonel—and went up there especially on Sunday to do so—about my unfortunate experience yesterday with the general. The colonel, as a good colonial and good artilleryman, told me I was wrong to attach any importance to the matter. "Let these people worry about it themselves!" was his conclusion, so that's the end of the incident as far as I am concerned. I must be very sensitive indeed, to have let it disturb my night's rest.

Before the memories fade, I'll continue my summary of the events of that tragic week.

June 12: At dawn we left Étampes, which was crammed with people fleeing, both military and civilian, and had received machine-gun fire during the night, I was told. Had a glimpse of Senator Breton and his scholarly [. . .], an old man of eighty, who had slept in their car on the church square. The procession continued down the road. Chaplain,[4] my lieutenant, and my men, who had risen at dawn, were policing the road out of Étampes to keep busy while waiting for me. . . . No news at all. We succeeded in getting gasoline for our vehicles by showing my marching orders. For a time our road ran alongside the railroad where convoys of locomotives were passing, fleeing the capital. Next to it the road was black with cars, moving in five lines at walking pace. Fortunately no military convoy was trying to go up that way in the other direction! It really felt like the collapse of everything—absolutely no police, not a single officer.

At noon, six kilometers out of Orléans, to which all access was completely blocked, I had the idea of bearing left, falling back to the Loire River toward Meung. An excellent thought. The road was free of cars. We had lunch at Saran, thanks to the D system [possibly a reference to the Allied D plan whereby the French army was to defend the area between the Dyle River and the Meuse] and the kindness of a group of British soldiers. From there we took the road along the Loire, where we found little congestion. We stopped at Mer, where I made a brief visit to my elderly aunt Lucie and my cousin Marcel's wife, who were surprised at my pessimism. . . . We crossed the Loire at Mer. Then we drove through Blois, and after nightfall arrived at Candé-sur-Loire where I caught up with Commandant Pascot and the Eighth Headquarters people. They breathed easier on seeing us, because the colonel in charge was biting his nails about leaving us behind in Paris. (I found out later that the truck assigned to us had been used to move his wine cellar and personal baggage and had been

4. This officer had become a close friend of RRL's when they worked together in Edouard Herriot's office in the 1920s. See especially RRL's letter of October 10, 1943, to Brener, below.

the first to arrive at Candé. Such a mentality on the part of a high-ranking leader explains a lot of things.)

The office, which had been evacuated to Candé nine months earlier, had not had time to attend to lodgings; without protest from Commandant Pascot, Chaplain and I spent the night outdoors. . . . Finally a mattress was found for each of us in an abandoned house, where several NCOs (non-commissioned officers) had made themselves at home. (At a little inn the next day I managed to find a small room with running water; I paid plenty for it. The following day Quartermaster Le Cogniec was going to give me his room in a painter's home, but I decided not to take it for just one night.)

June 13: Waiting at Candé, where the offices were waiting, expecting a further evacuation. The news reports grew worse and worse. Fighting along the Loire was expected. Even on the smaller roads there were cars and military convoys passing day and night. The cadets from the officers' school at Fontainebleau, riding on armored supply carriers, got as far as Poitiers. Surveillance by the Boche aircraft was beginning. The other directors' offices of our ministry and the general staff of the army were billeted in all the villages around us. They were having the company from Madagascar dig a trench in front of the chateau.

June 14: Waited all day. The village children were being evacuated. In the evening, orders came for the commandant, Chaplain (as a younger officer), and the lower-ranking officers on active duty to be sent to the Courtine Camp. They were to leave at 2 A.M. from the Montrichard railway station, twelve or fifteen km away. Chaplain was furious! I took over command of the technical section, which was being evacuated, along with the headquarters staff, to Bordeaux-Songe the next morning. The officers were in a hurry to get moving during the night. I knew it was wiser to leave by daylight, and, having my own means of transport, decided to get a good night's sleep before departing. At two in the morning we were awakened by circling aircraft that were strafing the entire region. I stayed in bed, feeling sorry for those who had to be on their way.

June 15: We took our departure, and, having complete freedom to plan the route, I chose roads that I knew, avoiding national highways. We were to spend the night at Bellac, to the astonishment of Simone and my dear boys. A unit heavier than ours was not to leave until the next day, so I was given gasoline. My men were more devoted to me than ever. The roads were a little less crowded. Horse-drawn carriages with rustic loads predominated as far as the Indre River. For lunch at Châtillon we had great difficulty in finding provisions; the bistro was being run by Leonard, the former valet of Robert de Rothschild. Fifteen km before arriving there, we lifted onto the truck a young woman who had been wounded and took her as far as the village to rejoin her companions—they were a group of workers who had fled Paris by bicycle. Versailles and St.-Germain had been taken. Orléans was already in flames.

We passed through Le Blanc and Le Dorat and arrived at Bellac in time for dinner. The town was full of convoys. What joy, tinged with melancholy, for Simone and me! How I wanted to take my sons and my wife with me, since I feared from now on anything might happen to them. . . . But they were still far away from the Loire here, and I swore to come back and get them if necessary. I was beginning to believe in our defeat and to expect an armistice, for I could see that from a military standpoint we were at the end of our rope. There was no more going forward, and the retreat was disorganized. I found lodging for my men at the hospital, since refugees were already sleeping in the streets.

June 16: A very emotional goodbye. I was reminded of my mother's dreaded farewell kiss whenever I left after my holidays, years ago. . . . The sight of my little Tony was heartrending for me, and I cut the farewells short. . . . No more convoys on the road. A pleasant lunch at Vayres, where there were neither refugees nor other soldiers. We moved on rapidly to Riberac, where I stopped to greet Madame Pascot. Dinner was at Montpont, where the mayor tracked down a room for me, dirty but well aired. My men found a relatively comfortable barn for the night. There were more and more refugees' cars on the road.

June 17: By way of Libourne and the bridge over the Dordogne River, we arrived in Bordeaux. For the first time since Paris I was asked to show my papers. The streets were completely jammed with military and civilian convoys. But the sun was shining and the shopkeepers' accents inspired confidence. . . . The office in the square was totally disorganized. I had to report there, but they couldn't confirm that the Eighth Headquarters were at Songe, twelve km south of the city, at the Colonials' camp. As they assured me that I would find no place to stay and nothing to eat in Bordeaux, I decided to go on—after lunch, and after a threatening storm. My vehicles were parked in front of the market. Lunch with my men in a little dump of a café nearby, where we could hear TSF [radio] through the open window. Pétain, president of the Council, was requesting an armistice. . . . It was terrible, but despite this crushing blow we breathed easier! We could hardly realize it was true. . . . We reached Songe by daylight. I was given lodgings in a dirty room, where another officer soon joined me, but the bed was clean and there was (running) water. . . . My men found whatever they could. I was given two offices for our section, but we waited to unpack anything. The night was less feverishly hot, but the planes were coming as far as Bordeaux.

June 18–19: Waiting in the camp at Songe. Not a word from Simone. Fighting still continuing. . . . I was beginning to worry about my wife and children. No traffic allowed on the roads—so I couldn't think of going to Bellac to fetch them—and there were also my parents-in-law and Jacques.[5] . . . I had to hope the negotiations would be concluded before Bellac was within the range of

5. Jacques Lambert was RRL's elder brother.

operations. . . . I remembered my mother's anxiety during the other war. I couldn't think any more.

June 20: Commandant Pascot and Chaplain—the latter to take over a unit in the camp—came back from the Courtine camp, which had been hastily evacuated. I turned over the command of the section to Pascot again. I was happy to see them, because the solitude weighed heavily on me. Pascot shared my anxiety, for Riberac in his case. Chaplain had left his wife in Paris. . . .

June 21: Waiting in a somber mood. The enemy was obviously dragging out the negotiations in order to occupy three-quarters of the country. I didn't even think to be critical of the repulsive filth of the camp, the swarms of flies or the thirty thousand Senegalese for whom there were no weapons. More and more convoys of refugees were arriving. We were beginning to complain about our headquarters being assigned to such a crowded camp, and we waited apprehensively for announcements on the TSF.

June 22: Day of most dreadful anxiety for me. At 2 P.M. it was announced that the Boche had reached Châtillon on the Indres, at 9 P.M. they were in Poitiers. What was Simone doing? If only she didn't get the idea of fleeing with the children on these roads—but I couldn't sleep for a second, going over the dangers in my mind: bombing, inability to get provisions, fighting in the streets, followed by occupation. . . . I didn't want my wife and sons placed in danger on the very eve of the armistice.

June 23: At 8:30 A.M. I heard that the armistice with Germany had been signed but would not take effect until Italy had also signed. What of Bellac? Nothing else interested me, and I didn't have a word of news. At 6:30 P.M. we heard that Rochfort and Royan were under occupation. . . . With a map, Pascot tried to convince me that, from Poitiers, the Boche would prefer to push on to the sea and avoid the mountains of the Massif Central. . . . We were now the ones who would be in danger if the signing did not take place. I admitted I would prefer that. But, together with my men, I studied the roads to the west through the forest, in case we were threatened. Otherwise grumbling was beginning in the camp. Chaplain was leaving with the detachments of local troops.

June 24: Evacuation of the camp continued. The colonel in charge had gone to Montauban, as usual running off ahead of everyone else. Expecting to leave at any moment, we burned all the files no longer needed. The camp stores were opened, and everything they had was distributed. It was the disorder of defeat. The newspapers announced the signing of the armistice with Italy. So the next day the killing would be over.

June 25: The hostilities ended at midnight. A national day of mourning was declared. What had become of our joy of November 11, 1918? Even if the Boche were in Bellac—which I doubted, wishfully perhaps—Simone would be breathing easier, whatever our anxieties for the future. I was lucky to hear the news that, as of June 23, Bellac was still free.

June 26: I left with the commandant in a Simca to find lodgings for the heavy units around Agen, since our camp was included in the zone expected to be occupied. We had a very pleasant trip by way of Casteljaloux and the valley of the Garonne River, where we saw the mess left behind by military convoys.

(We were charmed with the Simca. Two days earlier, eight cars of this model had arrived in the camp, all [. . .] with drivers from depot 321. The factory [. . .] had to evacuate and gave them to Rueil. They arrived at Songe ahead of the depot, which had reached [. . .]. Since it did not follow, it was surely taken prisoner.)

We looked in vain for lodgings in Agen for the Eighth Headquarters. What were the general and the prefect thinking of? . . . There was neither [. . .]. The town had been invaded by refugees and military personnel. There were six thousand men at the general artillery depot, where the colonel invited us to have coffee with him, at [. . .]—invaded by pilots and their families—where we met by chance. By chance as well we obtained a room with two beds for Pascot and me. [. . .] to telephone more to the south, in the Gers, at [. . .]—Pascot told me there are plenty of chateaux in the region. . . . The sub-prefect, whom I thought I knew, was a charming fellow. At 6:30 P.M. he asked us for an hour to find something. I called him back at eight and he said come back tomorrow morning. . . . We notified Songe and slept [. . .] . . . The streets were full of trucks inhabited by soldiers of all the different armed forces.

June 27: We arrived in Condom, a delightful town. The sub-prefect, Dubieck, received Pascot and me like old friends. He was flattered to have an inquiry from the ministry. We found everything we needed there but had a little more difficulty with rooms for the officers. By persistence, not to mention shouting, I obtained eight beds in the hospital, which was empty of patients, for the lieutenants and second lieutenants. . . . Pascot was to sleep at the mayor's house, the quartermaster at the subprefect's house, and I on Agen Road in a green part of town, at the home of the sub-prefect's secretary, who had three small children. . . . The Eighth Headquarters offices were in the chateau of Monteleone on the same street. The officers, who arrived at noon, were rather astonished at our success. We would have been better off if gentlemen of the health service—from nurses to the colonel—and gentlemen of the air force hadn't taken up all the free houses in the town and for twenty km around it for their families and girlfriends. . . . If I hadn't had Tony along, I could have done the same! . . . The Boche would say that our military rearguard all had tribes [*smalah*] like Abd al-Qadir's [the Algerian who led the opposition to the French invasion of Algeria from 1830–1847]. . . .

June 28–29 to July 1: Waiting and resting at Condom. I took my meals with Pascot, who was really becoming a friend. We talked about sending the reserve officers, who were to be demobilized, back to the depots of their various branches. . . . I was now receiving letters again, which reassured me.

July 2: Quartermaster Le Cogniec invited me to lunch. I was planning to leave for Montauban with a commander from the First Headquarters office who was at loose ends like me.

July 3: I packed my tin trunk without sadness. I would be happy to return to this area, so pleasant and fertile. The sub-prefect had spent the previous evening with me. We have friends in common and similar ways of thinking.

July 4: Left at 8 A.M. by car for Montauban, by way of Lectoure, a picturesque route. Besides myself there were four other officers. Four "marines," three of whom were to leave us at Narbonne to go to Rivesaltes, the fourth to head for Marseilles. The other member of the artillery, Commandant Souder, had already left the previous evening. We had a quick lunch at the buffet restaurant at Montauban. I took the first train to Nîmes via Toulouse and Béziers. Arriving at Nîmes, the office in the square assigned me lodgings at the Hotel Terminus; the room had no window but a soft bed and running water. Like Agen, the city was overrun with people.

July 5: I reported to Depot 55, Colonel Blancart. From then on it was the tedious life of an officer waiting to be demobilized. For the sake of order, I was assigned to the PHR [?]. From the 8th, the day on which the first demobilization measures were announced, I stayed at the Hotel Lisita, in a room facing the street [. . .] . . . On the 9th I finally had a letter directly from Simone. . . . On the 10th, Colonel Grünfelder—now a general since the day before—visiting the depot, told me I would not be released until the end of the month, and this was later confirmed. So I went on waiting, not very patiently.

July 24, 1940

I heard this morning in our quarters that I would probably be free in three or four days. . . . What luck! I shall finally be back again with my dear wife and my three darlings, Tony, whom I hardly know, and the two big rascals. The future may look dark, the ordeals to come ominous enough, but I feel I have the courage to face anything, if only I am with my little family. I am not going to close this diary yet, because I can see that it still will be useful for getting things clear in my own mind.

Bellac, August 14, 1940

Through friends of my cousin Sasha Krinsky, who lives in the apartment below us, I discovered that the Boche have sealed my apartment [in Paris]. I assume this is so that I will be obliged to report to the German authorities in case I return to Paris. I can't yet envision that in fact all our furniture, our memorabilia, everything resulting from twenty-five years of study and of caring for our home, have come to naught for us. . . . I don't accept it, and that is why I am not yet outraged.

To forget my own worries I think about the cataclysm that has come upon my country by surprise. By surprise—that is all there is to explain it, apart from any political passion. We were a people put to sleep by censorship; we couldn't understand it. We were conquered by Germany in the course of ten days. May 10: Belgium was invaded. May 11: they broke through the Ardennes in Belgium. May 12: bombing of the roads in Belgium, with fleeing civilians hindering troop movements. New tactic: target first the nerve centers from which morale and motivation stem. May 13: the Germans crossed the Meuse [the Belgian border with France]. May 14: capitulation of Holland; motorized divisions were advancing on all fronts without waiting for the foot soldiers. May 15: the Corap Army [the Ninth Army under General André Corap] was devastated. An immense gap was opened between France and the armies in the north. Defeat was now inevitable. In France we were told nothing of the truth about this. May 16: the gap was widening. Our leaders no longer had the initiative anywhere. May 17: "German vehicles are advancing along the roads of France with their tops open and men in black overseas caps playing the harmonica" (*Paris-Soir*, August 10, byline xxx). May 18: the Germans made a leap to the Somme. May 19: a torrent of refugees clogged the roads. The northern army was cut off. We could no longer be fighting for anything but our honor. Why didn't we ask for an armistice on May 11?

Marseilles, October 2, 1940

One of the most depressing memories of my life. This morning I read in the newspaper: "The Council of Ministers continued study and finalization of the *Statut* on the Jews. . . ." So it is possible that within a few days I shall see my citizenship reduced, and that my sons, who are French by birth, culture, and faith, will find themselves brutally and cruelly cast out of the French community. . . . Is this possible? I cannot believe it. France is no longer France. I repeat to myself that Germany is in charge here, trying still to excuse this offense against an entire history—but I cannot yet realize that it is true.

Luchon, October 9, 1940

I am in Luchon on an assignment for the refugee committee, since I have again taken up social work in order to earn my children's daily bread.

Here I found about a thousand unfortunate Jews from Holland and Belgium, in poverty and anguish, but the future for them looks even more fearful than the present.

The papers this morning published the decree, signed by Pétain, that has abrogated the Crémieux Decree.[6] The Jews of Algeria are no longer French citizens. . . . The Marshal has dishonored himself. What shame and what infamy! In Algeria a father who lost his son in the war is no longer a French citizen,

6. The law of October 7, 1940 (published the next day in the *Journal officiel* [*JO*, sometimes referred to as the *Officiel*], the government publication listing new acts, laws, etc.), abrogated the Crémieux decree of October 24, 1870, which granted to almost forty thousand Algerian Jews full rights as French citizens. It was named after Adolphe Crémieux, the indefatigable defender of Jewish emancipation, who was then justice minister in Léon Gambetta's Government of National Defense and was instrumental in preparing the law.

because he is Jewish. . . . So this is the armistice with honor. I am incapable of realizing that such an injustice is done, I am so ashamed of my country. Ah! if I didn't have a wife, three sons, and graves to care for on this soil that is still French, how well I would know the way to action, to revolt and struggle for what makes life precious!

Since Nîmes I have read quite a few books, a bit of everything without being very choosy or methodical, to keep my mind alert; Jean-Pierre Maxence's *Histoire de dix ans* [*Ten Years of History*], a remarkably lucid critique and a living testimony to be preserved; Paul Claudel's *Ainsi donc encore une fois* [*Thus, once again*] . . . some poems of '14 and '39 collected in a brochure, courageous lines that the censors missed; Jean Schlumberger's *Stefan the Proud*, a critique of military heroics, in the form of a Yugoslavian fable, but quite literary, quite cold; a work without passion and too coldly composed. Marcel Aymé's *La Table aux crevés* [*The Table for the Dead*] is a good, realistic novel. Colonel Ordon's *Le Siège de Varsovie* [*The Siege of Warsaw*] gives an arresting picture of heroism and of destitution. When I think of my friends in London just now, I am a little ashamed of the cowardice in Paris. J. J. Tharaud, *Quand Israël n'est plus roi* [*When Israel Is No Longer King*]: memories of Hitler's rise to power in 1933; the attempt to make the story colorful deprives it of the slight shudder the humane reader expects. André Maurois, *Voyage au pays des articoles* [*A Voyage to the Island of the Articoles*] is an excellent, brief story after the manner of Swift. And finally, Louis Marlio's *Dictature ou liberté* [*Dictatorship or Freedom*] is a book flowing with the juices (a sequel to his *Sort du Capitalisme* [*The Fate of Capitalism*]) which can help to understand these terrible times of ours and yet, in spite of all, offers hope.

Marseilles, October 19, 1940

I found out yesterday morning from a press release, dreadful forewarning of injustice, and yesterday evening from the text itself printed in the *Officiel*, what the *Statut des Juifs* says.[7] The Marshal and his team, on Hitler's orders, have my person and the future of my children in their hands. . . . The Jews of France, even those who died for our country, have never been assimilated. Racism has become the law of the new state. What boundless disgrace! I cannot yet take in this denial of justice and scientific truth. . . . All my illusions are crumbling around me. I am afraid not only for myself but for my country. This cannot last, it's not possible. But in history this 1940 abolition of the Declaration of Human Rights will look like a new Revocation of the Edict of Nantes. . . . I shall never leave this country for which I risked my life, but can my sons live here if they are not allowed to choose freely what career to follow? Because of my blood I am no longer allowed to write, I am no longer an officer in the army. . . . If I were a secondary school or university teacher, I should be dismissed because I am a Jew! I cannot believe it yet. . . .

Two hypotheses are possible: either Germany will be conquered by the Anglo-American forces, and humanity will be saved; or, if Germany wins, a century-long night will descend on Europe. Judaism will maintain itself, as it did during the Middle Ages. But how we shall suffer from undeservedly becoming second-class citizens, after all the freedoms we have enjoyed. . . . Where is freedom of thought now, in France, where is it sleeping, the [. . .] of Descartes and Hugo?

Yesterday evening I wept, like a man who is suddenly abandoned by the wife who has been the one love of his life, the one guiding light of his thinking, the one leader whom he has followed in his actions.

7. The *Statut des Juifs (Statute on the Jews*—herein, *Statut)* was passed October 3, 1940, but was not published in the *JO* until the 18th. Drawn up by the Vichy government, which defined the status of Jews by race (anyone with two grandparents of the Jewish race), the law banned Jews from holding public office and public posts in culture and communications. The *Statut* also provided for a *numerus clausus* on Jews in the practice of the professions. See Michael R. Marrus and Robert O. Paxton, *Vichy France and the Jews* (New York, 1981), pp. 3–21.

November 6, 1940

A friend wrote to me: You don't pass judgment on your mother, even when she is being unfair. You suffer and you wait. Thus we, Jews of France, are supposed to bow our heads and suffer. I agree. I still cannot believe that all this is definite, final. Even in the Free Zone we are living under German rule. The press is being told what to do. No free spirit has any way of being heard. The war goes on. Let us wait but, while never ceasing to be French people, let us accept this ordeal and never renounce our Judaism in any way.

I have read a collection of Armand Lunel's stories, *Occasions* [*Opportunities*]—quite artificial and quite removed from real life, and a facile book by Armand Robriquet, *Daily Life in the French Revolution*. This picturesque view of prosaic details helps me understand our time a bit better; the restrictions under which my wife suffers (very little actually) in getting food for the children, the fact that no oil or potatoes are to be had in the market, etc. That is what defeat in war means for the *vulgum pecus.*[8]

And the official radio broadcasts of my country continue to preach hatred of Jews. . . . All those formulations, current in Germany since 1933, have now been adopted in France. Is it possible to believe a word of it? What would I do if I were a Christian? I think I should still have the same thoughts, the same loathings, and the same hopes.

It is symbolic to see the censors cut out several sentences about Descartes from a purely literary article.

December 20, 1940

If I had carried on with my studies and become a university or secondary school teacher, today I should find myself dismissed as an unsavory character, despite having served in two wars, because of my Jewish background. It's beyond belief.

8. Ordinary mortals, the ignorant.

I have received from Commandant Pascot, my former boss, to whom I had written of my sorrow on the day after the *Statut* was published, an admirable letter which I must copy out here: "My dear friend, your letter—which took a while to reach me, since I have been transferred a number of times—*moved me deeply*. I am very much with you in my thoughts, my dear friend, in the painful circumstances you are enduring. You may be certain of this, both you and your family. If anything can be a comfort to you, then let it be this fact, and please also know that we are many who take this attitude toward you and sympathize with you in your grief. Consider this law that affects you as nothing definitive, that it does not correspond to the deep sentiments of the French people, which are liberal and humane. Have patience. This only increases the friendship I feel for you. I am thinking of you and your dear children, whom I should be so happy to see again. Please excuse this brief letter. I hardly know what more to say on such a painful subject. With very best regards from your devoted friend. . . ." Commandant Jep Pascot of the Colonial Artillery has been made assistant to Borotra[9] at the National Sports Authority.

I have been putting more emotion and energy than ever into reflecting on the Jewish question since this *Statut* was decreed; it has really shaken up my inner life. . . . It is so true that I am still completely French in my heart, in my mind, as a family man, in the love I had for my mother and that ties me now to my sons! But this is precisely what makes this such a tragic situation and makes me doubt the future, even though I am still convinced that this represents only an eclipse, an interruption, of the freedoms that are necessary for modern man. . . . I am French in my

9. Jean Borotra, a tennis champion from the Basque country, was brought into the Ministry for Youth, the Family, and Sports in July 1940 by his Basque compatriot Jean Ybarnégaray. Four months later, when the ministries were reorganized, Borotra's department was absorbed into the Education Ministry, and he was in charge of general education, physical education, and school sports. His moral reeducation program through sports was closely monitored by the Germans, and when Laval returned to power in April 1942, Borotra was forced to resign. He appears to have retained some of his ideas until at least the 1970s. See his remarks on the subject in *Le gouvernement de Vichy 1940–1942: Institutions et politiques* (Paris, 1972), pp. 285–288.

culture, in my blood, and by inclination. I am being made less than that. It hurts me terribly, but it makes me suffer even more when I realize that there are truly stateless Jews, both at the top and the bottom of the social ladder. The unfortunate pariahs who escaped from eastern ghettos and wandered about central Europe, who are now wandering or are interned in France, have never succeeded in becoming integrated into the nation where they have been temporary guests. They are still living on the margins of our society. On the other hand the leading capitalists, who are kings of their banks and industries, felt like internationalists and made a cult of wealth, of the Golden Calf, of "titles," rather than becoming attached to any soil. . . . If I was an internationalist it was in a dream of humanitarianism, it was my Judeo-Christian culture, catholic in the etymological sense of the word. But through the bones of my ancestors, which have been mingled for more than a century with this ground, I feel closer to the French serfs, to French artists and French writers, than to any others. So I shall have to suffer and to wait.

I have been traveling quite a bit in the past few weeks: Perpignan—Pau—Toulouse—Gaillac—Nîmes. I have read a great deal: Edouard Herriot, *At the Wellsprings of Liberty* (how moving for today!); François Mauriac, *Thérèse Desqueyroux* (a novel of the first order); Robert Aron, *La fin de l'après-guerre* [*The End of the Postwar Period*] (cruel truths. I am still a socialist in the humane and constructive sense); Alfred Fabre-Luce, *Journal de la France* [*The News from France*] (a first attempt to explain our defeat; truths and prejudices in detail); Dostoevsky, *The Double* (Slavic psychology surprises and shocks me a little); Marcel Aymé, *Maison basse* [*A Low House*] (to read on vacation); Francis Jammes, *De tout temps à jamais* [*From All Time, Forever*] (a lyricism both simple and profound, which washes away the impurities of daily life).

1941

January 26, 1941

In recent weeks I have read André Maurois' *The Thought-Reading Machine*, an excellent story after the manner of Swift; R. P. de Maillardoz, *Le decalogue de l'autorité paternelle* [*Ten Commandments for Fatherly Authority*], a little educational Catholic breviary, not very profound but a clever presentation of elementary truths (useful in my attitude toward the demands, needs, or affections of my sons); René Benjamin, *Charles Maurras*, rather feeble and superficial, so that frankly one can admire neither Maurras nor Benjamin.

February 17, 1941

A historical fact to remember. Italy "decided to break with France, when the Italian ambassador in Paris communicated to Rome the import of General Weygand's pessimistic report to Mr. Paul Reynaud, which he [the ambassador] had found out *through an indiscretion*" (*Journal de Genève*, February 2, 1941).

At the most critical moments in every country, there are indiscretions, or leaks, which amount to betrayals. Who could have betrayed this military secret? A minister, or perhaps a stenographer? Is democratic government responsible for this? I don't think so; it's much more likely that those responsible are men in power today who, even in the middle of a war, have been flirting with our enemies, declared or potential.

February 24, 1941

I've been told that on the day the *Statut des Juifs* was published the government spokesman, who receives the foreign press every day at the "evacuated" Quai d'Orsay in Vichy, answered a question from an American journalist by saying, "The *Statut* was neither demanded nor imposed on us by the occupying authorities. The government takes full responsibility for it. It was decided upon, after mature reflection, in response to the needs of the nation." It was useful to identify this historical point, and we shall know enough not to forget it. It appears that this comment, when received in New York, was considered sufficient cause for demonstrations and protest meetings. Poor France!

Thus I have been led to wonder, what are the causes of such an iniquity, what are the deep reasons why an armistice regime would deny, in such a brutal fashion, a humane tradition going back more than a century; for a soldier to forget the innumerable sacrifices, for thinkers to forget [Henri] Bergson and a whole galaxy of fine minds. . . . Since our calamity in June 1940, the Jews of France have had neither the leaders nor the defenders they deserve. The spiritual leaders have lost their voices and their courage.[1] . . . And the defense began too late and was ineffective, because defeat disrupted everything. . . . Let us look for the causes:

1. The moral influence of German propaganda, through imitation. Without admitting it, people are adopting the conquerors' methods without stooping so low as to accept any of their myths that are condemned by science.

1. RRL refers to the fact that numerous leaders and well-known community figures had fled France following its defeat, leaving the Jewish community disabled. He returns to this theme several times in the diary. See, for example, his comments on Helbronner below, November 30, 1941.

2. The financial activities of the German propaganda services, which have succeeded in poisoning the minds of certain journalists, consciously or unconsciously, during the past eight years by resurrecting and distributing the pernicious works of Céline, Chateaubriand, the *Gringoire* campaigns [a nationalist, anti-Semitic journal], the "Rothschild" and "Mandel" slogans, etc.

3. The explicit demands of *Action française*, which for the past forty years has been calling for discrimination against Jews in France. (Charles Maurras is said to be the Marshal's counselor in matters of doctrine.)

4. Certain facts that unfortunately have seemed to justify an apparently moderate racism: the actions of Léon Blum and the Popular Front, which were called Jewish; the presence of too many Jews in the press agencies (Robert Bollack), the film industry, banking, and behind the scenes politically, and, it must be said, their inborn exuberance; the too-hasty immigration of autocrats; the high percentage of Jewish names among citizens naturalized since 1918 (as a result of immigration from central Europe).

5. The inability of the French administration, despite all warnings received from those who were thinking clearly, to complete a *Statut des Etrangers* [Law on Foreigners] and to have an immigration policy. . . .

To sum up, France has taken revenge on the Jews for the [French] blindness and inability to understand, since the more or less disguised closing of the United States to immigration from Europe, that France could profit from these human resources if it would manage and select them—before assimilating them.

I have read *Bubu of Montparnasse* by Charles-Louis Philippe. How [. . .], and sometimes artificial, this naturalism appears to me, despite certain pages that are brilliant and moving. . . .

February 25, 1941

Another voice is heard on the subject of the *Statut*. Helbronner,[2] vice president of the Consistory (and who, during the first war,

2. Jacques Helbronner, born in Paris in 1873, the son of a well-known attorney, became a member of the Council of State in 1927. During the thirties he was involved in

belonged to Painlevé's cabinet, which nominated Foch and Pétain [as marshals of France]), is said to have received assurance from the Marshal that this *Statut* already had been imposed on France through secret clauses in the armistice treaty. A possibility, but not a certainty. In that case, why such methodical severity in implementing it, why the gratuitous comments, and why these odious campaigns? Let us hope that history will provide us with the whole truth on this point.

I remember the stories about food shortages at certain times during the French Revolution. We are living in a comparable period. Food is becoming scarce, and I wonder what working-class people are doing, and families who don't have much money. Part of the population no longer has enough to eat. With the ration cards and the complementary tickets, every housewife must become an accountant. Simone has to be at the butcher's at 7 A.M., and for three weeks this winter my children had no fresh meat to eat. Yesterday I paid two hundred francs for a turkey. No more butter, seldom any eggs, and, above all, no potatoes! In front of tripe and butcher shops and the grocers, the lines are lengthening, looking like the engravings of the siege of Paris in 1871. If Simone didn't have a priority card for a large family (the only gift we have had from the new regime), she would have to spend whole days just waiting in line. On Saturday she managed to get two eggs, and for this meager ration women were waiting in line for two hours. Housewives and the women in the market are be-

---

Jewish communal affairs and upheld the position of the more conservative elements in French society on the refugee question. He and Lambert were at loggerheads on this issue, and their mutual animosity intensified as the refugee problem grew during the 1930s. This split took on an even sharper dimension during the war. After assuming the presidency of the Central Consistory in 1941, Helbronner saw himself as the representative of French Jews and continued to maintain close relationships with high-ranking French officials. A personal acquaintance of Pétain, Helbronner met him often during the first two years of the war. Helbronner was arrested on October 19, 1943, and sent to Drancy, from where he and his wife were deported to Auschwitz a month later. For the thirties, see Vicki Caron, *Uneasy Asylum: France and the Jewish Refugee Crisis, 1933–1942* (Stanford, 1999), passim; for extensive treatment of Helbronner's activity during the war, see Simon Schwarzfuchs, *Aux prises avec Vichy: Histoire politique des Juifs de France (1940–1944)* (Paris, 1998).

ginning to grumble. The Boche requisition two-thirds of what is for sale even in the Free Zone. And our population, despite official TSF broadcasts, does not think for a second of deploring the English blockade, though we are the first to suffer.

Yesterday on the Canebière [the main street in Marseilles] I met a group of *Compagnons de France.*[3] They were trying to sing together. . . . What a pale imitation of the German youth organization—no order, no harmony or discipline, no collective faith! The French are still individualists (and therein lies my only hope). The variety of their uniforms, which ought to have been identical for these fifty young men, their hairy legs, dirty hands, badly shaved cheeks—all made this manifestation of the new order a sorry spectacle. Another sad sight was a demonstration on Sunday by the Veterans Legion in the streets of Marseilles. A regime that looks to the street for its mystique will not be able to build anything lasting.

March 7, 1941

I received by a dependable messenger the following letter from Chaplain in Paris. Dated March 3, it is a most moving document, made to give me confidence in the future.

"My dear friend, I am happy to jump at this opportunity to come, or rather, alas! to send, and have a chat with you. I don't need to tell you how impatiently I'm looking forward to seeing you, but we'll have to content ourselves with more modest pleasures.

"I surely hope you and your family are as well as can be expected in these fateful times. As for us, things go on as usual, if I

3. The *Compagnons de France* was the first official youth movement to be established after the debacle, in July 1940. The movement was intended to revive France, both materially and in terms of morale, through aid to refugees and prisoners. Because of its emphasis on regeneration, it was banned in the Occupied Zone by the German authorities. From its inception, Compagnons was both anti-liberal and anti-capitalist, but it repudiated totalitarianism; its membership reflected every nuance of the political spectrum. See R. Hervé, *Les Compagnons de France* (Paris, 1965); Halls, *Youth of Vichy France*, Chapter 10.

dare say so. One of the things I still enjoy the most is speaking of you with people who [. . .] you.

"I don't know what life is like for you, but here it is difficult, provisions are hard to find, undependable and available at odd times of day. We have no meat or almost none, no potatoes, no fish, no pastry, and our bread rations have just been tightened. Since the beginning of winter I have been able to get [. . .] kilos of coal, so that, warmly [. . .] Diderot-style in my old bathrobe, [. . .] enjoying oyster-bread when there was nothing else. This must be the revenge of that poor Princess of Lamballe,[4] and we have gotten used to sweet buns.

"But these are minor matters; what is essential is that the people of France, in our captive zone, are neither collaborating nor fraternizing. We keep our distance from the Germans, and one even sees women with them only on exceptional occasions. And Déat[5] himself is forced to admit that collaboration isn't productive (when I think that, in my innocence, before the 'flood' of course, I used to defend this guy in our conversations! *sacrosancta simplicitas!*) His Rassemblement National Populaire is a fiasco, the trade union types are keeping out of it, and the fact that the former chief of the 'Cagoulards' ['hooded men'] has joined will not make the RNP more attractive to the masses. To the ex-socialists Déat is a renegade, and to the civil servants Laval is still the man who brought us deflation. So Déat is trying to regain a 'platform,'

4. Marie Antoinette's dear friend who was eventually killed during the French Revolution in the days of the Terror.

5. Marcel Déat had a lopsided political career with peaks and valleys. With only a village grammar school education, he eventually taught philosophy in a high school in Reims before being elected to the French parliament, the Chamber of Deputies, and appointed minister for aviation in 1936. Politically he evolved from socialism to an authoritarian neo-socialism, which led him to propose to Pétain, in 1940, that a single-party system be established. After some political maneuvers against Laval, Déat was arrested in December 1940 but was imprisoned for only several weeks. A month later he founded the RNP (Rassemblement National Populaire [National People's Union]), which was strongly tainted with a form of National Socialism. He remained on the periphery of political developments during the war until Laval appointed him minister for labor in 1944.

and I'm afraid that some imprudence of the government, however well meant, may yet give it to him. Anti-clericalism is being stirred up again, and one of the most recent headlines in the *Oeuvre* announced, 'Anti-clericalism [is] not dead.'

"Working-class youth are hostile toward the invaders, an attitude apparently due to a fresh upsurge of activity by revolutionary communism; as for the youth who are at school, at least four-fifths of them favor the actions of de Gaulle, and all the reasoning in the world won't change that. Even anti-Semitism doesn't sway them, and at this age, so characterized by untrammeled generosity, students find it scandalous that a [French] Jew who has served in one of the two wars should be stripped of his honor by the occupation authorities while a Greek, Hungarian, or Bulgarian Jew thrives under the protection of his legation or embassy.

"The Germans themselves are rather painfully surprised by this apparent indifference which [. . .] more or less plainly a vigorous hostility. They [. . .] that they would bring Paris to its knees with their rigorous measures, and thus have not taken long in losing all the [. . .] which their initial conduct had gained them. They are searching even harder in Paris for the names of those whom they then make [. . .] by force of arms, since their unhappy experience at the time [. . .] of Bonsergent,[6] when they had to call out the entire police force of Paris to stand guard over their posted notices day and night for a week.

"In any case, perfect unanimity has been achieved against the Italians, and I think that even the Germans are informed of our opinion. The problems in Africa have, moreover, led to offers of work for yours truly, glowing with all the "technical" prestige of the S.T.T.C. [a department serving the colonial troops?]. I turned down these flattering proposals and, following the courageous example of Thiers, have returned to my cherished studies.

6. An engineer by trade, Jacques Bonsergent was the first Parisian civilian to be killed by the German occupying forces in 1940.

"Speaking of the S.T.T.C., you said you had seen Jep. I wrote to him but haven't had any reply. I would be happy to know what has become of him and the work he was given to do.

"I would also very much like to have news of the second lieutenant who came through our place like a meteor before going to join our former director.

"As for us, please know that any news of you is precious to me, and that you can count on my firmest friendship toward you always, under all circumstances. [. . .]—it's a shock to your modesty, there is only one voice [. . .] counts when the marines who were in contact [. . .] you get together.

"Please present my compliments to Madame Lambert, and best regards to your family, and be assured that you have a warm and true friend in R. Chaplain."

And he gave me an address in Lyon at which I can reply to him.

This letter did me good, more than I can possibly say. This is the true France, my country that I love, the reason for all my hopes.

March 8, 1941

For several months I have been thinking about the reasons for our military collapse, and I am trying to search out elements of truth among all the official communications that fill the newspapers and magazines. I am finding that a few scattered sentences in the Swiss papers sometimes contain revelations that are unexpected but, I suspect, accurate. We are living under an authoritarian regime, controlled by Hitler's Germany and, where it is not directly controlled, fearful of any German reaction. . . . What, under these conditions, becomes of honor and dignity? What can the true representatives of the French nation, and of humane culture, be thinking? Duhamel wrote the other day, in the *Figaro*, that all one can do is read, meditate, and write down one's reflections for oneself; that says it all.

The causes of our defeat seem to me (according to the information I believe I have in March 1941) to be of three kinds; those having to do with the military order, with the political order and with the moral order. I shall outline quickly here the basis of what would make a useful historical essay.

1. *Military order.*

I. Total superiority of the German armies with regard to equipment. The war moved in on us as it did in 1870, as in August 1914. It was a disastrous surprise, as at Crécy.

II. Lack of preparation, which was the leaders' fault: bad instructions given to officers and troops, neglecting possible battlefield conditions; in winter they were talking about soccer balls for the soldiers, the "phoney war." . . .

III. Incompetence at headquarters, where imagination was lacking and the warnings of a de Gaulle or a Giraud about the possibilities of mechanized war were ignored. The report of the second office, in January 1940, on the German operations in Poland with their criminal outcome, said something like: "Such operations are inconceivable on the western front due to the character of the terrain."

IV. Lack of will on the part of leaders and of the spirit of sacrifice among the troops. Huge numbers of prisoners. Numerous generals captured without a fight.

V. In the field, lack of liaisons of every sort. Destruction of a division headquarters led to the rout of the division even if it held the line.

2. *Political order.*

I. War was declared without *willing* it, hoping it wouldn't have to be done. Ignorance of the real power of Germany. Hitler was bluffing with a full deck.

II. Lack of collective will and enthusiasm in the country. No energy at all among the leaders. No figure such as Clemenceau or Poincaré.

III. Inadequacy of the leaders; all second-class men. Laval made the government totter with a mere flick. Lebrun = 0.

IV. Panic among the people. The roads became choked with civilians. The time came when orders could no longer be carried out. The reign of irresponsibility opened the door to *total* fear.

V. During the war a group of politicians were speculating on defeat, wanting it and preparing for it (Montigny's book). Fifth column's activity.

3. Moral order.

I. A country incapable of the burst of energy that could have saved it from total disaster. A country weary and left in ignorance of the true danger.

II. No one gave any thought to defining an ideal or creating a mystique, the mystique of individual freedom. What has become of the time when Baudin died defending parliamentary government?[7]

III. Total absence of a heroic view of life. People were speculating on everyone's desire for the good life. The Marshal personified the country, which preferred defeat to total occupation, even if only temporary.

March 9, 1941

I have been reading the *Poems* of Léon Deubel, whose death in poverty caused a great sensation in 1912 when I was in my next to last year at school. Somewhat for snobbish reasons, people sought afterward to make of him an unrecognized literary genius. There

7. In 1851, having failed to bring about a vote to revise the constitution in order to extend his term as president of the Republic, Louis-Napoleon dissolved the Assembly by coup d'état. In opposition to the coup, several republicans built a barricade in the suburb of Saint-Antoine, where Dr. Baudin, a member of the Chamber of Deputies, was struck down. His memory was not forgotten. In 1868 when the laws restricting the press were relaxed, several journalists, notably Delescluze, started a fund to build a monument in his memory. Brought to trial by the government, they were defended by a rising luminary of the bar, the young lawyer Léon Gambetta, later to become a major figure in French politics.

are hints of Samain, of Verlaine, even of Banville, but mostly there are promises and high expectations. A talent more or less faded. But I remember this lovely verse:

> And you shall be the one who thinks
> you have recovered, in the flowers
> germinating at the hands of silence,
> the lost gold of your happiness

and this sensual image:

> Those beautiful naked slaves, your sleeping feet.

I also read *Le kiosque à musique* [*The Bandstand*] by Franc-Nohain, a collection of topical rhymes.

May 10, 1941

For weeks I have been tormented by witnessing these most somber events of our century (and perhaps of my whole life); it enrages me to belong to a nation that is so powerless today. . . . There are moments—when one reflects upon Hitler's flag flying over the Acropolis—of doubt that we shall ever see the victory so longed for by all free spirits. Yet there have been centuries in history when evil triumphed, when independent thinking was asleep, when moral and material progress were halted. So it is possible that Europe is now on the eve of such an age of obscurantism and misery. It seems that nothing on land is capable of standing up to the mechanized strength of the Reich. What then? The decision will only come on the sea or in the air, when the time comes that the United States and the British Empire can bombard the industrial centers of central Europe, day and night, until its peoples beg for mercy. I don't see any such possibility for at least two years. And I tell myself, without being pessimistic, that it is not an absolute certainty.

The old world will not be reborn. Perhaps the victory of the evil forces will give birth, after a long time, to a new world. Can the tiny cell that my family represents survive that long, in the midst of chaos?

So I fear for the future of my children, and my fears are particularly those of a Frenchman, a French Jew. Fortunately my sons are not yet adults. What means should they be given to defend themselves in four or five years? I accept this suffering for myself, because I hope in spite of all to see the dawn of freedom once again, but for them—I don't want them to suffer, and I just assume they will not face debasement and discrimination. It's a problem—such grievous cruelty that I refuse to be resigned to it for the moment. I'm either an optimist or a coward.

In view of the persecutions being initiated by the new order in France, against foreigners in general and foreign Jews in particular, in light of what has happened elsewhere, in view of racist laws and the "Commission on Jewish Affairs"[8] being run in Vichy from Berlin, I wonder whether this collaboration won't bring about a yet more rigorous *Statut*. A history of racism in France from 1939 to 194* will have to be written. . . . There are days when I don't dare listen to the official bulletins on the radio; they wound me, because I still feel French and call myself a Frenchman. If I didn't have my wife and my three sons, I should be sorry not to have "died honorably in action," or sorry to have survived my mother.

May 11, 1941

In the last few weeks I have read: H. G. Wells, *The War of the Worlds*, a prophetic description of what must be happening at cer-

8. On March 29, 1941 (published in the *JO* on the 31st), Xavier Vallat was appointed commissioner of the Commissariat-Général aux Questions Juives (General Commission on Jewish Affairs—hereafter the Commissariat). For months the German authorities had been pressing the French to set up such an organization, but in the end the Vichy government made an independent decision, appointing a person who was definitely not to their liking. Between the wars Vallat was known for his strong anti-German and anti-Semitic positions, upholding a patriotic French nationalist stand. For more on Vallat, see Marrus and Paxton, *Vichy France and the Jews*, pp. 75–119. See also William D. Irvine, *French Conservatism in Crisis: The Republican Federation of France in the 1930s* (Baton Rouge & London, 1979), passim.

tain times in England and of the disaster on the highways of France; Jules Renard, *Natural Histories*, full of wit and hair-splitting; Henri de Régnier, *Le bon plaisir* [*At Your Pleasure*], a delicious story to read on the train, but concern for style takes precedence over psychological truth and feeling for real life; Francis Jammes, *Le deuil des primevères* [*Mourning for Primroses*], like an affected and weary La Fontaine, but infinitely wholesome; Julian Huxley, *What Dare I Think?*, profound speculations which give you courage for present trials and expectations for the future; Francis Jammes, *M. le Curé d'Ozeron* [*Reverend Father of Ozeron*], too Catholic for me, but moving in its honesty; E. Estaunié, *L'Ascension de M. Baslèvre* [*The Rise of Mr. Baslèvre*], an admirably constructed novel, a bit artificial but quite charming. The one lacks artistry and depth and the other smells too much of the late nineteenth century.

May 16, 1941

Yesterday evening on the TSF I heard the most depressing news we have had since the armistice. A heavy blow for any soul still concerned about our independence! It began with a brief message from the Marshal, empty and vague, announcing "collaboration" and calling for absolute trust in this dark night. Then an announcement from London that France has surrendered the airports of Syria to the Germans, which gives them access to Iraq.[9] . . . What an infamous act! What will the Americans say, and what will the British do? Wretched people of France, who are so deep in lethargy that they do not even sense this affront to their entire history, and to our generation of the Great War.

9. After Hitler's interview with Darlan at Berchtesgaden on May 11, 1941, an agreement was signed in which France surrendered to Germany its airports and military depots in Syria in order to help Rashid Ali who was fomenting a rebellion against the British in Iraq. Darlan tried, through collaboration with the German authorities, to obtain concessions in the armistice agreement. On this question and the declaration broadcast on the radio by Pétain, see Robert Aron, *Histoire de Vichy* (Paris, 1954), pp. 424–433.

The future looks pretty dark. . . . Swiss newspapers are no longer allowed in. Hitlerism is being implanted further and further into every area of the new France.

Besides, not a day goes by that the newspapers do not publish some threat to Jews. In the "Free Zone" (so-called) a more rigorous law is soon to be imposed. I am beginning to rebel quite seriously against an order that from now on, for no reason at all, will disrupt my daily life. Certainly I must stick it out. But I am beginning to understand the Protestants who took their silver and left for Berlin after the revocation of the Edict of Nantes [1685], and I wonder, in my anguish, whether the forces of evil may possibly uproot my family, some day, from this country where we have lived for two centuries. I can't imagine being able to live and be content somewhere else, but do I have the right to force my sons to accept a life that demeans them? All this is very disturbing. . . . I envy those who have a personal faith, or who have come to terms with the futility of human efforts.

June 4, 1941

Roosevelt's speech a week ago,[1] which in practice makes all the American industrial potential available to the British Empire, encouraged my hopes. But the withdrawal from Crete, France's political about-face, now makes me doubtful about the future. We should no longer consider our desires to be elements of reality. I think British imperial power has been severely shaken—and I wonder whether the monstrous forces of the Axis will not sweep us all away. . . . It is possible that we shall soon see compromise negotiations between America and Hitler-dominated Europe, thus shifting the British Empire's center of gravity from London

1. On May 27, 1941, Roosevelt took a resolutely pro-Allied position in a speech that was heard in Vichy. He declared that the United States would use all its power to prevent any attack against the Western Hemisphere. It represented a new effort on his part to try to tear France away from German influence and bring it back into the Allied camp. Roosevelt's speech was fiercely criticized in the French press. See William D. Leahy, *I Was There* (London, 1950), pp. 44–48.

to Montreal. . . . In that case, farewell to our dreams of freedom and all our past joys! That would mean a century-long night in Europe, unless a few oases of independence can maintain themselves in the midst of the torment. . . . This struggle is indeed beginning to look like a physical and planetary catastrophe. War could go on for generations.

In this last case, with the rising tide of racism, I wonder whether life will be possible for my sons in Europe in a material sense. So I am taking the first steps toward finding temporary asylum in New York. It pains me to do so, but do I have the right not to assure my sons a future? I shall remain French until my death, but if the French nation legally expels me from its bosom, do I have the right to decide that my sons should be pariahs?[2] The worst anxiety at this point—one which I don't think I have deserved (not after slogging through the mud, nor at the Chemin des Dames,[3] nor through the modest and respectable life led by my ancestors for more than a century)—is that of opening the paper morning after morning and evening after evening and seeing how the draconian *Statut*, already in force in the Occupied Zone, is now being applied in the Free Zone . . . as an accused person who knows he is innocent awaits a verdict of condemnation. Only an earthquake or a miracle could now restore his honor and his freedom to him. The Christians who had to wait like this in the Catacombs had at least the consolation of prayer.

2. Some international Jewish organizations had made efforts to obtain temporary entry visas to the United States for RRL and his family. (See, for example, YIVO: § 245,4, XII, France, C-4 letter of May 17, 1941, from Oungre to Gottschalk, letter of May 23, 1941, from Oungre.) But it is not known for certain whether the visas were in fact obtained or why RRL decided not to leave France. The course of events in his career seems to have been the decisive factor.

3. The memory of the Chemin des Dames is evoked several times in the Diary at poignant moments. Several important battles in World War I took place on this stretch of French land to the north of Paris. In 1917 the French army under the command of General Robert Nivelle recaptured the Chemin des Dames after suffering heavy losses, which led to Nivelle's being replaced by Pétain. In the spring of the following year, General Erich Ludendorff launched a German offensive between Soissons and Reims along the Chemin des Dames. On the first day the French had to retreat twenty kilometers.

Read an odious brochure published in Paris, by Drieu la Rochelle, *Ne plus attendre* [*Don't Wait Any Longer*]. It advocates blind submission to the conqueror, with fake accents in the manner of Barrès. Such an attitude can cause one to doubt France. Having been this unfaithful to its secular mission and to the Christian significance of its history, France could simply disappear or go to sleep for a long time. It's terrible, but it could happen. This mechanized war would have crushed the spirit of Descartes. I did read an excellent book about the war, simple and moving, *L'officier sans nom* [*The Nameless Officer*], by Guy des Cars. The first account to have any lasting value.

June 15, 1941

Day before yesterday evening on the TSF and yesterday morning in the papers I finally learned the details of the new *Statut des Juifs*.[4] Another body blow! I could never have imagined this. It's a dry run of the St. Bartholomew's Day massacre![5] With one decree, what took seven years in Germany, seven months in Austria, a few weeks in Prague, is now being done in France. . . . It's inconceivable that French people have dared to sign such orders, a hundred and fifty years after the Declaration of Human Rights. What shame it brings on our country! Is this the armistice with honor and dignity? Here I am, my sons, my brother, my family, and me turned into "pariahs" in the country for whose sake I came close to being killed, many times over. From now on, anything is

4. The second *Statute on the Jews* was adopted on June 2, 1941 (published in the *JO* on June 14). It excluded Jews from the few public offices still open to them, and from a host of private professional careers, as well as providing for complementary legislation that was to deprive Jews of their occupations en masse. Although there was a measure of indulgence for veterans of the war, and for especially eminent Jews of the oldest families, the Law set a quota of 3 percent for Jewish students in higher education. For a discussion of the law, see Marrus and Paxton, *Vichy France and the Jews*, pp. 138–141.

5. RRL alludes here, as elsewhere, to the treatment of French Huguenots in prerevolutionary France. The infamous massacre of the Huguenots in Paris and the provinces took place in 1572 and led to further warfare between the Catholics and Protestants.

possible since talk is being heard of internment on the orders of the prefect, as a penalty for being Jewish, even if you are French-born. . . . I wonder if I am dreaming, and it doesn't help to remind myself that Hitler is in command; I feel no less contempt for the leaders of this country in which I have been fated to have my roots—an immense and profound contempt.

After taking such measures, which betray its historical mission, can France become itself again? After having been a protectorate of Hitler, can it become anything other than an American colony? Like ancient Greece in its time, perhaps France has reached the end of its career. . . . I no longer know whether to wish to live a long life or to regret not having fallen at the front in Champagne,[6] in the days when all Frenchmen were brothers.

As for the future, I cannot think of it without anguish. What shall I do for my sons if this *Statut* remains in place? The universities will be closed to them. They will be less than they should be. . . . Shall I have the right, in the near future, to buy them a little piece of land? I doubt it. . . . We must wait and see. . . . Either Germany triumphs, which for all free spirits (even in America) means servitude and unhappiness, or Germany must be defeated and then, somehow or other, life will become worth living again.

June 22, 1941

On this day last year I was in the worst possible state of anxiety, fearing that my wife and my three sons had been bombed and

6. Three decisive battles took place in Champagne during World War I, two in 1915 and one in 1917. The first two, including General Joseph Joffre's major offensive, which lasted six weeks (September to November), had no significant effect on German emplacements. The third took place in the spring of 1917 as part of Nivelle's offensive against the Germans. Apart from the conquest of the Chemin des Dames, smaller attacks were launched on the Champagne front. RRL recalls these battles several times in the Diary. Here again, as often occurs in the text, he speaks nostalgically of this period and the symbiotic spirit that existed between Jews and Frenchmen in the sacred unity of the nation.

were lost in the turmoil of total defeat. . . . Is my suffering today any better, now that we have been legally cast out of the French community? Perhaps, since on reflection I still trust there is an underlying justice. There are things which now, in the twentieth century, can no longer be considered absolutes. The individual human spirit has inalienable rights. Bloodlines can no longer make kings. That would be the denial of all spiritual evolution.

On the day after the new *Statut* appeared, Mr. Helbronner, president of the Consistory, went to see the Marshal, who said these measures had been imposed by the Germans. He said he was trying to resist them, as far as possible, but in vain: "These are dreadful people!" Such an admission sheds light on plenty of things. But doesn't it amount to a condemnation of the armistice and the entire policy of collaboration?

This *Statut* of June 1941 is draconian. It includes provisions to ensure that it will be enforced with great severity and that the consequences for French Judaism will be terrible. It consolidates within a single text measures that were applied in stages over a period of years in Germany, of months in Austria, and of weeks in Czechoslovakia. It is a true condensation of all racist legislation.

French Judaism has become spiritually paralyzed. Members of the community are treated by definition as pariahs. This should result in the formation of a true moral ghetto. The text does not dare to base itself on racist arguments—for fear of repercussions in the colonies—but rather on arguments that are properly considered religious.[7] As paradoxical as it may seem, this focus shows

7. The two first points of the *Law* of June 1941 made the following stipulations: Article 1. A person is considered Jewish if:

1. He or she, whether belonging to any confession or not, is descended from at least three grandparents of the Jewish race, or from only two if his or her spouse is descended from two grandparents of the Jewish race. A grandparent who belonged to the Jewish faith is considered racially Jewish.

2. He or she belongs to the Jewish faith, or did so on June 25, 1940, and is descended from two grandparents of the Jewish race. The status of not belonging to the Jewish faith is to be established by proof of having joined one of the other confessions which were recognized by the State before the law of December 9, 1905. Disowning a child, or the annulment of one's recognition of a child who is considered a Jew has no effect upon the above provisions.

15.2.2007 = start

30.11.07

BA 19 Oct 06 12-31-06

4 Aug 07 - ~~[illegible]~~

Paha 5 Aug 07 - 12-31-07

10 March 08

1-1-08 - 10

~~file under 2008 taxes~~
~~no longer excludable~~
~~because didn't~~
~~meet phys presence test~~

2007

a certain cleverness, since it counts on the old, underlying anticlericalism of the French people to overlook measures that should offend every free spirit. The sanction, the threat of the concentration camp appears for the first time in this text and on religious grounds.[8] From an economic viewpoint, the consequence of this decree will be the total asphyxiation of French Judaism if the regulations announced for each profession are carried out in the same spirit.

One has the feeling that even the details of the law are inspired or dictated by the German authorities—since from now on the Reich will consider France's resolution of the Jewish question as the criterion of its sincere participation in collaboration policy.

The commissioner for Jewish affairs, Xavier Vallat (disabled by the *Action française*) had promised everyone, in private conversations, to spare veterans of the war, but this promise means nothing since he is not free. The armed services are to be brought under a real ministry, with all the dangers that involves for individuals who are the object of these measures. Furthermore we shall have to reckon with ill will on the part of junior officers who, under surveillance by certain elements in the service of the occupying power, will make sure not to demonstrate any sympathy toward us.

The conditions that have been set for dispensations mean that, in practice, it will do no good to apply for them. It is in fact impossible for Jews from Alsace or Lorraine—whose ancestors were emancipated in 1791—to trace their ancestry back five generations, if the search has to be made in archives in what is now a prohibited zone.[9] Furthermore there is the particularly iniquitous fact, under this new regime which makes "the family" its watchword, that any dispensations granted would be on a purely individual basis and would not revert to one's children. In the case of

8. Article 9 of the *Statut.*

9. RRL refers here to Article 8 of the *Statut*, which exempted certain categories of Jews from the effects of the new law.

some officials, dispensations may make it possible to save at least a small number of persons.

The consequences of this legislation are unfortunately foreseeable. It will mean economic death for French Jewry, and not just by stages unless at least the young people can be saved through a mass emigration, in the event this German period in European history lasts a long time. French Jewry, still confident despite these trials, has decided to hold on and wait.

"Anti-Semitic Propaganda in France Since the War[1]

"Since August 1939 there has been a development of anti-Semitic propaganda in France, which has taken different forms at different times. In judging its methods and effects, three very distinct periods should be considered.

"I. *From September 1939 to the armistice*

"As soon as war was declared, certain circles in which the extreme right parties had already been at work, and which had even been infiltrated by Germans just after Munich, intensified their efforts to spread the usual anti-Semitic themes and to influence public opinion, which had become more sensitive after the general mobilization. This extremely insidious activity had no effect on the masses during the hostilities; it was only certain individuals who could be persuaded or shaken by such statements as 'The Jews' war. The Jews, the only ones who profit from the war . . .,' etc. Such ideas were being pushed daily in French-language broadcasts by German radio and by leaflets dropped behind the lines by enemy aircraft. But the great majority of fighting troops resisted such incitements and, except for a few very rare incidents outside the Polish legions, no anti-Semitic attitudes were reported among the troops. There were just a few officers, members of *Action française*, who made their antipathy toward their Jewish

1. The following passage was published in *Le Monde Juif*, No. 25 (1969), pp. 7–9, without citing the source.

colleagues obvious; a colonel, when a Jewish captain reported to him during the mobilization, asked him, 'Well, are you happy, now you've finally got "your" war?'

"II. *From June to October 1940*

"The defeat, the collapse of the republic and democratic institutions by the end of June 1940, at which point freedom of expression became impossible, facilitated the development of anti-Semitism, which from then on took its most violent forms.

"The reversal in foreign policy gave strength to the slogan 'Allied Judaism' or 'Judaism dominating Britain.' In every speech, in all notes and publications coming from official spheres as well as in TSF commentaries, efforts were made to associate, in the eyes of the French people, the three forces that were held responsible for the war and guilty of our defeat: Judaism, Freemasonry, and communism. Of these three enemies of the new France, Judaism was attacked in the most vulgar form, and even through caricature. At the same time public opinion was being prepared for the publication of the *Statut* by arguments renewed from the time of the Dreyfus Affair and drawn from Drumont.[2] Xenophobic passions aroused by our defeat and the restrictions in force were exploited, and Jews were considered incapable of being integrated into the French community but rather seen as individuals who are eternal foreigners in every country.

"It is clear that the presence of Armistice Commissions throughout France and the infiltration of the conquerors into every administration have only intensified all these actions.

2. A journalist, Edouard Drumont was a leading figure in the anti-Semitic campaign in France at the end of the nineteenth century. His *La France juive* (1886) constituted a challenge to the ethics of republican society and claimed in myriad ways that Jews had overcome France. It has been republished in more than 250 editions. His newspaper *La libre parole* pursued a relentless anti-Semitic agenda and vilified Alfred Dreyfus, the Jewish captain in the French army who was accused of treason in 1894. His conviction sparked a major political controversy in French society (the Dreyfus Affair), which came to an end with Dreyfus's full rehabilitation in 1906. On Drumont, see Pierre Birnbaum, *Anti-Semitism in France: A Political History from Léon Blum to the Present*, trans. Miriam Kuchan (Cambridge, Mass., 1992).

"III. *From October 1940 to June 1941*

"Following the publication of the *Statut*, anti-Semitic propaganda in France took on the methodological and scientific aspect that it has had in Germany so far. The official authorities themselves—from the Havas Agency to the local police stations—have accepted and directed it.

"Not a day has gone by in which the press did not publish an article or a news bulletin on misdeeds in free France, or on the history of Jewish individuals or families, whether they concerned the black market (without a word, of course, about the actions of non-Jewish merchants), or illicit speculation, or violations of government instructions on residence permits, etc. The censorship even shows a certain puerility in its instructions; for instance, when Bergson died it was forbidden to print in the obituaries that he was a Jew of Polish origin who was naturalized as a special favor after being admitted to the Ecole Normale Supérieure [the prestigious post–high school institution].

"At the same time propaganda through posters, leaflets, and images has doubled its intensity. Jews are now being depicted as hostile to the work of national reconstruction. 'Judaism and Gaullism' [support for Charles de Gaulle] are being associated and mixed together. As in Germany, propaganda through books is increasing, especially through distribution of brochures published in the Occupied Zone. Propaganda through films, greatly reinforced by suggestive posters printed in Germany, is also on the increase (The Jew Süss).[3] Finally, mention must be made of certain symbolic actions carried out by Germans or the police (broken windows in Marseilles, in Nice, in Limoges; bombing of the synagogue in Marseilles, with a ban on publication of the condolence letter from the bishop to the chief rabbi, bombing in

3. RRL refers to the anti-Semitic Nazi film *Jud Süss*, directed by Veit Harlan (1940), portraying the life of the court Jew Joseph (Süss) Oppenheimer, who rose to a position of much influence in Württemberg in the 1730s. Oppenheimer was later tried, found guilty, and publicly hanged in 1738. The film was shown in various occupied countries to disseminate the claim of Jewish domination.

Grenoble as well, etc.); all this to prepare public opinion for the second, aggravated *Statut* in June.

"The consequences of such propaganda in the Jewish community itself are especially to be feared, through the shock to the authorities in turn and the effect on the masses which may after all be perceptible in the long term.

"In this way a depressing atmosphere is being created for the Jewish community itself. New suicides are being reported, desperate decisions, people giving up. Even more than from these measures, which we hope to see reported one day, Jewish families are suffering from the official commentaries. In relations with the authorities, moreover, I am often painfully aware that assertions from the anti-Semitic propaganda are being cited as truth 'based on experience' in conversations that should be technical in nature, and are being used to justify, after the fact, the most severe and unjust measures.

"If one can say that in a general way this propaganda has not yet poisoned the public mind, still it must be feared that in the course of time its action will do further harm. In the Occupied Zone an understanding is emerging in the minds of most French people, namely that racism is an import from Germany; but in the so-called Free Zone this truth cannot appear so clearly. The Jews, as they are affected by the *Statut*, always meet with sympathy as individuals among their compatriots, but public opinion remains indifferent to the overall problem. The silence in the press can be explained by censorship, more draconian than ever on this point, but word is being passed around of infinitely comforting reactions within certain groups (Catholic church, Protestant consistory, former liberal parties, etc.). On the other hand, the discriminatory measures have been applauded in certain economic circles, particularly by certain representatives of banks and chambers of commerce.

"France these days has been struck down by lethargy. Those individuals who no longer enjoy any freedom, living under an empire, are thinking only of how to get food, and it is more difficult every day. So the Jewish problem in France cannot be solved, in the sense of greater justice, until the country is cured of the cancer that is eating away at it. The rebirth of spiritual freedom is only one especially painful part of the deliverance of Europe from Hitler's rule."

This morning at dawn Hitler declared war on Russia. This is of major importance and could have unforeseen consequences. . . . Everyone looks happy and is trying to grab a paper, the extra editions, under the heat of the Provençal sun. . . . Either Russia will surrender and be rapidly tamed, like France last year—which will only delay the final outcome—or Russia will entice the huge German army into its even huger steppes, for a replay of 1812. One thing is certain: Hitler fears the moment when America, already virtually at war and in possession of two-thirds of the gasoline in the world, will have finished equipping itself to intervene effectively in Europe. The mirage of the East has always been the downfall of conquerors. . . .

From Georges Bernanos, a most profound judgment on the works and philosophy of Barrès: "The respect that I feel for the memory of Maurice Barrès cannot deter me from writing that nationalism was invented in order to resolve moral dilemmas more literary than political, to provide people with a humane faith, a humane religion, people in the humanities who are de-Christianized or, to put it better, dehumanized (it is the same thing) down to the roots of their souls" (*Scandale de la vérité* [*The Scandalous Truth*], p. 49).

My recent reading: an infamous brochure by Puységur in which I have the honor of being quoted. L. F. Céline, *Les beaux draps* [*Beautiful Linens*], pornography, pretty depressing. Simenon, *Maigret and the Concarneau Murders* (which introduced me to a great novelist, a definite talent; the naked truth, in a clear and self-controlled artistry. Flawless. One lives with the characters). Jean de Baroncelli, *Vingt-six hommes* [*Twenty-six Men*] (a quite remarkable war novel, very moving. It will endure, like *Les Croix de bois* [*Wooden Crosses*] for the previous adventure [World War I]). Pierre Benoît, *Le désert de Gobi* (Poor. This academician is getting old and repeating himself). Marcel Aymé, *The Grand Seduction* (excellent—a fine escape from present worries). Jean Cocteau, *Morceaux choisis* [*Selected Works*] (almost nil). Georges Bernanos, *Scandale de la vérité* (brochure written right after Munich when Bernanos decided to flee to Brazil; the masterpiece of a prophet; the infuriated testimony of one of the great minds of our time. Flashes of insight on the past and present of our poor country and its betrayal by its patriots. Worth rereading.)

July 6, 1941

I returned yesterday from a trip to Vichy, where I made contact again with the authorities. . . . I saw and heard a great deal, and learned a great deal, during the five days there, and I've come back quite optimistic. I shall make notes of it all in two or three days, when I have digested it all.

I read *Le Troisième Richelieu* [*The Third Richelieu*], by my friend Fouques-Duparc, a remarkable monograph, very lively. One can negotiate with conquerors, when one has been conquered, without submitting to them, without putting oneself under a yoke. How different this is from Admiral Darlan, whom the Parisians call "Admiral Bow-and-Scrape"! Also read De Garcia Calderon, *La Périchole*, a romantic biography, brilliant and lighthearted. And finally an excellent collection of philosophical and political essays, published at a time when one had the right to one's thoughts, *La France et la liberté*. Readings like these (Valéry, Francis Delaisi) give one faith in the future.

That is really what we need just now, especially when, like me, we must meet with officials whose opportunism too often makes us feel sick.

When there is peace again, I'd like to work with others on resolving the problem of foreigners and immigration in France. I have some experience here. It is certainly necessary, though sixty years too late, to put an effort into solving this problem—because the deeper cause of this war is stopping human beings from migrating. There is a sense in which one could say that the United States admitted its guilt, along with the other new nations, the day it closed its doors to immigration.[4] . . .

In Vichy I heard about that sentence from Roosevelt's speech last May 10—which of course was kept secret from us: "I refuse to believe that the French people freely agree to collaborate with a country which is crushing them economically, morally and politically. . . ."

July 7, 1941

Read this sentence in the *Candide* [a right-wing journal], which will be remembered in future, a new proof of the plot that destroyed the freedom of the republic (issue of June 25, 1941), in an article by Pierre Lancien (?) on the *Homme de l'Elysée* [*The Man in the Elysée Palace*]:

"He [Mr. Millerand] refused to engage in battle, period; after that the occasion for battle presented itself only twice; once on February 6, when it was lost; and once more, when it was won, but that was after the defeat and in the turmoil of the invasion."

In order not to forget, I am noting here the list of internment camps for foreigners in France (where 60 percent of them are Jews), as I have it as of May 1941, particularly according to information compiled from all the aid organizations, from the Red Cross to the YMCA. First of all, in the Occupied Zone there are 47

4. In 1924 the United States set quotas on immigration. During the 1930s, when thousands of refugees were seeking a haven, even the quotas allocated to each of the European countries were rarely filled. Several scholarly studies have dealt with various aspects of American policy and have come to similar conclusions, reproaching the Roosevelt administration with indifference to the situation of the refugees. See, among others, Henry Feingold, *The Politics of Rescue: The Roosevelt Administration and the Holocaust, 1938–1945* (New Brunswick, N.J., 1970); Saul S. Friedman, *No Haven for the Oppressed: United States Policy Towards Jewish Refugees, 1938–1945* (Detroit, 1973); David Wyman, *Paper Walls: America and the Refugee Crisis, 1938–1941* (Amherst, 1971).

camps, of which the largest are: Pithiviers (3,000 Jews), Beaune-la-Roland (2,000 Jews), Saint-Denis (700 British), Drancy (700 British), Vittel (500 British women), Clairvaux (250, all nationalities), Troyes (250), la Lande (700), la Motte-Beuvron (300), Linas (150 Gypsies), etc., etc.

Then, in the Free Zone, we have this moving overall picture, destined to be as dark a blot on French history as the persecution [of the Huguenots] by the dragoons:

A. *Camps for political prisoners:*
- Vernet, 2,000
- Rieucros, 450
- Brélant-Marseilles, 100

B. *Camps for British nationals:*
- Sault, 400
- St.-Hippolyte-du-Fort, 300

C. *Refugee detention camps:*
- Gurs, 6,200
- Argelès, 3,000
- Noé, 1,550
- Récébédou, 1,800
- Rivesaltes, 9,000 (including 3,000 children)

D. *Deportation camps:*
- Les Milles, 1,100
- Bompard, 180 (women)
- Terminus-du-Port, 130 (women)

E. *Camp for demobilized troops:*
- La Lègue-Fréjus, 400

F. *In North Africa:*
- Djelfa, 1,200
- Boghari, 4,500
- Colomb-Béchar, 2,000
- Bou-Hafa, 500
- Oued-Zem, 240
- Agem-Our, 200

Previously run by the military authorities, since December 1940 these camps have come under National Security, thus are being ravaged by the "Fouchés" of the New Order).[5] The situation there is indescribably depressing. The internees are subjected to a regime like that of prisoners of war. Family members are separated from one another, the women being confined separately. Most of the camps are only barracks, open to the winds; too often the internees have to sleep on straw, and the straw is never changed and is swarming with rats and vermin—otherwise people sleep on the moldy floorboards or even on the ground. Hygienic conditions are pretty basic, there is not enough to eat, sanitation is deplorable, and the death rate is high. There is not only a lack of food but also of clothing, medicines, and milk for babies.

All the aid organizations, regardless of religious affiliation, are trying to remedy this indescribable misery, but private charity finds itself powerless faced with the scale of the problem, complicated by the economic problems of the country and the general difficulty in getting supplies. . . . In the midst of the catastrophe shaking the world, how many individual tragedies there are, what vast undeserved suffering!

July 8, 1941

Not a day goes by without a new decree on the *"numerus clausus"* affecting the Jews in all areas of activity nationwide.[6] Yesterday it concerned only students' admission to universities, today they're talking about lawyers. To deceive public opinion, which is amazed at all this, they're calling it rights of priority granted to veterans of the war. Just like Romania, just like Poland; what has become of the days when Poincaré, in 1923, reproached our allies in the

5. For a complete list of camps, see J. Weill, *Contribution à l'histoire des camps d'internment dans l'anti-France* (Paris, 1946).

6. RRL's forecast was correct. During the next six months decrees were adopted applying the *numerus clausus* in different areas.

East with committing a crime against humanity, with their *"numerus clausus"*? A depressing sign of a new era: in *Le Temps* of July 5, a small advertisement says that an industry is seeking a first-rate employee, with the notice "Isr. s'abst. [Jews need not apply]."

For the census,[7] which was foreseen and must be taken care of before July 14, I went yesterday to the prefect's office, where the classical disorder of official bureaucracy holds sway. An office for "Jewish affairs" has been opened next to those for "Gun permits" and "Permission to hold public dances." The young man in charge of the office received me in quite a friendly manner, a bit embarrassed—"don't know anything precise yet"! In the corridor I met a lady from Marseilles who, like me, had come in response to the new notice. She protested loudly against such discrimination: "My husband served at the Dardanelles, and my four sons were drafted in 1940. . . . The Marshal has dishonored France, but God will punish him, because no one has the right to make the innocent suffer. . . . My husband was a guard at an administrative office, and they've just fired him, it's shameful! And nobody's bothering the Italians who are eating our bread!"

July 16, 1941

I have just spent a few days in Vichy, staying in contact with my friends in the public administration. I was most warmly welcomed by Lieutenant Colonel Pascot, the right-hand man of Borotra in [the Ministry of] Sports. I was rather astonished by the atmosphere in the ministries. The New Order cannot be firmly established as long as, even in the offices of the ministers themselves, people know and say that their bosses follow the precept of servitude—a sign of the times, the same as during the transitory

7. The census of Jews in the Free Zone was announced by Vichy on June 2, 1941 (published in *JO* on the 14th). It required Jews to present themselves within a month (later extended until July 31, 1941) "at the prefect's office of their département or the sub-prefect's office of their arrondissement," and to submit a declaration "indicating that they are Jews in the eyes of the law, and mentioning their marital status, their family situation, their occupation and the goods in their possession."

era of the first Restoration [of the republic]! So this is now the capital of a country like France, installed in a spa town with its flashy luxury palaces, the changing of the guard across from the park in new Hitler-style uniforms, uniforms all over the place despite our defeat; all this reminds me of a little pre-1914 German principality.

With my friend Pierre Bloch, the young socialist deputy from Aisne, the above-mentioned Colonial officer who escaped, I went to see Xavier Vallat, commissioner for Jewish affairs, who received us cordially.[8] A strange conversation! To have accepted such a position one cannot be a philo-Semite, nor can one have a strong conscience to be able to take—four days a week in Paris!—orders from Germany. Xavier Vallat considers the two of us as comrades-in-arms, but, as a good follower of Maurras, he no longer wants any Jews in the administration, in politics, or in banking. . . . He doesn't know anything about the issue but seems relatively sensible, well brought up and very much the "war veteran." Concerning our children's future, he advises us to wait, and to steer them toward manual trades or working on the land. He promised us that in the Free Zone our goods will not be confiscated, but he asked me for information about the [social work] projects; he asked to see me again and was touched by the picture I painted of the internment camps, but he told me he has nothing to do with police work.

At Foreign Affairs I saw [Charles] Rochat, director of the admiral's office, whom I knew from the days of Delbos[9] and Geneva. He is still the same. He must disapprove of this regime and particularly of the *Statut*. He speaks quite sincerely against the inhumane regulations that have been imposed on foreigners . . . but

8. On November 17, 1943, Jean Pierre-Bloch (born Jean-Pierre Bloch) former socialist deputy from the département of Aisne, was named assistant commissioner at the Interior Ministry of the Free French government in Algeria. He described his resistance activities and his other tribulations during the war in *Le vent souffle sur l'histoire* (Paris, 1956). A description of this meeting is included in the memoirs of Pierre Bloch, *Jusqu'au dernier jour. Mémoires* (Paris, 1983), p. 185.

9. Yves Delbos served as France's foreign minister from 1936 to 1938.

what can be done about it? When I was an official under the Occupation, I took action, in a less important job, because my conscience "couldn't accept" what I saw. . . . I saw Guichard, the main private secretary, whom I knew as a ship's lieutenant in Bonn and as a fellow member of Writers in Combat. He complained about his job and said he disapproves of the *Statut*, but he sounded more like a disgusting opportunist. I also saw Leydoux, the deputy head, always friendly, but just as obsequious. . . . Only Fouques-Duparc,[1] who refused to be posted to Chungking, has kept a clear conscience and sound judgment; he understands that our leaders today are risking their necks. He believes the Americans will defeat Hitler but is afraid there will be a bloody revolution and remains concerned about the future of our country. I share his fears but believe the future will be healing.

At the Ministry of Interior, Fourcade[2] seemed shiftier and more opportunistic than ever. The atmosphere there is like that of a police headquarters.

At the headquarters of the Colonial Troops, General Blairot received me with the warm welcome I expected from him. The *Statut* hasn't changed anything here—long live the Colonial! The general is going to publish some more fascicules or a magazine on the TC (Troupes Coloniales—Colonial Forces); he asked for my help with it. . . . General Bührer will retire in September. I had the idea of proposing to him that all former officers be included in "Imperial Study Societies." He is away from Vichy;

1. Jacques Fouques-Duparc spent almost his entire professional career in the Ministry of Foreign Affairs. Born in 1897, Fouques-Duparc was a delegate to the League of Nations and was posted to Berlin and Madrid during the 1920s and 1930s. RRL's estimation of Fouques-Duparc proved correct: he was dismissed from his job by the Vichy government and joined the resistance in 1943. After the war he was taken back into the Foreign Service and named ambassador to Rome. RRL saw him several times in 1942 and 1943. They had known each other since they had both attended the Collège Rollin.

2. Fourcade was inspector general of the Interior Ministry and took over as interim secretary general of the Police during the deportations from the south of France in August 1942. He had also taken part in the failed negotiations with Jewish and international organizations to arrange to send Jewish children to the United States. See Serge Klarsfeld, *Vichy-Auschwitz: Le rôle de Vichy dans la solution finale de la question juive en France—1942* (Paris, 1983), passim.

I shall go back to see him next month. It would be useful to organize an action outside official activities, useful even for the future, in peacetime.

At the Chamber [of Deputies]—or rather at the hotel that lodges the rare members of parliament who pass through here—the opposition leader is Louis Marie, of the Catholic right. He's very good. The superior of the Dominicans at Beirut, and Cochet, the air force general, have been arrested for "subversion." Ah, if only we had a free press!

I saw Spanien[3]—my friend from school and Tour d'Auvergne Street—who is defending Léon Blum. He told me what is going on behind the scenes in this matter, and it won't work. Blum is in contact with Roosevelt, who sent him a telegram on his birthday.

We recite to one another the text of the two letters addressed to the Marshal. The one from Mandel,[4] in regard to the circular letter from the Chamber [of Deputies] asking him whether he was Jewish, said: "In fulfilment of the decree that you have signed, I have the honor to inform you that I am a freethinker, but that I have never concealed my Jewish origins. The first time I addressed the Chamber from the platform, in 1924, I made a point of referring to my ancestry, so that there would never be any mis-

3. Samuel Spanien was one of the three attorneys who were to defend Léon Blum in his court case at Riom in 1942. The Vichy government attempted to try leading figures from the Third Republic in order to place the blame on them for France's decline and defeat. The trials were halted in May 1943 due to the international support accorded Blum and others. Spanien, a young socialist lawyer, had begun gathering documentation for the trial in 1940 while Blum was imprisoned in the castle of Chazeron. See Henri Michel, *Le procès de Riom* (Paris, 1979). Spanien and Lambert had also been students together at the Collège Rollin.

4. Georges Mandel, who was head of Clemenceau's office (1917–1920) and his right-hand man, was later appointed minister for colonial affairs and, after the onset of World War II (from May 18, 1940), Minister of the Interior in the disastrous Reynaud government. Mandel opposed the armistice with Germany and strongly recommended that the government be moved to North Africa. He joined other deputies from the National Assembly in the voyage of the *Massilia* in June 1940 to North Africa and was arrested and imprisoned by Vichy upon his return. Mandel was later interned in Buchenwald by the German authorities. In July 1944, after having been surrendered to the French by the Germans, he was killed by members of the Vichy Milice. See John M. Sherwood, *Georges Mandel and the Third Republic* (Stanford, 1970).

understanding about it; moreover, my purpose on the platform was to ask that the French embassy to the Vatican be reestablished. I further wish to remind you that from 1917 to 1919 I was head of Clemenceau's office, *and that he won the war.*"

The other, from Paul Reynaud, following Admiral Darlan's declarations in which he proclaimed the need for collaboration to the point of servitude, said: "You will remember, sir, that it was at my personal insistence that the president of the Republic asked you to take over as president of the Council, on the night when it was decided to ask for an armistice, which you promised to request and to accept honorably. Today I have realized that you have not kept your word. Since it was I who insisted, I have no other choice, in the sad circumstances in which I now find myself, but to ask the forgiveness of my country and the forgiveness of God."

July 17, 1941

Yesterday it was three years since Mama died, three years since the most horribly painful experience of my life. I cannot weep any more, but the feeling of emptiness is still the same. Every day and almost every night I feel the presence of her to whom I owe everything, and I miss her love, which was so gentle and understanding. How much has happened, to the world and to me, since that terrible evening! . . . I have begun writing a book, *Une mère* [*A Mother*],[5] in which I shall record all my memories, first of all for my sons, and for fear that my memories may become dull as I grow older.

I read *The Hopkins Manuscript* by R. O. Sheriff, a Wells-style novel about the end of our civilization, rather long, but witty; *Le Poème des Griffons* [*The Poem of the Griffons*] by Tristan Derême, who is wrong to imagine that his poems' seasoning intrigues us, or that he is a second Lamartine; and the *Carnets de Schwartz Koppen* [*Journals of Schwartz Koppen*].

5. This manuscript has never been found. RRL several times expressed his deep attachment to his mother.

July 28, 1941

The war in Russia has been going on for five weeks, and the Bolshevik army has yet to be destroyed. It's the first time Hitler hasn't had success with his blitzkrieg. The world must be amazed at the Russian resistance, and I really think that this time the fortunes of the Nazi conquerors will turn. Besides, America is practically in the war now, on the British side. I think I shall see Paris again by the autumn of 1942. British bombing raids on Germany are multiplying while the newspapers, according to the Swiss press, are full of obituaries that say "fallen in Russia." It is clear that the German people, totally puffed up as they are, will begin to suffer as well.

In the *Weltwoche* [*World Weekly Review*] from Zurich, I read two detailed and valuable articles. In France our press has become so Germanized that one can't find out anything from it, and we snatch up the few Swiss papers that get through to us. Even these, since the war started in Russia, show a hatred for bolshevism that looks remarkably like synchronization [with the Nazi line]. . . . I learned: (1) that, through the monitoring of the mails in Bermuda, the British found out that Hitler was preparing to attack Russia; (2) that in their blitzkrieg, instead of the "hooch" they used in the other war, the Boche dope their shock troops with "*Weckamine*" [amphetamine, "wake-up" pills]. The use of these pills explains the performance of the men in the tanks and their insensitivity to the noise and heat in those machines. Surely history will record the importance of this chemical factor.

The Vichy government has just ceded Indochina to the Japanese for purposes of military control. . . . If you understand the imperial mission of France, the culmination of its entire history, its *raison d'être* as a European power, it's enough to make you weep! We have truly been betrayed. Roosevelt can say that the Vichy government has covered itself in dishonour. . . . All this will be over some day—but I am more and more fearful that there will be some settling of accounts in blood in our country.

They have also had Marx Dormoy[6] assassinated, or allowed it to happen; he was Blum's Minister of the Interior.

Readings: *Sacred Hill* of Barrès, in which the story did not move me as much as certain pages where I found the music I expected. *Pétain ou la démocratie* [*Pétain or Democracy*], a brochure by Georges Suarez, who was a talented journalist but here shows a contemptible conformity. *Freedom and Authority in French West Africa* by Robert Delavignette, a perfect book that should be basic for all training for the colonies. Finally, a sign of the times, Charles Lesca's *Quand Israël se venge* [*When Israel Takes Its Revenge*]. The editor of *Je suis partout* [*I Am Everywhere*],[7] who was arrested by Mandel a few days before our collapse—too late—tells how prisoners witnessed, and were the victims of, the disarray on the crowded roads from Paris to Gurs. . . . Through certain details he frankly admits, while declaring himself innocent, that *Je suis partout* has been an instrument of foreign propaganda. There is something brutish about his anti-Semitism. Even during the hostilities, the editors of this paper were preparing for civil war.

August 2, 1941

No longer a week goes by without a decree, appearing in the *Officiel*, putting finishing touches on legislation to exclude Jews from the country's economic life. My sons now have, as a choice of careers, rock-breaker, agricultural worker, or peddler—and even this last may be closed to them tomorrow, because they would be "in contact with the public."

6. Minister of the interior under Léon Blum in 1937–1938, Dormoy was under close arrest at Montélimar when a bomb exploded in his hotel room on the night of July 25, 1941. His assassins belonged to the Cagoule terrorist organization, which he had kept on a short leash as interior minister.

7. At the end of the 1930s *Je suis partout* was one of the main organs of the anti-Semitic press in France. Under the editorship of Robert Brasillach, it brought together fascist kindred spirits such as Lucien Rebatet, Louis-Ferdinand Céline, and Brasillach himself. See Zeev Sternhell, *Neither Right nor Left: Fascist Ideology in France*, trans. David Maisel (Princeton, 1996).

As part of my job, I had a two-hour interview yesterday at the Prefecture with the head secretary in the bursar's office of the regional police; a Mr. Ozanneau, a former marine officer, *Croix de Guerre* [decoration for bravery in combat] 1940; he looked cultivated and intelligent, the very type of the young New Order official. After the questions about my work (getting my foreigners included in work units), we had quite a candid exchange of views. He openheartedly confessed to me his thoughts on the Jewish question, which "needed to be resolved."

I was struck by the lack of qualities of spirit and of humanity in such a man. It's a sign of the times, and it makes me quite pessimistic about the immediate future, if the war continues. While there may be a certain freedom of judgment at the head of the Vichy government, the people who carry out its policies at the local level show an appalling sectarianism. Based on [my] experience, they accept as truth whatever the Germans say. They reproach the Jews for their international solidarity; for being at the head, always at the head of professions and governments; they even reproach them for their religious particularism and their whole history, leaving out the persecutions and even denying them.

Ozanneau asked me what my feelings are about the *Statut*. Of course I did not hide the reasons why I am bitter about it. And the solution? When there is peace, I said, there must be a territorial solution for those who are stateless, as Palestine offers only a partial solution. And you? he asked me rather cruelly, what will you do? Why, I am and shall remain French, I replied. And I waited in vain for a word of agreement, which would have proved to me that there was not, between these people and ourselves, a wall of incomprehension built by the tenacious actions of the Germans.

I had a visit from Emile Kahn, secretary general of the Human Rights League, who gave me some reassuring news. He had just the right word: this is Ubu the king's regime.[8] Herriot and Jeanneney[9] are holding firm in the Resistance, and there will be bloody days ahead in the streets. He gave me the text of an admirable letter from General de la Laurencie to Darlan. This general, who was arrested today for saying he believes in freedom, had been the Marshal's deputy in the Occupied Zone and was dismissed as if he had been a cleaning lady, on orders from Berlin (at the time of the Laval affair, he had Déat arrested in Paris, on the orders of Peyrouton, who was then fired from his job by Abetz). All these facts will be made known some day.[1]

Emile Kahn also showed me a fine protest letter against the *Statut*, to be signed by teachers and submitted by Jeanneney to the Marshal; it is an appeal from freethinkers of Jewish origin who are not recognized as such by the *Statut*, since it obliges them to declare that they are of the Jewish "confession."[2] With regard to this protest, which illuminates all the judicial aspects of the problem—and concludes that the liberation of France will be our liberation—note should be taken of the protest letter of July 1, 1941, which Helbronner[3] submitted to the Marshal, in the name of the Central Consistory, and which sums up perfectly all our thoughts:

"Your Honor:

"At a time when rigorous, exceptional measures are placing a minority of French citizens outside the law because of their religion, it is the duty of the representative of their religious associations to raise a solemn protest.

8. The reference is to the play by Alfred Jarry, *Ubu Roi*, that was first performed in 1896. It depicts the personality of an obese, uncultured, and evil figure, Ubu, who usurps the throne by intrigue and is later dethroned himself.

9. Edouard Herriot was prime minister three times and was a member of various French governments in the 1930s. In 1936 he replaced Vallat as president of the Chamber of Deputies and remained at his post until July 1940. Jules Jeanneney was his counterpart, as President of the Senate. Both opposed the armistice.

1. For the Laval affair, see Robert O. Paxton, *Vichy France: Old Guard and New Order, 1940–1944* (New York, 1972), chapter 1, also pp. 199–200.

2. RRL is perhaps referring to the letter of protest that was sent to Pétain in April 1941 by several distinguished Jewish figures in Paris. See Adam Rutkowski, ed., *La Lutte des Juifs en France à l'époque de l'occupation (1940–1944)* (Paris, 1975), pp. 49–50.

3. The letter that follows was published in part in ibid., pp. 52–53.

"You have declared, in your proclamations to the French people, 'I hate the lie that has done us so much harm' and 'I fight against injustice wherever I encounter it.'

"Why must these noble words be brutally denied by actions that constitute the worst of injustices, based on lies?

"Do not the new laws promulgated on June 14 in fact constitute an attack on persons and their goods? Do not the statements made to the press by the general commissioner for Jewish affairs officially represent in an aggravated version the slanderous attacks, always in a vague and collective form, which constitute the worst sort of humiliation? Yet in terms of both laws and statements, the declarations made in the name of the government by Mr. Baudouin, the minister for foreign affairs, in October 1940, had given us guarantees that we had to believe were valid in view of their source.

"But is it still possible to speak of guarantees or of rights, when the simple fact of being a Jew is enough, in most cases, to legitimize the most arbitrary decisions of the administrative authorities and the heads of private companies?

"Our dignity as French nationals, since as far as we know our status as citizens has not been officially revoked, makes it our duty to protest against the terms of Article 9 of the *Statut*, and those of the last paragraph of the Law on the Census. The offensive and infamous penalties indicated there for transgressors provide among other things for *internment camp even for those who are French*. Thus the Law is not aimed at Jews, whether French or foreign, but rather, in servile imitation of the occupying powers, takes cognizance only of a Jewish flock whose nationality, even when it is *French*, is only an accessory fact and has no value or impact.

"What then is the legal status of French Jews today? If they are still French, what is the meaning of citizenship rights, emptied of almost all their content and inferior even to those of the native citizens and subjects of many of our colonies, who do not even speak our language?

"Is the government's aim in fact that French Jewry should disappear, and are the words 'measures of justice and not of persecution' not the expression of the truth?

"The Bible is the only book that Jews hold sacred; are its teachings pernicious when they are followed by Jews but considered as the expression of the divine Word for Christians, since, under the name 'Old Testament,' they constitute one of the sacred books of the Catholic and Protestant Churches? 'We are all the children of Abraham, sons of the Bible,' in the words of H. E. Cardinal Verdier. So why must those who practice the ancient faith of Israel become, today, pariahs in their own homeland?

"Alas! It is by appealing to the basest passions of the human soul, to its cupidity, its envy and jealousy, that the foreign proponents of racial theories that are denied by science and condemned by the Church have found accomplices in our own country.

"The French Jews thus would have no choice but to submit, with the resignation and courage they have shown throughout the centuries, and with the help of their faith, to the ordeals that lie ahead of them.

"They will try to suppress the feelings that are all too natural, of contempt and hatred for their persecutors, whether foreign or French.

"They will preserve nevertheless their faith in the destiny of eternal France, that they may someday obtain their just recompense for the rights that are being violated today.

"In closing, we assure Your Honor of our profound respect and our absolute devotion."

August 3, 1941

On thinking it over, I expected Mr. Lebrun,[4] president of the Republic, to bear very heavy responsibilities. He allowed the regime

4. Albert Lebrun was the weak and ineffectual president of the French republic from 1932 to 1940.

to be destroyed by the Laval-Pétain-Weygand conspiracy. I was talking about it the other day with Emile Kahn. He replied that Lebrun had redeemed himself with a single sentence. "How," he asked at Bordeaux, "could we make war with generals who didn't want to fight?" And Lebrun, a graduate of the Polytechnique, an artillery captain in the other war, was hardly an anti-militarist! But two anecdotes will illustrate the intellectual competence of this man who was chosen as our head of state. Despite all his faults and his bourgeois dogmatism, Poincaré could have saved our ship.

At the opening of the Exhibition of 1937, Léon Blum and Jean Zay[5] were showing Lebrun the priceless treasures gathered in the Palais des Beaux-Arts—paintings, sculpture, the art of goldsmiths and silversmiths. As they stood in front of a display case full of jewelry, Léon Blum said jokingly to Lebrun—alluding to the campaigns of Maurras and Béraud—"Here's *my* famous silver!" and they continued their rapid tour. Wanting a closer look at these treasures in peace and quiet, Blum decided to come back alone with Jean Zay that evening after closing time. When they stopped in front of that same display case, they noticed that the guard was having a fit of the giggles. With difficulty, promising that he would be well paid for it, they made him confess what amused him so much. That morning, before leaving the hall, Mr. Lebrun had quietly taken him aside, without being noticed, and asked him in a low voice, "Is it true that this is Mr. Blum's own silver?"

During a Council of Ministers session in 1936, Delbos, the foreign minister, was giving a speech on the less than brilliant diplomatic situation. The actions of Germany and Italy were bearing fruit: Belgian neutrality, the turning of the tide in the

5. Zay was minister of national education from 1936 to 1939. He joined a small number of deputies from the National Assembly in June 1940 in their abortive attempt to resettle the French government in Algeria by sailing there via the *Massilia*. Shortly thereafter he was arrested and imprisoned, and was assassinated by the Vichy Milice in June 1944.

Balkans, Moscow smiling on Berlin. . . . "I am sorry," Delbos said in conclusion, "to paint such a discouraging picture." The ministers were dismayed. Lebrun could find nothing better to say in conclusion, clapping Delbos familiarly on the shoulder than "Well, old chap, we certainly know that your job has something to it!"

Jean Zay—whose defender, Varenne, got him a place in the political regime—told this to Emile Kahn a few days ago. Speaking of political trials, the most infamous was that of Mendès-France, who was ordered condemned even though all his military chiefs had him completely covered.[6] What acts of infamy there will be to blot out later on!

August 16, 1941

On August 13, Marshal Pétain made the most serious of all declarations on the TSF. He admitted that the French nation is no longer behind him at all, and announced the most draconian measures ever. Darlan is to take charge of the army, air force, and navy. The police force is to be strengthened. This is absolute dictatorship in its most dangerous form. . . . I am afraid the Marshal has not understood, for himself, the bloody consequences such words portend for the future.

On August 14, Churchill and Roosevelt published a joint declaration of eight points, which will give courage to the free people of all countries and all races. "Hitler's tyranny" is doomed to death. . . . It makes me think of the immense hope I felt in the days when, at the front, I heard of Wilson's Fourteen Points. Despite the shameful commentary that the French press, synchronized with Hitler, dares to publish today, one has the feeling that there is something new in the air.

6. Pierre Mendès-France, of Jewish origin and conviction, had served as finance minister in Blum's government in the 1930s. He too was part of the voyage to Algeria (see above note). Like Zay, Mendès-France was also arrested shortly after, tried, and committed to six years' imprisonment for treason. But he succeeded in escaping to England in 1942 and figured prominently in French politics in the postwar period.

Pétain attacks the Communists and the [capitalist] "trusts," but the official commentary names "international Jews" as responsible for the barbaric acts that have continued under the New Order in the past year. This time it is the Freemasons who are mentioned as being excluded from public employment. . . . What a strange regime and a strange armistice! The Legion [Légion française des combattants—the French League of Veterans, or LFC] = now the French SS! and even Gestapo. What does the future hold for us when restoration comes? Never in the history of France has a regime been able to maintain itself by the use of police terror and informers. We can no longer talk in the street or in restaurants, we can no longer write anything in our letters.

Food is becoming extremely difficult to find. We stand in line to buy tomatoes and zucchini. There were disturbances at Toulon and Lyon. But the Russians [have not been] crushed yet, even though Odessa and Kiev probably will fall.

August 27, 1941

After the Marshal made his speech, we had one by Pucheu[7]—that teachers college student who became a businessman and politician in the style of Doriot, who dreams of playing Fouché [Napoleon's minister of police] in the Interior Ministry. It's really police terror—and he who sows the wind [shall reap the whirlwind] . . . emergency courts, death sentences for expressing the wrong opinions. Ah! if only the Germans were not in Paris! I don't think people will stand for this form of servitude very long. In Paris the passive resistance is becoming active. Where are we going with all this? Yesterday we were happy to hear that Laval and Déat had encountered gunshots at Versailles. . . . Tomorrow and the next day there will be celebrations, with portable stages

7. At various times during the Vichy regime, Pierre Pucheu was minister of industrial production and minister of the interior. In this latter capacity he established the Police for Jewish Affairs (PQJ) in the autumn of 1941. On this new institution in France, see Marrus and Paxton, *Vichy France and the Jews*, pp. 135–137; Joseph Billig, *Le Commissariat général aux questions juives (1941–1944)*, 3 vols. (Paris, 1955–1960), passim.

and large numbers of partisans on the move, for the anniversary of the LFC. I am afraid there will be incidents, even in Marseilles, where cinema audiences are beginning to hiss at the Marshal when he appears on the screen.

Furthermore wine is to be very severely rationed, as has already been done with tobacco. How will working people react, and peasants, and even soldiers? I remember that during the suffering in the trenches in '14–'18, a quart of wine meant more than anything. Without it we wouldn't have won the war.

I read a book of memoirs by Robert Brasillach, the sectarian writer who was running *Je suis partout*, about the *Before the War*. It explains how people were educated to accept defeat and the new regime. Second-rate graduates of teachers colleges were jealous of those who had assumed leadership of the country. Without ideals and without faith, which was somewhat the fault of teachers who didn't know how to get hold of them and look after them, they went over to the *Action française* and fascism, which gave them the illusion that they were building something new. None of them had any heart. This wily young provincial was unfit to understand humanism.

I also read, by that pretentious man of letters who was a minister, de Monzie,[8] a book monumental in its foolhardiness, *Ci-devant* [*Formerly*]. De Monzie publishes the details of the moral betrayal that was the downfall of our country. After Munich, as a minister under Daladier, he received visits from Abetz in his garden. In the midst of the war he was telephoning Rome. At the time of the armistice he thought only of his own village, forgetting about the nation and the empire. Two more details: in July '38, Weygand gave a speech in Lille declaring that the French army had superior equipment. At the tragic meeting of the Council of Ministers in June 1940, where Weygand painted the picture of oncoming defeat, Marshal Pétain had only one regret—that

8. Anatole de Monzie had been minister of public works in the Reynaud government of March 1940 until the cabinet reshuffle on June 5. He was known for his sympathies toward Italy and regarded his own deposition as another victory for Léon Blum. See his journal *Ci-devant* (Paris, 1941), with entries for June 1940.

passenger pigeons had not been used to ensure contact among the various armies. One doesn't know whether to laugh or cry.

September 7, 1941

The situation is becoming dramatic in the Occupied Zone. Six thousand Jews from the 11th arrondissement have been interned,[9] and the French lawyers who submitted a request for dispensation to Vallat have been arrested. . . . Emergency courts and executions; this is political terror in addition to the rigors of the military occupation. How can one imagine that, under such conditions, Vichy would continue to believe in collaboration? The Free Zone is sagging, but I am told that in Paris there are just two worlds, on one hand the French and on the other the Boche and their agents. These agents, even though they are in power, will pay in person for the errors and crimes they commit.

Last Sunday there was a tumultuous celebration for the anniversary of the Legion of Honor, copied from Hitler's assemblies: forests of flags had been ordered up, but there wasn't much enthusiasm. Now, when the Occupied Zone is suffering more than ever, the Marshal makes the grossest psychological mistake he could by organizing an artificial July 14 [the French national holiday commemorating the storming of the Bastille], when no one is free or happy any more, or able to enjoy anything. People who had come from Paris wept for shame in their hotel rooms. Flyers were distributed that said "A year of the Legion, a year of misery!" The Parisian slogan was repeated here: *Pétain au dodo, Darlan au poteau, de Gaulle au boulot* [off to bed with Pétain, to the scaffold with Darlan, to work with de Gaulle]! Unfortunately it will take a civil war, I believe it more every day, to finish the military's war and the German occupation.

9. RRL is referring to the internment of Jews from the 11th arrondissement in Paris on August 15 and 20. Other arrests in other arrondissements in Paris took place from August 21 to 23. The total number of Jews arrested and sent to Drancy came to 4,232. The French police played an active role in these arrests.

In Nîmes[1] I went to see the representatives of American and Christian charities that are working to aid the interned foreign nationals here. It is comforting to talk with Protestant pastors and with Jesuits. It gives one hope for the future, and faith in the truth. In Paris the R.P. Riquet,[2] who was in charge of drawing up a statement on racism in action for the Bishops' Conference, began it with this sentence: "The *Statut* on the Jews is a scandal for Christian consciences and defies the intelligence of the French." Worth remembering. New measures are continuing to be published with Germanic thoroughness. Yesterday we had the *numerus clausus* for doctors.

When I went to my bookstore for the books by Barrès that I want to reread, I was told they are out of stock. A few days ago they sent the *Culte du Moi* [*Cult of the Ego*] and the *Roman de l'Energie nationale* [*Novel of National Energy*] to Georges Mandel, who is interned in Vals. That I was glad to hear.

I read Paul Eluard's *Love, Poetry* (null for me. I still can't understand poetry composed of unconnected words. Empaytaz[3] and I used to call that "phoney," and we were right), and Jules Romains' *Chants de dix années* [*Ten Years of Songs*] (trying a new form until he ran out of steam, with dubious results, not very musical).

1. The Coordinating Committee for Aid in the Camps (Nîmes Committee) began its functions in the autumn of 1940 and was officially recognized by the Ministry of the Interior on November 30, 1940. It consisted of Catholic, Protestant, and Jewish relief organizations, directed by Donald Lowrie of the YMCA. Meetings of the Committee were held in Nîmes.

2. Before the meeting of cardinals and archbishops in Paris in July 1941, Reverend Father (R.P.) Riquet called for a protest against the June *Statut*, saying it was "a scandal for Christian consciences as well as defying the intelligence of the French, an exceptionally sectarian and oppressive law against a religious confession." The assembly of Catholic leaders took little notice of Riquet's appeal. See J.-M. Mayeur, "Les Eglises devant la persécution des juifs en France," in G. Wellers, A. Kaspi and S. Klarsfeld, eds., *La France et la question juive, 1940–1944—la politique de Vichy, l'attitude des Eglises et des mouvements de résistance* (Paris, 1981), p. 154.

3. Frédéric Empaytaz was sub-prefect of Saint-Dizier during the war. He had been Lambert's close friend since school days at the Collège Rollin; they shared the same literary interests and views on many social and political issues.

October 3, 1941

In the last month I have been twice to Vichy, temporary capital of the "New Order." I made my rounds of administrative offices and saw friends, and now I have more confidence in the future than ever. In fact I brought back from Vichy a profound impression of a temporary situation in which nobody believes. The ministers have their offices in hotels with hastily written signs, sometimes even handwritten, like those of an occupation army headquarters. In the corridors the carpets have been taken up for fear they will be worn by too many visitors. The secretaries keep their files on top of the bidets in bathrooms, which have been turned into filing cabinets. Typed notes hang on the walls, since paper has become the all-determining resource. In this mess of a requisitioned palace, every floor is guarded by porters, but if you come during working hours you have only to look a bit self-assured to get in anywhere, see and read anything, and even take it with you. . . .

I have been reading a lot. I went back to Loti's books to remind myself of the musical orgies of my spiritual puberty, but at my age now these exotic symphonies seem poorer. The epithets are not thoughtfully chosen. I reread *Aziadé et les Désenchantées* [*Aziadé and the Disenchanted*]. Simenon is always a good distraction for me, especially while traveling. One right after the other I read *The Burgomaster of Furnes, Chez Krull* [*At Krull's House*], and *Les inconnus dans la maison* [*Strangers in the House*]. A very confident touch and bitterness in portraying certain settings. These novels will last like those of Alexandre Dumas.

Read two brochures, one on the Rothschilds and the other, by André Gide, *Découvrons Henri Michaux* [*Discovering Henri Michaux*]. I shall do so. A long novel translated from English, just the thing for an officer in the Colonial army, *No Arms or Armor* by Robert E{He}nriques. Then a rather feeble witness account of '14–'18, *La guerre à sept ans* [*After Seven Years of War*] by Jean Maxence. A fiery critique, *Aux fontaines de Barrès* [*At Barrès' Springs*] by Roland Engerrand. The latest by Giraudoux, a bit dense, a bit quirky, but quite charming in spots, *Choice of the Elect*. Although the exception proves the rule, I go to French springs to quench my thirst.

I had a long visit with Xavier Vallat in response to his summons.[4] Very correct. The man in charge of his office, Colonel de Jarnieu, is a stupid cavalryman who spent half an hour on a personal phone call when he was supposed to be receiving me: it was about a shipment of oats from one of his properties in Puy-de-Dôme to another at Saint-Laurent-du Var! Vallat told me that in the Occupied Zone the situation for Jews will only become more critical by the day. He looks as though he is annoyed with the Germans for gaining sympathy for us with their excessive persecution. He has the idea of creating a unified Jewish Community, with two sections. Thus our charitable work in the Free Zone can continue with commissioners if, as he is planning to do, he gives us money to aid the poor . . . out of the confiscated funds [of Jews]. But we cannot refuse since the important thing is for the social workers to carry on. I accept it from him since he is the legal authority. But I hope this will put me in a position, some day, to preside over the liquidation of this Commissariat, that it won't last any longer than the longer ministries we had in the olden days.[5]

When I joined Simone and the children at Cannes for a few days, I saw Nice again. A rather depressing scene. Too languid,

4. Jarnieu to RRL, September 23, 1941 (Brener Collection, Paris). The meeting took place on September 27 with the approval of the president of the Committee on Aid to Refugees (CAR), Albert Lévy.

5. It should be noted that Vallat had already informed RRL of his intention to establish this organization in the two principal zones in France; this had not been part of the German authorities' original demand. At this stage RRL did not seem to comprehend the significance of the organization, since his response was fairly placid. After their meeting, RRL sent Vallat a list of Jewish leaders, corresponding to the Jewish welfare societies, as possible candidates for a board of directors of the new organization. He included his own name among them "to facilitate the liaison and then withdraw, if you find it preferable, at the appropriate time." CDJC, XXXI–144 (September 27, 1941).

too much music, too many buttonhole intrigues. All this is going on at a far remove from the suffering and defeat. What has become of the dignity our ancestors showed after [the Franco-Prussian War, in] 1871?

October 5, 1941

Seven synagogues were blown up in Paris the day after the Day of Atonement.[6] I would never have believed the time would come when, in my own country, fanaticism would manifest itself in such a way! The future will judge and compensate us. Like the sorcerer's apprentice, those who govern us have sown the whirlwind, I hope for their sake that they didn't realize it. . . . From now on, anything is possible: the next thing they could do is desecrate our cemeteries.

But Germany has not crushed Russia. Winter is coming. From a military viewpoint, I don't think a German victory is at all possible. But it's going to take a long, a very long time. Will we be able to live through this long wait? Blessed are those who can still fight!

In the *Figaro* I read this fine thought by Paul Valéry: "There are some people whom one must wish that they may have the worst opinion of us in the world. For, in a warped mirror, it is better to look ugly." Since no thought may be freely expressed in France any more, we are reduced to consoling ourselves by reading between the lines.

6. In the night of October 2–3, 1941, seven synagogues were destroyed or heavily damaged in Paris by anti-Semitic groups. On October 15 the Association of French Rabbis adopted a declaration of protest in which they stated: "As we are moved and caused anguish by human victims, so also by these stones hallowed by piety, these tabernacles that enclosed the scrolls of the Torah. Where will this fury of sacrilege end? Will all the synagogues of France, like those of Germany, be turned into ruins, like those of Galilee where Jesus prayed?" Rutkowski, *La Lutte des Juifs*, p. 67; Jacques Adler, *The Jews of Paris and the Final Solution: Communal Response and Internal Conflicts, 1940–1944* (New York and Oxford, 1987), pp. 40–41.

October 12, 1941

The German offensive in Russia appears to be succeeding, but one cannot imagine that a decisive resolution could be gained militarily on the ground. . . . The date for a possible peace was pushed further ahead the moment Roosevelt drew up his message nullifying the neutrality law. At the same time the heroic opposition in all the countries occupied by Germany proves that Europe, though under its orders, will never accept Hitler's yoke. . . . In an article in *La Gazette de Lausanne* I am reading views that seem to me disturbingly true with regard to our immediate future, such as the opinion of the prelates in the Vatican on this war: "The whole of humanity has entered a tunnel and cannot see to the other end. It is a struggle between two hemispheres. We are already in a time of famine. Millions of people are suffering. Unless the unexpected happens, many of them will endure a harsh martyrdom, as at various times in centuries past. Because of the blockade, Europe will be the most severely affected. The military war may be over one day, perhaps sooner rather than later, but that will probably not mean the end of the economic war."

So if the Russians fall back to the Urals, even if Moscow is burned, if the German troops get as far as the Caucasus, as long as they don't get hold of the oil, nothing will have changed. This is my conviction as well. But what will become of France, and of us Jews—what will happen to us in the meantime? It is clear that in this huge inferno, Jewish concerns are only one element in the general anxiety—we all have to wait. This calms me at least with regard to my sons' future, since the Poles, the Belgians, the Dutch are no more sure of tomorrow than I am. . . . As I have said to myself many times in the past year, we must have the energy to endure. I myself may perhaps not see the new world to come. Our individual lives are counted in years, but what are twelve months in the lives of peoples, and in the evolution of humankind?

I read René Benjamin's *Sous l'oeil en fleur de Madame de Noailles* [*Through the Mature Eyes of Madame de Noailles*] (excellent criticism, in the form of a chronicle like Anatole France). Some more Simenon, whom I treasure because he lets me escape from the worries of the day: *A Wife at Sea* and *Unlucky Star*.

November 30, 1941[7]

I have been back to Vichy twice to see Xavier Vallat.[8] I am sorry to realize that he trusts and consults me as the social worker who knows most about the Jewish agencies, and as the least suspect person from the French point of view. He is under strong pressure from the occupation authorities and has really agreed only to carry out their orders. The Union des Juifs [Union of Jews] will be created with us, without us, or against us. I am the only one capable of being its secretary general—a heavy and very serious task. With an eye to the future, I shall consult only my own conscience before accepting it.

Be that as it may, the Jewish agencies, the militants, the philanthropists, and those whom I call the "Jewish princes" are agitated, jealous, and already criticizing me. . . . Mr. Helbronner, who kept his head down before the *Statut* was published, when he should have been courageous, asked me indiscreet questions when I saw him in Lyon.[9] . . . But I am pursuing my course with a clear conscience and the clear desire to remain both an excellent Jew and an excellent Frenchman. I am rereading Maurice Barrès and Henri Franck.[1]

7. The long break between October 12 and this entry is probably due to RRL's intensive involvement in establishing the UGIF [Union Générale des Israelites de France], and to the central role he played in the negotiations. A detailed description of these events is found in RRL's report to Albert Lévy, UGIF president, YIVO Institute, New York, § 210, II-1. Extracts are included in Zosa Szajkowski, *Analytical Franco-Jewish Gazetteer, 1939–1945* (New York 1966), pp. 125–127.

8. These two meetings took place on November 7 and 21.

9. Helbronner and Chief Rabbi Schwartz saw RRL on the way to his second meeting with Vallat in November, and severely criticized his partisan activities. They implored him not to go on to Vichy, but RRL disregarded their criticism and went to meet Vallat. See the Introduction.

1. Henri Franck (1889–1912) was a French Jewish poet whose most noted poem, *La Danse devant l'Arche*, was published in 1912. The fact that RRL mentions the two together in the same breath expresses yet again his inner duality as a Frenchman and a Jew.

Xavier Vallat telephoned me this morning. The historic decree[2] will be issued Tuesday. He wants to see me again on Friday, alone. Another trip—this is getting to be a habit. Should I rejoice or bemoan it?

These trips have given me time to read plenty of books these last few weeks. For a recharging of my energies, and beautiful language, *L'ennemi des lois* [*The Outlaw*] and *Colette Baudoche*. Two Giraudoux that disappointed me; what superficial stuff this is, nothing but expensive schmaltz: *The Trojan War Will Not Take Place* and *Les Aventures de Jérôme Bardini* [*The Adventures of Jerome Bardini*]. Books on current affairs: *L'Etat-major s'en va-t-en guerre* [*The General Staff Goes to War*] by Georges Bonnancy (excellent—Dorgelès, 1941) and *Les causes militaires de la défaite* [*The Military Causes of the Defeat*] by Colonel Alerme (the best defense for Blum and Paul Reynaud); finally, Daniel Halévy's *Trois épreuves* [*Three Ordeals*] 1814, 1871, 1940 (or the art of cooking history to the Marshal's taste). As a pastime, a whole series of Simenons, which are never boring, never fail to amuse me: *Justice, The Man Who Watched Trains Go By*, *Ceux de la soif* [*They Who Thirst*], *Les sept minutes* [*Seven Minutes*], *Le coup de vague* [*The Breaking Wave*], *Monsieur La Souris* [*"Mr. Mouse"*], and *Malempin* [*The Family Lie*].

Nîmes, December 2, 1941

Staying at the Hotel Imperator—in this peaceful city where I have been thinking over the causes of our disaster, not foreseeing what would be my personal ordeals as long as my officer's uniform was relieving me of ordinary worries. . . . I am here to attend the interconfessional conference of the aid agencies working in the camps,[3] chaired by Donald Lowrie of the YMCA, a distinguished American and very much the "social worker." I leave again early

2. Refers to the establishment of the UGIF by the French government on November 29, 1941 (published in the *J.O.* on December 2). For the complete text of the law, see L. Czertok and A. Kerlin, eds., *Les Juifs sous l'occupation: Recueil des textes français et allemands, 1940–1944* (Paris, 1945), pp. 102–103.

3. Refers to the Nîmes Committee, see above.

tomorrow for Marseilles, where I am to confer with my other colleagues—Vallat's future victims: leaders, "appointed by decree," of French Jewry.

Xavier Vallat did in fact call me at home on Sunday. The decree creating the Union des Israélites de France, as a racial grouping to be distinguished from the Consistory, is to be published today. I know the names of the nine Council members for the Free Zone, of whom I am one. I succeeded in delaying the appearance of the names in the *Officiel*,[4] and I am to see Vallat again on Friday in Vichy. They are good choices since they are the most qualified leaders of the agencies.

But the decree itself is terrible. Its publication has been accompanied by radio commentaries designed to humiliate us. Can we accept being the executors of those in power? Can we refuse, with all the personal consequences this may have for us? This is the moral dilemma for us. However the war turns out, the job of secretary general, to which everyone is already designating me, will be heavy, very heavy to carry. . . . I shall answer the call according to my conscience. But I think we cannot accept being the representatives of the Jews of France in anything other than social welfare and philanthropic issues, that we ourselves cannot impose taxes on others of our faith, that we ourselves cannot distribute funds confiscated[5] from our people and that, in any case, the fact that we are doing this technical work should not suggest that we accept the principle of such exceptional legislation.

The Marshal met with Goering yesterday.[6] Certainly the decree in question must have been published, or at least announced,

4. RRL's statement that he was responsible for delaying publication of the names of the nine candidates who had been nominated is confirmed by the sources. The list was published in the *J.O.* on January 9, 1942. See Czertok and Kerlin, *Les Juifs sous l'occupation*, p. 133.

5. RRL refers here to the Solidarity Fund established by a French law of July 22, 1941 (published in *J.O.* on August 26, 1941), which allowed the Jewish community to use a certain percentage of the goods confiscated from Jews to aid those in need. The Council in the south never made use of these funds because of the moral implications. The July 22 law, which set up the legal structure for the organization of Jewish property, had a devastating effect on the community. For an analysis of its impact, see Marrus and Paxton, *Vichy France and the Jews,* chapter 4, passim.

before he left. I realize more clearly every day that, with regard to the Jewish question in France, Berlin is calling the shots.

On the train I reread *Les diverses familles spirituelles* [*The Faith of France*] by Maurice Barrès. It is very fine and especially moving for me at this time. I remain convinced that, in the zone under siege, one can no longer speak of the will of the French people. To hold on and to stay the course remains my plan, the rule for my actions.

Lyon, December 11, 1941

Written December 11 on the train between Orange and Valence, and recopied in a modest room at the Hôtel de Russie, reserved for me for one night by my former assistant on the National Committee, Bernard Schoenberg,[7] a rabbi from Lyon. I am returning to Vichy, after just having left there on Monday with Simone, who had come with me because she wanted to see our provisional capital before the birth of our fourth child, expected around the 12th of February.

I am now a central figure in French Jewry, which means I am discussed and attacked by some and flattered and encouraged by others. But I am acting, and that is what matters. I am strengthened, matured, and impassioned by action, and I must take on heavy responsibilities. I should write down the details of this comedy, for myself and for the future, as I did with the ups and

6. Pétain met with Goering on December 1, 1941, at Saint-Florentin, southeast of Paris, and there submitted to him the conditions for France's collaboration in economic, political, and social matters. But Pétain did not offer what the Germans wanted most: military assistance in North Africa. The "Jewish question" was apparently not on the agenda for this meeting. See Eberhard Jäckel, *La France dans l'Europe de Hitler* (Paris 1968), p. 300; Otto Abetz, *Das offene Problem: Ein Rückblick auf zwei Jahrzehnte deutscher Frankreichpolitik* (Köln, 1951), pp. 213–214.

7. Bernard Schoenberg was a young rabbi who served as an assistant to Chief Rabbi Sèches of Lyon. He had been in Paris in the 1930s, where he had contact with RRL as they were both working for refugee aid organizations. Drafted into the army in 1940, Schoenberg was demobilized in August 1940 in Lyon, where he resumed his prewar work. In 1943 he was arrested in Lyon but released, then rearrested at Amberieu in May 1943 and deported to Drancy. He died in the Ponowitz camp in February 1944.

downs of the actions I took before leaving Bonn to move to the Quai d'Orsay [in Paris]. If you know what you want, and are clear about wanting it, everything is there for you.

Before I left for Vichy that week I had understood how much I was envied for my courage and for the esteem in which I am held by our country's leaders today. A Central Commission of Jewish Aid Organizations[8] was set up a year ago, under the authority of the chief rabbi, of which the secretary general is the chief rabbi of Strasbourg, my friend René Hirschler.[9] But the authorities did not recognize this organization, which got no further than its pretensions, only organized some discussion sessions, and accomplished nothing. It was I who, for personal reasons and because of my experience (I have been known to the ministry people for ten years), was summoned by Vallat to act as an unofficial liaison agent or technical expert. From there it is only a step to saying that I am Vallat's man. The evil tongues really let themselves go.

My train last Thursday left for Vichy at 11:30 A.M. At ten o'clock a little Jewish parliament met at the Central Commission office.[1] They asked me not to go to Vichy. I did not accept this as an order since I had solemnly promised Vallat to answer his summons alone. I was treated as a dictator, and it was Pierre Dreyfus, the colonel's son, who threw this insult in my face. I permitted myself some imprudent words and went to Vichy anyway. I was

8. On October 30–31, 1940, the main Jewish organizations met in Marseilles to set up an umbrella organization, the Central Commission of Jewish Relief Organizations (Commission Central d'Ouevres Juives d'Assistance), to coordinate the community's relief activities. Under the aegis of the chief rabbi of France, Isaïe Schwartz, it operated rather ineffectively for more than a year, until the UGIF was created.

9. Rabbi René Hirschler, the former rabbi of Mulhouse and Strasbourg, took the initiative to establish the Central Commission and was its guiding spirit. After it was dissolved he remained an active participant in the relief work and founded the General Chaplaincy in March 1942. He remained at his post as general chaplain until he was arrested by the Gestapo on December 23, 1943. He was deported to Auschwitz on February 23, 1944, at age thirty-nine. See Serge Klarsfeld (ed.), *Le mémorial de la déportation des Juifs en France* (Paris, 1978), convoy no. 67.

1. This meeting took place on December 4, and, as RRL noted, the mood was one of great agitation and hostility to further private meetings between him and Vallat.

bitterly reproached for going alone since, it was wrongly asserted, I was involving everyone else against his will.

The results of my trip exceeded what I had hoped for. I obtained from Vallat a verbal communication addressed to me,[2] in which he agreed to negotiate on the points at issue, and summoned three negotiators to appear with me tomorrow, namely Oualid,[3] possible president of the Union, Joseph Millner[4] and André Weil.[5] (I'll give a portrait of each of them some time.)

I was truly overjoyed. Last Sunday I left Simone in Vichy and went to the Consistory session in Lyon, where I gave an account of the conclusion of my mission and the results obtained. I received no thanks for it. I can only pity these elderly people who set themselves up as leaders of the Jews. Helbronner, the pontificating president who is going deaf, told us about an astonishing letter from the Marshal's cabinet. At the moment Vallat was

2. See RRL's report, appendix 6, YIVO: § 210, II-1. The verbal communication defined the responsibilities of the UGIF with regard to certain controversial matters. The UGIF could inherit the functions and assets of welfare organizations; the UGIF could use the Solidarity Fund but could also receive funding from voluntary sources; its imposition on the community was temporarily dropped.

3. Originally from Algeria, William Oualid was an eminent attorney who had become a leader of French Jewry in the 1930s. He was intensely involved in many community and refugee activities. Following the death of the president of the Alliance israélite universelle in 1935, he became one of its vice presidents, an office he occupied until 1942. A respected member of the Central Consistory, Oualid was actively engaged in several refugee committees in the prewar period. See Caron, *Uneasy Asylum*, passim.

4. Joseph Millner was a central figure in the OSE (Ouevre de Secours aux Enfants—Children's Relief Charity) and was RRL's confidant during the negotiations with Vallat. Their association stemmed from joint cooperation in the management and editing of *L'Univers israélite* in the 1930s. Nominated by Vallat to the UGIF Council, Millner was nevertheless quickly removed from his office after being denaturalized. He continued to look after the OSE until the end of 1943, at which time he recommended that the children's homes be closed and their residents dispersed.

5. We have corrected RRL's spelling of his name—Weill—to what appears in various sources. André Weil was a very active member of the Central Consistory during the war and took an active role in the community's discussions on the establishment of the UGIF. He was also one of the executive officers of the Central Commission. For Weil's widespread activity during the war, see Simon Schwarzfuchs, *Aux prises avec Vichy*, passim.

telephoning me in Marseilles to tell me the law was about to appear, the Marshal's cabinet was insisting that the law must not be published without the advice of the Council of State, and was coming up against the Commissariat's opposition. . . . This is the very apex of hypocrisy! Why not admit that the Marshal did accept the law, and that he knows that Germany gives the orders, from Paris, directly to the Commissariat of Jewish Affairs, the same as to the press and the information service? Whom do they think they're fooling?

So this was a painful session for me,[6] all the more because I was informed, while I was speaking, of the sudden death of Gastalla, my comrade in arms, the former assistant secretary of the Consistory, who lived in the apartment next to our meeting room. The President took note of my verbal communication, and it has been distributed. It was immediately followed by a tirade from the chief rabbi of France, who attacked me personally and reproached me for overstepping my competence, contending that the names I had proposed to Vallat were those of all my friends. . . . I did not dignify this with a reply. With the maturity of life and experience, I now know how to contain myself, and from now on am making efforts to choose irony over verbal offensives. But some friends made me feel better. They repeatedly told me that the chief rabbi is an old fool and gets jealous when he sees himself being eclipsed by courageous members of the laity; that he was talking like a village preacher. Moreover, I don't accept his criticisms.

Then I returned to Marseilles, where some confidential explanations have put things back on track. I have to watch out for myself left and right. Vallat, tomorrow,[7] must not be allowed to make me look suspect. I have to remain clear-minded. I have to

6. This meeting took place on December 7, 1941.

7. This refers to the meeting between Vallat and three representatives of welfare organizations (RRL, Oualid, and Millner) and André Weil, on December 12. See Diary entry for December 28, 1941.

remember, every time I am listening to an adversary or someone who contradicts me, to think, before responding, about what might be the ulterior motive for their attitude. I am expecting a struggle, and I am ready for it. Vive la vie, et vive l'action humaine [Long live life and long live human action]!

Marseilles, December 21, 1941

In *L'Alerte* a week ago I read this story in Roger Vanjour's Paris chronicle! It would make a good plot for a novel: "During the exodus from Paris, one family had piled into their car everything they owned, including an elderly grandmother, eighty-seven years old. When they reached the banks of the Loire there was a heavy bombing raid. The family members scattered into the woods, leaving the grandmother in the car, entrusting her to the Lord. When they came back after the Stukas [German aircraft] had gone, the poor old lady had died of fright. The family devoutly emptied the laundry basket and laid her in it, then continued on their way. A hundred kilometers farther there was another air raid. Again the occupants of the car abandoned it. But when they came back this time, they found it ransacked. Thieves had taken everything, including the laundry basket with the elderly lady in it.

"This must have caused plenty of trouble for both sides, if I may say so; the looters because the corpse must have been quite an embarrassment to them, and the heirs because they no longer had any proof of the death of their ancestor."

Read Simenon's *Quartier nègre* [*Negro Quarter*]. A good exotic novel.

December 28, 1941

These last days of the year have seen events that will be most important for the outcome of the war, which is now no longer in doubt: the attack by the Japanese—the beginning of a victorious resistance by the Russians—the British victory in Libya—Hitler, as commander-in-chief, linking his fate to that of the German armies. Victory is certain; it is even possible in 1942.

I am going to Vichy again tomorrow because all is not going as well as I could have hoped. I must quickly write down for the record what has been happening with Xavier Vallat since my last interview with him. I must be precise in remembering, because individual people are jealous and mean. One cannot judge properly if one does not know the extent of the problems or the need for action.

December 12: Visit to Vallat by the Agencies' delegation. Oualid reads out a rather rambling statement explaining the reasons for our refusal . . . unless Vallat gives us assurances regarding the domain of the UGIF Council's competency (we are social workers only and not the representatives of "the Jewish people" in France); on the moral impossibility for us to be the managers of the Solidarity Fund; on the possibility of receiving specially designated funds; on offering the chairmanship to one of the French charities; on the desire for the administrators not to be paid; on looking for a secretary outside the Council (this was aimed at me!). Present at this interview, besides myself, were Joseph Millner, who remained silent as agreed, and André Weil, a neophyte in philanthropy, former secretary of Maurice de Rothschild, who made the mistake of speaking, claiming that the agencies could by themselves raise all the funds they would need, and brightening his intervention with quite unhelpful details such as his family's five generations in France. . . .

Vallat replied frankly and firmly. He gave his word of honor that he would never call upon the UGIF in the Free Zone for any purpose other than that of the agencies. He underlined that it was impossible for him to change a single word of the law because of the "conqueror's requirements." He decided, and we agreed, that he would ask for an individual agreement from each of us before nominating us. We would respond by sending him our reservations in writing, and since nominations would not be made until after our responses had been received, he would let us know that our reservations had been accepted, and he would see the resignation of any of us, in case it were necessary, as justified. He said he would never think of asking the UGIF Council to fulfill policing functions!

When we came back, apart from André Weil, Oualid, Millner, and I were in favor of accepting this offer. We met Gamzon[8] of the Jewish Scouts of France, and he too wanted us to accept.

I met with Vallat alone before and after this meeting. He wanted me to be on the Council and was thinking of appointing me as delegated administrator rather than secretary general. I must say that he proved his loyalty to me by maintaining to the others that I had made no commitments on anyone else's behalf.[9]

Dec. 13: Meeting of the Central Consistory in Lyon. I decided not to attend, after writing to Oualid my personal point of view; I wanted to accept my appointment to the Council, with reservations about its competency; but our acceptance should be a collective one. After the usual disorderly session, the Consistory agreed to advise the nine of us to accept, and proposed a text for a letter of acceptance with reservations.[1]

8. Robert Gamzon was the son of an immigrant engineer from Eastern Europe and the grandson of a chief rabbi of France, Albert Lévy. In 1923 in Paris he founded the first Jewish Scout movement to provide Jewish youth a new identity, loyal both to Judaism and to France. The *Jewish Scouts of France (Eclaireurs Israélites de France)* had a strong influence on Jewish youth in the 1920s and 1930s. Gamzon was its driving force throughout those years and during the war. RRL's remark here contradicts Gamzon's own assertion in his journal, which was edited and published posthumously *(Les eaux claires: journal 1940–1944* (Paris, 1981), that he joined the UGIF only later, and for tactical reasons. Other documentary sources corroborate RRL's remark. See Alain Michel, *Les Eclaireurs israélites de France pendant la Seconde Guerre mondial* (Paris, 1984), pp. 101–108.

9. RRL's diary is not perfectly clear, at this stage, on the nature of his commitment to Vallat, and whether it overstepped the limits of the UGIF. RRL mentioned earlier that he feared Vallat might divulge incriminating information, and happily reports here Vallat's denial that he had coaxed the others to accept. It is certain that a relationship of trust had been established between the two men. This placed RRL in a very complicated situation with regard to other leaders in the community.

1. The text was completed by André Weil after a marathon deliberation that lasted more than seven hours. Weil's text stipulated the shared objections to participation, and based acceptance on Vallat's official promises that the organization would not be called upon to fulfill police functions.

Dec. 15–18: The eight letters arrived. Those chosen are Oualid, Albert Lévy,[2] Gamzon, Jarblum,[3] René Mayer,[4] Olmer,[5] Millner, and I. André Weil is thus out of it before it begins; that's all right, he's too chauvinistic for my taste, critical and a supporter of worst-case policies, but he forgets the viewpoint of the persons in need, which to me is the only thing that matters. On the 18th we met at Oualid's home. The letter drafted by the Consistory was a tissue of poor terminology. Oualid prepared a new text, which we submitted to Helbronner in Lyon.

Dec. 21: Vallat telephoned me to ask if the letters had arrived, and informed me that the ninth candidate is a Marcel Wormser

2. A distinguished member of the Jewish community in France between the wars, Albert Lévy was active in the Central Consistory and, from 1936 on, in the CAR (Comité d'Assistance aux Réfugiés [CAR]—Committee on Aid to Refugees), which he helped found. As a result of his high profile in the community and his connections with the American Joint Distribution Committee, he was considered a good candidate for UGIF president, and he was willing to accept the position. It would appear that he was informed about all of RRL's negotiations with Vallat and seems to have supported Lambert's orientation. Deeply troubled by the internal frictions within the French Jewish community, Lévy resigned from the Consistory in March 1942. He was able to escape to Switzerland at the end of December 1942.

3. Marc Jarblum, originally from Warsaw, arrived in Paris in 1907 at age twenty. Engaged in left-leaning Zionist political activity, Jarblum became one of the leaders of the East European Jewish community in France in the interwar period. He was one of the fiercest opponents of the founding of the UGIF and influenced a number of members of the community to think likewise. In 1942 he took part in resistance activities in southern France and was then forced to flee to Switzerland in the spring of 1943. There he played an essential role by sending aid to Jewish organizations outside the UGIF.

4. René Mayer, born and raised in France, was the head of the leading international Jewish emigration organization, HICEM (an acronym of three Jewish migration associations that established it in 1927) in France. At one point Mayer thought of joining the UGIF but ultimately decided against it in order to preserve the effective operation of his organization. Mayer suggested that Wladimir Schah take his place on the Council, thus promising HICEM influence in the UGIF. After the UGIF was established, Mayer intervened with RRL to delay the dissolution of HICEM. (See Mayer to RRL, March 14, 1942, YIVO: § 210, civ-4). HICEM was officially dissolved in 1942.

5. Professor David Olmer was born in Marseilles in 1877. An accomplished physician in pathology and clinical medicine, Olmer divided his time between research and clinical work. His activity in the Jewish community was devoted to the Central Consistory, in which he emerged as a leading figure. A member of its permanent section from the 1930s and through the war, he was also president of its Commission on Social Welfare and an overseer of the army chaplaincy in the camps, run by the Consistory. He survived the war. See Schwarzfuchs, *Aux prises avec Vichy*, passim.

who is known to the Foreign Affairs Ministry, from Alsace, has connections to the United States, an industrialist who now lives in Vichy.

Dec. 22: Helbronner has given our letter his approval. We had a new meeting, but it turned dramatic: René Mayer and Olmer had each personally decided to refuse to serve. Oualid and Jarblum then followed them. . . . Albert Lévy, Millner, Gamzon, and I could not possibly accept under the circumstances. So we decided to go along with the others, and all of us signed the same letter declining the office. I am convinced that this is an imbecilic step to take, but we'll see what happens! Oualid had a failure of nerve. . . . I wrote a personal letter to Vallat to notify him of this collective refusal, since I am the only one who has any power to save this thing any longer—I'm right about that.

Dec. 26: Telephone call from Vallat, saying he hasn't had any answer, and he can't wait any longer: time is running out. I told him what has happened. He was disappointed and annoyed and asked me to come without further delay. I asked to have Millner come with me, and he agreed. I shall make the report, and we leave tomorrow.

1942

Vichy, January 8, 1942

I am copying this out in the salon-office of the Hotel Albert I, after writing it yesterday on the train between Valence and Lyon. Since I am on my way to Vichy once again, I should note the events of the days just past: a week of Jewish diplomacy. Perhaps one day I can use my notes to write *Ten Years of Jewish Diplomacy* (recollections from Geneva, London, Amsterdam since 1933, with critical portraits of big shots and of little bugs, of victims and of those who profit. I must keep it in mind).

I have been letting my diary drift. With the new year I'm taking it in hand again. Left for Lyon on December 29, stayed at the Hotel Russia on Gasparvé Street, a modest refuge that Schoenberg introduced to me. Arrived at 6 P.M. and dined alone in this city made somber by the blackout and the black ice, at a narrow table in a bar where jazz music unexpectedly cheered me in my solitude. It was a good dinner, and three tables over I saw George Wormser, who was head secretary to both Clemenceau and Mandel. He was certainly discussing banking with a [. . .] who looked more or less Semitic, and refused to recognize me, making use for once of his poor eyesight. On the 30th, at 7:30 in the morning, I went on to Vichy. Bad coffee in the dining car and lunch at the Albert I, where the superintendent knows me by now and reserves a good room for me.

December 30, 1941. I must recall things in order, as on an agenda, so as not to forget anything. If I need to, I'll elaborate later with the obvious portraits (my friend Vallat—Joseph Millner—André Weil—Albert Lévy—Oualid, who is now senile—Gaston Kahn,[1] a faithful and clear-minded friend, etc.). I meet Millner for lunch at the Albert I. Vallat, busy with a ceremonial occasion at the Interior Ministry, has a colleague tell us not to wait but to come back at 6 P.M. We agree, and do so. I return to the hotel to warm myself, sitting on the radiator reading my Simenon. His complicated life helps mature my thinking and action in these negotiations, in which I have learned always to ask myself: Why is this person saying that? What is the ulterior motive for this attitude or that declaration?

At six o'clock, conversation with Xavier Vallat; as always very open and frank with me. Millner is just a witness, my Pylades whom I would prefer a little more silent and passive. Vallat is extremely unhappy about our collective refusal to serve. It represents lost time. This business has been dragging on since December 12. He still trusts me because I at least understand the demands that defeat imposes on us and the difficulties of the

1. Gaston Kahn's career within the French Jewish community reflects new directions in the orientation of French Jews. Born in Wingersheim in 1889, Kahn devoted himself almost entirely to relief work. Before World War II he was a member of the Comité de Bienfaisance Israélite, the Jewish Charity Committee that was established in 1906 in Paris, and from 1936 he was actively involved in CAR with RRL and Albert Lévy. His involvement in the UGIF was thus a natural outgrowth of his prewar activities and his close relationship to Lambert and Lévy. The director of the UGIF's 5th department, he was in constant contact with RRL and also took part in the 1943 founding of the Center for Jewish Documentation. Following Lambert's arrest, he succeeded him as the head of UGIF-south for several months. Although the source of incriminations after the war, Kahn was decorated twice; he received the Medal of Resistance in 1946 and was made a Knight of the Legion of Honor in 1953. His postwar work reflected his previous career; he was Joint delegate to the French Jewish charitable organizations and a member of the Central Consistory and the Paris Consistory.

situation. I ask that he understand the scruples of these eminent figures. Yes, he says, but after the conversation with Oualid he had expected the whole group would accept. Our reply to his letter was to be yes with reservations regarding the competence of the council *in the Free Zone*. Having received our letter and then nominated us, he was therefore prepared to accept our reservations, and if it came to cases, a letter like ours would justify our resignation.

In view of these events, Vallat can't wait any longer. He is leaving for Paris on the 5th. Besides Mr. Marcel Wormser, whom he chose himself and who has accepted, he will choose eight Jewish individuals not involved in our social work. He will have an easy time finding eight "mercenaries," he says, people living in Vichy who know nothing about our organizations but will be happy to have a role in them, if only because this will give them the authorization to stay.

I insist that he reconsider, that he make one further gesture to persuade those who are willing, and see for himself which of the eight had decided to accept (Gamzon, Millner, Albert Lévy, and myself), since I cannot name names to him officially. He asks for my advice. I make the suggestion—which he accepts—to send a telegram to all eight persons, confirming his promise (he himself prefers the word verbal *commitment*. A good point.), and I draw up a text for him. He is thinking of sending the telegram that very day, but Millner has a better idea: since he is asking for replies by telegram, to put the two of us on the same basis as the others he will wait on our return down south on Friday, January 2. Vallat accepts.

Our mission has been a total success, and I now think all eight will say yes. As for me, this time I shall not wait around for the chitchat [. . .] and shall take up my responsibilities. I return to the hotel. Vallat has given me a list of organizations that should be incorporated into the *Union*, and he would like information about them. This is childish! They are the associations registered with the police headquarters in Paris. I shall bring him the information when I come back on the 8th with Millner. But we shall tell the others that he telephoned on Sunday, January 4, and asked us to come, so as not to give away our very useful strategy.[2]

Before we leave, Vallat informs us of some sad events in Paris—ninety-seven executions, arrests of six hundred people concentrated around Compiègne[3]—and bows respectfully in speaking of André Baur,[4] who will be vice president of the *Union*,

2. This partisan action by RRL and Millner raises the problem of collaboration to its full extent. These two figures—and Lambert was the pivotal one—were joining forces with Vallat against other Jewish leaders to force them to accept their nominations. They had completely bowed to Vallat in the face of his threat to appoint "mercenaries" to head the organization. RRL believed in "[his] friend Vallat," maintaining that he was not bluffing about the pressure from the Germans. RRL's behavior in this delicate matter reveals his disdain for many of the other leaders of French Jewry, especially in the Consistory. To a certain extent this followed from the bad blood that existed between them from the interwar days, but also to RRL's personality. Lambert trusted his instincts and relied on his experience in the French bureaucracy, and suffered no self-doubt or timidity. Personal ambition was far from the sole motive behind his action. Tired of "parliamentary chitchat" and confident in his own clear-sightedness, Lambert was driven by his commitment to save the charitable organizations from being dissolved. For the wider historical ramifications of his behavior, see the Introduction.

3. RRL refers here to the intensification of German action against the Jews in the Occupied Zone in December 1941. On December 12, 743 Jews, who were French citizens, were arrested by the German and French authorities. In order to obtain a thousand hostages, the number set by the Germans, 300 more Jews were taken from the Drancy camp and all were sent to the Compiègne camp, near Paris. On December 15, 95 hostages (including 53 Jews) were executed on Mount Valérien. The day before, the German military authorities had announced that a fine of a billion francs would be demanded of the Jews in the Occupied Zone. See Klarsfeld, *Vichy-Auschwitz,* p. 32.

4. Born in Paris in 1904, one of eight children, André Baur was the son of a prominent and established Jewish family. He was the grandson of Emmanuel Weill, the former chief rabbi of France, and was related to leading members of the Central Consistory. A banker by profession, he was elected president of the Reform congregation on Copernicus Street in Paris in the 1930s. Through his web of professional, communal, and family connections, Baur had many contacts within French society. Due to these relations and his personal commitment to Jewish community affairs, he was coopted into the Coordinating Committee in Paris in May 1941. His involvement in this committee made him a likely candidate for the UGIF, to which he was appointed vice president on January 9, 1942, and the head of its northern division. He remained in this capacity until his arrest in July 22, 1943. He, his wife, and four children were deported on December 17, 1943, to Auschwitz, where they all perished. A collection of Baur's personal letters to family members, from his imprisonment in Drancy to the day before his deportation to Auschwitz, was published privately by Gilbert Manuel in 2006. See André Baur, *Lettres à Odette. Drancy 26 juillet–3 septembre 1943* (n.p., n.d.).

but in Paris. He is sorry that Baur could not have come to tell us to accept. Regarding the billion-franc fine imposed on the Jews by the Germans, through the *Union*, he tells us that he found out this news from *le Temps*, as did we. In confidence he tells us further that the French government will advance this sum to the *Union* in Paris and, in order both to obey and to cover this amount, will confiscate the Jewish apartment houses in the Occupied Zone and take out ninety-nine-year mortgages on them. "Until then . . ." he says. A fine thing, and very important.

On the 31st, after a short night at the hotel, I leave Vichy again at 5:20 in the morning, and by evening I am with Simone and the children in Marseilles. I get there at 6 P.M., record time, a quick trip on which I congratulate myself. Taking action is intoxicating and satisfying.

During the trip I have read a good history book by M. A. Fabre, somewhat biased, *Vie et Mort de la Commune* [*Life and Death of the Paris Commune*]—and two good Simenon mysteries, *The Country Doctor* and *The Long Exile*.

On January 3, 1942, I, like the seven others, receive my copy of the official telegram, the text as I wrote it without even a comma added. "Confirm hereby receipt your letter of 24th. I can only confirm verbal commitment given you in conversation with Oualid. Request you inform me by telegram whether you still refuse. If so I must find candidate among persons unconnected with charities."

Albert Lévy, Gamzon, Millner, and I have decided to accept, but put off sending our telegraphic acceptance until the next day. Telephone calls and chatter on the 3rd and 4th in Marseilles. At the instigation of Jarblum, who still talks as if this were a socialist congress, Oualid accepts, but writes in his telegram about the *totality* of the *Union*. I protest against both the procedure and the act, since I know that in Paris the Germans give the orders and Vallat can't do anything. Oualid refuses to understand and goes on talking straight nineteenth century. Then there's Olmer, who wants a meeting with Vallat before the decree is passed. Tactless!

As for René Mayer, he says no and proposes, in his place, a technician from HICEM, Mr. Schah unfortunately,[5] a colorless and flavorless naturalized citizen.

These poor old fellows are still thinking in prewar terms and forgetting that a minister under an authoritarian regime has asked them to reply by telegram. I compose telegrams for myself and Albert Lévy without mentioning the totality of the *Union*, to show that we understand. Gamzon and Millner come round to our point of view. After six hours of useless quibbling, each of us sends his telegram on Sunday after lunch. To prevent any hitches, I also send Vallat a personal, explanatory telegram. Then I wait.

January 4: I announce that Vallat has asked me to come to Vichy with Millner on Thursday, before having received all the replies.

January 5, 9:30 A.M.: Disaster. Telephone call from the head secretary. The minister does not accept the qualified replies from Oualid, Olmer, and Jarblum. He asks me for other names, which I send by telegram on the 6th.[6] I announce that I am going there and prepare to leave. . . . Oualid and Olmer say they are sorry. After criticizing me roundly, now they're asking me to stop the whole thing and sort it out—that's sweet revenge! But I don't think I'll bother to sort anything out. We shall just get along without people who dither too much and refuse to understand that in the Free Zone we have to place our bets on the sincerity of

5. Wladimir Schah, who was born in Russia, was an active official in HICEM. Although aware of the controversy over the founding of the UGIF, Schah decided to enter the council to maintain its continuity with the charitable services. Two weeks after accepting the nomination, he expressed his reservations to a HICEM official in New York. He admitted that he was joining the UGIF against all his principles and entertained no illusions that his participation would be effective. Furthermore, he declared, "if there is serious pressure from our current masters, the Council members may be of no use for any purpose except to serve as hostages, and in case, in spite of promises, the Council is called upon to do things outside the domain of our charitable work, I shall resign, whatever it costs me." (January 15, 1942, YIVO: RG 245.4, XII, France, B-19,20). Schah remained a member of the administrative Council until the spring of 1944.

6. RRL proposed three people: Raphaël Spanien, Laura Weill, and André Lazard.

Vallat, but in the Occupied Zone he and we can do absolutely nothing. The *Union* will be founded without these folk, and the Jewish community can only benefit.

Yesterday in Marseilles, André Weil was saying of me that I had wished Vallat a happy New Year. That's speaking with a forked tongue! The truth is that, as we were leaving Vallat's office on December 30, Millner said to him, "Your honor, I should like to wish you a happy New Year, but with your permission I'd also like to wish the Jews a less unfortunate year." Vallat listened in surprise, hesitated, and then said, "If you like, let us wish France a happy New Year, then everyone will be the winner."

Above and beyond my minor Jewish worries, there is the Marshal's message for New Year's Day. It's very important, an admission of bankruptcy. We can see that the power of Germany is beginning to be undermined. The Marshal admits that in his "partial exile" he is only "half free." Well then? He goes on to condemn those who, *in Paris as well as London*, are speaking and acting against French unity. But the text printed in the newspapers says *in France and abroad*. There's a nuance!

Marseilles, February 11, 1942

On January 27 at 7:30 P.M. a daughter was born to me—our fourth child—Marie-France, a name expressing affirmation and hope. Thanks to my wife I have been given perhaps the greatest joy of my life. Simone was amazing, both before and during the delivery, at which I was present, as is my custom; not a cry or complaint came from her. My daughter opened her eyes before she was born, since her head appeared a few seconds before her arms and body. I thought of my mother, who would have been infinitely happy. . . . As the father of three sons and a daughter, with a companion who is still as much woman as mother, what more could I want, despite the disappointments of life in society? Have I deserved this happiness in a world turned upside down? As I believe there is an equilibrium between good and evil, I tell myself that this is perhaps why my mother before me endured such suffering.

I have not noted here the conclusion of my personal negotiations with Xavier Vallat, nor that of my diplomatic activity, though I have summarized them in a "white book"[7] that I am keeping with my personal files. On January 8 and 9 I was back in Vichy, by way of Lyon where I dined and slept well. Joseph Millner came to join me in Vichy. On the 8th at 5 P.M., Xavier Vallat received us, with a moment's interruption in our talk to receive Mr. Lequerica, the ambassador from Spain, who came to ask him to exempt Jews of Spanish nationality from the *Statut*. We were amused.

Xavier Vallat was very cordial and quite satisfied with all my personal suggestions, and confirmed that he had accepted all my proposals—and that in fact it was I who had chosen the Council members. He confirmed to us that the decree appointing us had been published in Paris the day before. Colonel Jarnieu was to prepare a communiqué to explain it to the Vichy press, and I asked that he indicate precisely, for those competent in the matter, Free Zone or Occupied Zone next to each name. Vallat talked to us again about the telegrams and said he was sorry that his word had not been sufficient for the three who protested.

He gave us details on the mechanics of paying the billion-franc fine in Paris, on the appalling situation at Drancy, on the executions, on the deportations that were possible, and on the need for blankets at Royalieu, near Compiègne, where the Jews arrested during December were concentrated. He informed us more precisely about the financial administration of the *Union*. There were to be two separate accounts, for Paris and for the Free Zone. He proposed they be in the Caisse des Depôts [public deposit bank]. I insisted on the Bank of France in Marseilles; he accepted.

7. This document has not been found among Lambert's private papers.

Now that the decree has been published, I asked for a long period of time in which to prepare my plan for the organization of the UGIF. Since I cannot be away from Marseilles until the end of February, I asked Vallat not to summon me until then, and he accepted that. "I'll give you all the time you want, since you assure me that the agencies will continue functioning meanwhile." Now I am beginning to design the organization of the *Union*; for this minor task we are using a separate office at my Committee's [CAR] premises.

But there continues to be agitation and back-fence talk among the Jews, led by people who have nothing to do and are jealous of our useful action, jealous especially of the trust the authorities have shown in me, and even hostile in principle. Our president [Lévy] is a Consistory member, and now it is he who is being targeted. Mr. Helbronner is acting like a Jesuit father. The motion adopted on January 18 by the permanent delegation of the Consistory is a monument of hypocrisy. In particular, this motion "deplores the conduct of discussions by a person not mandated to do so" (this is half to do with me and half with Vallat), but this lamentation after the fact leaves me cold.

More serious is that the motion regrets the attitude taken by our president, stating—falsely!—that he did not include in his acceptance the conditions suggested by the Consistory, and it pays homage to those who "by the firm stand they took, preserved the honor of French Jewry"—when actually Oualid, Olmer, and Jarblum had not been honest enough to refuse. It's certainly true that as soon as one has to do with those who accept the dogma and worship [the members of the Central Consistory who speak in the name of French Judaism], one encounters duplicity and lies. Our president, and Helbronner, read out an acid exchange of letters (with which I am not unacquainted).[8] He demanded that

8. RRL alludes to the fact that he himself probably wrote the reply from Lévy to Helbronner. This was not unusual. The diary provides evidence that RRL often wrote Lévy's speeches, letters, and reports, offering the general impression that Lévy was strongly influenced by Lambert and had minimal impact during his short tenure as UGIF president in 1942.

this motion be annulled, or he would withdraw from the Consistory and the *Union*. I expect that, as usual, these Gentlemen of Religion will simmer down again. The next meeting is on February 28. But I am outside this rather tiresome circle.

I am considering the results of my conversations in Vichy for the Jewish community and will describe them fully later. I gained time; I succeeded in preserving the agencies' independence, and in preventing any Aryan commissioners from being named to the committees; I gained the right (very important for funds from America) for donations to be specially designated. I didn't give up anything that was a matter of principle, however; that area is safe. I accepted only collaboration at the technical level. Two endorsements are precious to me: Victor Basch[9] said in Lyon that "as soon as Lambert, my student, had accepted, our minds could be at ease about the charities and the Jewish community." And the big American organizations, the YMCA, the Unitarians, and even the Red Cross, speaking through their leaders, had urged me to accept—so had the French Protestants and the Catholics—since where there is danger there will be sacrifice, or courage at least.

I have been sent a fantastic document that proves that Pétain is now resisting the Boche demands for measures against Jews. One of its formulations is even supposed to have been borrowed from the secret clauses in the armistice, which almost certainly had the purpose of removing Jews "from public employment and from positions of authority in industry and commerce." What is notable is the delay in replying. I am copying it out here because it is too important not to be preserved:

9. Hungarian born, Basch (1863–1944), was strongly identified with the Dreyfusards in the late nineteenth century, figured prominently in the League for the Rights of Man from its inception, and served as its president from 1926 to 1940. A professor of aesthetics and art history, Basch published various scholarly studies on philosophical and cultural problems. He was an ardent supporter of the Popular Front in the 1930s and a member of the French Resistance Central Committee during the war. He and his wife were assassinated by Vichy officials on January 10, 1944. See Françoise Basch, Liliane Crips, and Pascale Gruson, eds., *Victor Basch (1863–1944): un intellectuel cosmopolite* (Paris, 2000).

The Vice-President of the Council
General Secretariat
Office ref. 387.SG

Vichy, January 21, 1942

The Admiral of the Fleet Minister,
Vice-President of the Council, to the General Administrator of the French Government in the Occupied Territories

"Re: Measures against the Jews
"Ref.: Note No. G78 of December 15, 1941, from the Commander-in-chief of the Armed Forces in France.

"Sir:

"1. By the communication referred to above, the commander-in-chief of the Armed Forces in France asks that a certain number of measures be taken with regard to Jews in the Occupied Zone, such as: the obligation to wear a distinctive symbol, being banned from frequenting public places, excepting certain premises particularly reserved for them, and the institution of a special curfew.

"2. I have the honor of informing you that I am not in agreement with these proposals.

"3. I feel that the various strict measures already in force to date against the Jews are sufficient for the intended purpose, which is to remove them from public employment and from positions of authority in industry and commerce in this country.

"4. There can be no question of going further without deeply offending French public opinion, which will see in these measures only humiliations without real efficacy, either for the future of the country or for the security of the occupying troops. The very excess of these decisions would certainly go against the intended purpose, and would run the risk of provoking a movement in support of the Jews, who would be considered martyrs.

F. Darlan"[1]

1. See CDJC: V-64. For a discussion of Darlan's attitude to the "Jewish Question" in this case and in other circumstances, see Marrus and Paxton, *Vichy France and the Jews*, passim and pp. 209–210. RRL's conclusion that a change of mind was gaining ground among the French was also advanced by Baur of the UGIF-north during a remarkable

I have had the opportunity to read the indictment against Blum, Gamelin, Daladier, etc. It is a monument of thoughtlessness and proves that the trial is jaundiced and not based on charges that will stand scrutiny. In normal times it would be laughable! The secret purpose is understandable: to absolve the active armed forces from the defeat for which they are totally responsible. I picked out this sentence, which all those who served in either war will find appalling: "The corps of junior officers in active service, despite a lack of practical training, was generally of good quality, but the troop strength was insufficient; the non-commissioned officers in the reserve, who were necessarily numerous, were mediocre overall."[2] How shameful to make such a statement!

Reading: Simenon, *Blind Alley*: a good tale, always the unexpected; slices of life; Chastenet (of the HCITR[?], later with *le Temps*), *William Pitt*, an excellent history book; helps one understand Churchill and the tenacity of the British, speculating on how long it will take; by Albert Josipovici (who, before the war, published *Goha the Fool* with Albert Adès, about whom Mirbeau was enthusiastic), *David chez les chrétiens* [*David Among the Christians*], a Jewish testimony, lively but too frank and too facile, very true-to-life Geneva settings; Henri Troyat's *Le jugement de Dieu* [*God's Judgment*], an excellent composition with echoes of Bernanos, Rabelais, and even Jules Lemaître, all put together with a real sense of harmony.

February 18, 1942

Current international events are not calculated to make us optimistic: the fall of Singapore, German naval victory in the Pas-de-

---

meeting held in Paris on January 28, 1942. (See Yad Vashem Archives [YVA]: P 7/8; Richard I. Cohen, "On the Establishment of UGIF in Northern France—An Unknown Document from January 1942," *Yalkut Moreshet*, 30 [1980], pp. 139–56 [Hebrew].) This private information, probably transmitted to RRL by Vallat, is symptomatic of the relationship he continued to maintain with the Commissariat.

2. The ruling of October 28, 1941, in this court case has been reprinted many times. See Pierre Cot, *Le procès de la République*, vol. I (New York, 1944), pp. 296–299; Paul Soupiran, *Bazaine contre Gambetta ou le procès de Riom* (Lyon, 1944), pp. 63–66.

Calais, and noticeable slowdown of the Russian offensive. . . . The British Empire will not recover from such shocks as these. A truly new world will emerge from this war, and of all Hitler's claims the only one to remain true will be that economic dominance by one bloc of powers will not be possible. The City of London will have had its day. . . . But I am wondering if it is not possible that the forces of evil will triumph, despite our hopes and the right being on our side. That would mean night in Europe for at least a century, and we would be damned like our ancestors in the Middle Ages. . . . I don't dare think of that for my children since, for my part, I would dare to confront anything. . . . But I have faith that Washington will take London's place and strike down Berlin, with help from Moscow—but it will take a long time. I don't see Europe at peace again until the autumn of '43. Are we going to have the physical strength to wait? It's all there.

Friday the 13th at eleven o'clock, I had a telephone call at the office from Vallat. He congratulated me most kindly on the birth of Marie-France and asked after Simone. This is very correct diplomacy! He also asked me how my organization plans are coming (they are finished), and will expect me next Friday.

Meanwhile the General Commissariat has demanded that the president grant official powers to the vice president, the treasurer, and the general administrator in Paris. This is proof that the [UGIF] section in the Occupied Zone will really have nothing to do with ours, and that its carrying out of the German regulations does not implicate the team in the Free Zone in any obligation.

On Monday the 18th[3] at 4:30 P.M.: another telephone call, from Colonel de Jarnieu, who asks me to act quickly lest "we have more regulations imposed on us from the other side," especially since they have been looking at member contributions. He asks

3. The previous day Vallat and Dannecker had a stormy meeting in which the effectiveness of Vallat's anti-Semitic activities was questioned. This meeting contributed to the decision of the occupying forces to remove Vallat from the Commissariat. Vallat remained in office until May 6, 1942, but his authority was severely curtailed in his last months. The pressure that Jarnieu put on RRL should evidently be seen within this context.

me to bring a special authorization for the opening of the accounts, in Paris at the Caisse des Depôts. I have the impression that this head secretary, just back from three weeks in Paris, is more under the heel of the Occupation than the minister himself.

So I am leaving tomorrow at 11:30 A.M. for Lyon, but this time invested with an official mission, fully conscious of my role and my responsibilities.

March 2, 1942

I'm writing this on Tuesday the 24th at 2:30 P.M. in my room at the Hotel Imperator in Nîmes, where I have come, for the last time in a long while, I hope, to attend the Interconfessional Conference on the Camps. In the rain, my Nîmes that was so brilliant in the summer of '40 has become a depressing place—narrow provincialism. In addition there was the problem, at 1:30 P.M., of finding a place to eat and then a place to have a bad coffee. . . . But newspaper effigies of the Marshal are enthroned in front of the closed "associations" premises and the stores selling official propaganda, sad symbols of France in these dark hours.

On the train I read a few pages of André Gide's *Journal*, which I have in fact been reading, in small portions, for more than a year. It is monumentally important, so full of lessons, so engaging in the details of his evolving thoughts that one cannot absorb it all at once. What a man this is, and what a fine book! I understand myself better when reading Gide, and I think he is the only one today who can equal Goethe, despite their dissimilarities.

Notes on my social and bureaucratic activities on Thursday, February 19: I left Marseilles at 11:30 A.M. on a train that I appreciated because my fellow travelers in the compartment did not talk. Lunch was very bad. I read *Monsieur Thiers* by Robert Dreyfus—an excellent book. The will of a stubborn, good citizen triumphs over the incompetence of the masses and saves a country that neither ideals nor a sense of honor could succeed in arming or disciplining (compare 1939–40). At Lyon I had a bad room at the Hotel Russia but a good dinner at the Restaurant Lamour, which is well known to the silk manufacturers, thanks to Lazard[4] who invited me there. On Friday the 20th, after getting up at dawn, I arrived in Vichy at the Albert I in time for lunch. The room, the hotel, and the city were numb with cold—no heat, or hardly any. Colonel Pascot and Moliner, whom I had invited to lunch at 12:30, arrived at 1:20, when I had already finished. They left because the table had already been cleared, and it was normally the waiters' time off.

Spent the afternoon at Vallat's office, in a long talk with both the minister and the colonel. Vallat told me in confidence about a threatening note he had received from the German authorities, complaining that the *Union* was not yet functioning in the Free Zone.[5] They gave him to understand they were ready to take measures to have the Paris section give it the . . . Vallat explained to me that if we got the *Union* going quickly in Marseilles, this would give our colleagues in Paris the opportunity to propose to the Germans a plan for technical activities that would allow some freedom of action. Vallat accepted, with a few changes in terminology, the details of my plan for the organization, which would preserve the technical framework of the existing charities. He informed me that, in view of the threats from Paris, he would have to publish decrees of dissolution for the charities during the month of March. I was able to arrange for the large charities to be dissolved in two lots—for the smaller ones we would make arrangements later. A special Union is being set up for Algeria, so it will not be within our jurisdiction.

Vallat asked me to see the treasurer, who agreed that the central account would be in Vichy and the trading account in Marseilles. The Alliance[6] is to be incorporated into the *Union*; for

4. André Lazard was a member of the administrative council of UGIF-south.

5. See letter of February 7, 1942 from Lischka to Vallat (CDJC: XXVIII-7), in Billig, *Le Commissariat général*, vol. I, p. 214.

6. The Alliance Israélite Universelle was founded in 1860 by seventeen French Jews with the aim of promoting the emancipation of Jews and raising the cultural level of

political reasons there will not be a section in Alsace. To ward off the German authorities' threat to require a *Union* membership fee for every Jew in France, Vallat will have to take to Paris a note on membership fees. According to the terms decided on by the *Union*, all members will be asked to pay an annual fee in proportion to their income, a family fee rather than an individual one, a minimum of 120F per year, payable in monthly installments, by everyone not subject to income tax. Indigent persons are to be exempt. In principle the amount will be one-sixth of the income tax paid by each member for the preceding year. The membership fees are to be sent directly to the *Union* without intervention by the authorities. Vallat promised to work energetically to have this scale accepted for the Occupied Zone.

After some visits and a frugal dinner at the grill in Chantecler, where the temperature in the restrooms is tepid since the Marshal is working in the hotel, I return to my icy room, where I realize that I'm getting older. What has become of the time when I used to take my bath exposed to every wind of heaven, during the other war? When I get up from my bed I feel the weight of two blocks of ice on my shoulders.

Saturday the 21st in the morning, a visit from Rudnansky of the Alliance, from Millner of the OSE, and lunch with Marcel Wormser, general treasurer of the *Union*.[7] I find him a satisfactory colleague; we understand each other, and there was a spark of sympathy from the start. That makes one more loyal ally on the Council. Wormser is not Vallat's man. I will give a portrait of him

---

Jewish communities outside France. The Alliance saw itself as a forerunner in the protection of Jews from anti-Semitic activity. During the Third Republic the Alliance became one of the main Jewish organizations in France, with extensive programs promoting the ideals of productivity, enlightened education, and French culture. It was particularly active in the Jewish communities in North Africa and the Middle East, where it developed an extensive school system that advanced an enlightenment agenda. One of its important functionaries at the end of the 1930s was Jacques Rudnansky, a personal friend of RRL. See Aron Rodrigue, *French Jews, Turkish Jews: The Alliance Israélite Universelle and the Politics of Jewish Schooling in Turkey, 1860–1925* (Bloomington, Ind., 1990).

7. Wormser, an industrialist, was to play a minor role in UGIF affairs.

at some point. A fine fellow. After lunch I see Vallat again. We agree to confirm the amount of the membership fees, and he approves my plan in all its details. So now it is time for the *Union* to start up, for its useful work to begin. The caravan will move ahead, and the dogs will bark more than ever.

Saturday night I had dinner at Chantecler with Millner, Moliner,[8] and a young official from the Finance Department, a certified public accountant to whom I will probably turn over my accounts office. The next morning, at dawn and in the cold, I had a very quick bath and left for Marseilles, via Lyon, arriving home at 6:30 P.M.

After being away four days I found Marie-France more beautiful. My sons celebrated my homecoming, and Simone is as strong as she was before the births of all the children. Happy *pater familias*!

In Nîmes I bought *Un esprit non prévenu* [*An Unprejudiced Mind*], an excellent short tract by André Gide. Read it straight through before going to sleep—excellent food for thought.

March 27, 1942

I'm writing this on the train between Orange and Lyon. (Have been so busy getting the administration of the *Union* organized that I have not been able to obey my desire to return to this diary. From now on I shall spend half an hour on it every morning before going to the office.) I am on my way to Vichy, called there by meeting of the Social Services Department for Foreigners. I shall take advantage of it to see Xavier Vallat instead of coming back at the end of the month. Action, action, long live action! and what responsibilities I have! It puts a smile on my face, and my smile convinces me that we shall succeed in the end. Helbronner said to Albert Lévy in Lyon last Sunday that I'm quite intelligent but a lightweight, not enough depth. . . . Out of the mouth of a

8. We have been unable to find any relevant information on this person.

mandarin from the last century, that reproach does me honor. My citation from the first war called me a "young officer with plenty of drive." I'm still the same, and I shall save the Jewish charities in spite of these old codgers.

But I get carried away by the action and no longer have time to write down my thoughts day by day. I hardly have anything more than the fifteen minutes or so in the bath to be introspective; I fall into bed at night, too tired, and at home I must be a husband and father. . . . I need the time alone while traveling to write down my observations and get back in contact with myself. So I do my writing before my reading. . . .

The conscious will is a miracle. I see these old men get excited and talk; I see people hold forth who aren't good for anything; I see people who are thinking only of their money, which they have certainly lost, sinking into foolishness. But 1943 or 1944 will not be like 1918. Other times, other methods. I understand that this is a world in agony, but I know that after the bloodbath and the economic upheaval some values will be preserved. I compare the endurance of my ideals to the persistence of certain features in the landscape, this sunlit kaleidscope unreeling past the window of my train compartment.

On February 25 the terrible news appeared in the press that "The steamboat *Strouma*, with 750 Romanian Jews on board, has sunk in the Black Sea." It makes one ashamed to be human. We weep for victims in the Parisian suburbs and mount lots of official demonstrations, but no one thinks of this nameless tragedy. With its 18 million inhabitants who were spared in the war, Turkey will bear the terrible responsibility for this inhumanity. Some Jewish professors, engineers, and property owners from Romania were able to flee Hitler's hell, which was ravaging their country, on a steamboat, thanks to the complicity of its Bulgarian captain. They spent four months marooned on their little ship. They were docked in a Turkish port, where mechanical problems kept the *Strouma* from continuing its journey. But the Turkish government had it repaired and forbade these 750 pariahs from disembarking. No country wanted these Jews, not even Palestine, and it was finally decided to send them back, outside territorial waters, in the direction from which they came. The boat was left to its fate, six miles off the coast in the Black Sea, where it blew up after an explosion. . . .[9] Only one person escaped! It was a mine, or suicide; a bit more Jewish blood spilled on Europe in its madness. No words are adequate. *Homo homini lupus*.[1]

The Riom Trial goes on,[2] a caricature of justice under one of the most abject regimes France has ever known. No freethinking person can be fooled. It is an illegal trial; the men facing judgment have already been condemned by the head of state[3] by virtue of powers that he has conferred on himself. . . . There were no weapons, the doctrine being followed by the top military command was outdated, but what comes out of all the depositions that have been filed? What emerges is that the entire responsibility for the lack of preparation for war falls on the military administration, and none on the civilians who had been in power only two years. They tell me that Daladier said in revenge, "If such a trial had taken place in 1871, Gambetta would have been

9. The *Strouma* was carrying 769 Jews from Romania. The British government pressured the Turkish government to deny the ship access to its ports, and refused to grant the passengers entry visas for Palestine, then under British mandate. Following an explosion, the ship sank in the Sea of Marmora with all its passengers except one who escaped. The *Strouma* was probably sunk, unintentionally, by a Soviet submarine torpedo. See Raul Hilberg, *The Destruction of the European Jews*, 3rd ed. (New Haven, CT: Yale University Press, 2003).

1. Humankind is a wolf toward humankind (Plautus, *Asinaria*).

2. The Riom Trial was part of the Vichy campaign to discredit the political leaders of the 1930s (Blum, Daladier, and Guy la Chambre) and to bring charges against the army's commander-in-chief from 1935 to 1940, General Maurice Gamelin. The trial opened at Riom on February 19, 1942, and twenty-four public sessions followed. On April 14, 1942, four days before Laval returned to office, the proceedings were suspended and never resumed. See Michel, *Le procès de Riom*, passim.

3. On October 16, 1941, Pétain had announced that the Council on Political Justice had submitted its findings to him, with its recommendations concerning Daladier, Blum, and Gamelin: they were all found guilty and deserved severe punishment. But, the Marshal declared, the Supreme Court at Riom would continue its judicial inquiry and would soon give its verdict.

thrown into prison and Bazaine made head of state."[4] As for the censors, they had received orders to be kept under wraps; the truth must not be revealed, at any price.

Heading back to Vichy again, I am hoping this time not to find it cold as it was in February, that glacial weight on my shoulders, the discomfort at night, like memories of war; my hands unable to write, hands even clumsier than when they were sapping in the wet at the Chemin des Dames.

My poor Aunt Lucie has died in Paris. It reminds me of the passing of my mother—which is not in my diary. But there is the book I am considering writing, *Une mère juive* [*A Jewish Mother*], for without my mother I would have been nothing, nothing at all from a spiritual point of view. Her memory takes the place of religion for me. Thanks to her I am a good husband and father. "Think," she used to say, "whenever you feel doubtful, that Simone has given you two fine sons!" And now I have four children. How satisfying it is to work for their happiness, and when I wake up as king of the household, to show my beneficent presence at the bedsides of my two eldest.

Life in French society of 1942, topics for further development: the shops three-quarters empty of merchandise—shoes with wooden soles—clothing without any style—the dentist crowning teeth with steel—no more mustard at meals—being hungry after lunch—elegant bars where one comes less to drink than to ask the waiter for contraband cigarettes, or silk stockings for two hundred francs a pair.

I console myself by reading André Gide's *Journals*, picking up pearls such as, "I am someone who does not believe; I am not impious." Yes, Gide has helped me to see within myself more clearly.

And suppose . . . suppose what is happening has a scope beyond our poor imaginations? Suppose France and Europe were to disappear from the Earth in the shapes in which we know them?

4. This is in fact a memorable line from the first speech that Daladier made during the trial. He was invoking the memory of Gambetta, who carried on the struggle in 1870 while Marshal Bazaine capitulated. See Michel, *Le procès de Riom*, p. 119.

Suppose our civilization of incompetents were to be snuffed out, bleeding and miserable, like Byzantium long ago, or Carthage or Rome? Suppose Judaism, like the eternal principles of '89, like Christianity, were to make way for a new gospel of a restricted community, in which the individual would be a connecting rod in an engine, part of a better organized whole? Suppose that I myself were not to see the last act of this tragedy? And suppose. . . . Well, too bad! Let us cling to our ideals, and if everything crumbles around us, let me preserve my will which enabled me to resist during the bombing raids long ago, and at my mother's deathbed, and in the midst of all of life's trials.

Notes on my trip to Vichy and my stay there in the "capital" on February [March] 10 and 11. On the 7th Vallat telephoned, while I was out of the office, to ask whether I was ready for the dissolutions of the organizations being incorporated into the *Union*—the first lot on March 8, the second lot on March 23. Most surprised that he asked for my agreement, I gave it to him by telegram. In this way I can ask him for all the time I want to carry out the formalities. I am not telling anyone about this telegram, since the old fellows are getting agitated again, particularly that fool Maurice Leven,[5] who is grasping the fact that the Alliance will escape his control. . . .

In Vichy I had discussions at the Social Services Department for Foreigners and at the Interior Ministry about the measures being taken against foreign Jews. I spoke with Vallat alone on the 10th and on the 11th (together with Wormser, our treasurer, whom I like very much). The issues were dealt with and settled to my satisfaction: all the necessary time will be allowed me, in the interest of the agencies, for the legal formalities of a corporation; I am to make contact personally with the Quai d'Orsay on behalf of the Alliance, over which I have control as the representative of the

5. Maurice Leven was then vice president of the Alliance. He had called an extraordinary meeting of the organization's Central Committee in March 1942, at which it was decided that the Alliance could cooperate with the UGIF. Leven was one of the six notables whom RRL originally proposed to Vallat as possible nominees for the Council.

Council; Millner, whose citizenship has been abrogated by decree, will have to resign. At the Interior Ministry I obtained agreement that the foreign Jewish work gangs no longer be called "Palestinian companies" but rather "Jewish companies." Another nuance.

Vallat told me that he is no longer sure of remaining as general commissioner. The Germans don't think he is sufficiently under their heel. Lieutenant Dannecker,[6] the "Führer" for Jews in Paris, has even threatened him with "not being in charge of Jews much longer," and the Germans tore up his pass.[7] So now Vallat is no better off than I am when it comes to traveling to Paris! Darquier de Pellepoix,[8] an anti-Semite seen at public meetings, known for his swindles and his illnesses, is already announcing himself as Vallat's successor and being mentioned in the press in Paris. What a disaster that would be! Vallat says so, and hopes that the Marshal won't give in. . . . I hope so too—the bird in one's hand is better. . . . I suggested a solution to Vallat: that he stay in Vichy and delegate his authority in Paris to someone there, since in any case he can hardly do anything more there. We shall wait and see. What will be will be. . . . Vallat told me, finally, that Stora,[9] my counterpart in the Occupied Zone, had sneaked into

6. Theodor Dannecker held the office of *Judenreferat* [special police unit for Jewish affairs] in the Gestapo in Paris from September 1940 to September 1942 and was the chief organizer of the massive deportations in the summer of 1942. See Marrus and Paxton, *Vichy France and the Jews,* passim; Klarsfeld, *Vichy-Auschwitz,* pp. 63–87.

7. Dannecker was instrumental in removing Vallat from office and in March 1942 confiscated his pass to enter the Occupied Zone.

8. Darquier replaced Vallat in May 1942 and directed the Commissariat until February 1944. For an evaluation of his character and activity, see Carmen Callil, *Bad Faith: A Forgotten History of Family, Fatherland and Vichy France* (New York, 2006).

9. Marcel Stora was born in Pithiviers in 1906. He began working with the Coordinating Committee in Paris in the spring of 1941 and later played an important role in the Administrative Council of UGIF-north. Stora's incognito visit to the south was arranged by Vallat's office. See Szajkowski, *Gazetteer,* p. 61, who incorrectly identifies the UGIF officer who met with Pétain as André Baur. RRL's comment confirms Vallat's remark, during his trial, that UGIF-north had arranged a secret meeting with Pétain to persuade him of the importance of keeping Vallat as head of the Commissariat. See *Le procès de Xavier Vallat présenté par ses amis* (Paris, 1948), pp. 146, 267, 272, 474–475. Stora's trip, and RRL's comments, clearly emphasize that the UGIF leaders considered Vallat a Frenchman who tried to alleviate the ordeal of French Jews.

the Free Zone to tell them all the harm that would come of firing Vallat. He had seen the Marshal. Stora was in Marseilles while I was in Vichy. I sent a telegram asking him to wait for me there.

When I got back, I found out that Stora is a fanatic who knows nothing about our agencies, and that he had talked only to the Jewish capitalists who were hostile to the *Union* and to my actions. He even slandered me, so watch out! He used my telegram of the 7th[1] as a pretext for saying that I was pushing Vallat to take this action. It's always the same story. Those who talk and blame others in this life are those who don't know what things are like on the ground.

I saw Fouques-Duparc in his lodgings-cum-office in the Ministry. We had a long and delightful conversation. He foresees a long war, with movements of populations here and there and political disturbances as in the time of the great [barbarian] invasions. Perhaps he's right.

March 29, 1942

I haven't been recording the tragicomedies at the Central Consistory, but this could be useful for me; it shows elements of Jewish psychology since, as usual, the old mandarins don't want to submit to the laws of life. . . . On February 28 our President let himself be manipulated. . . . At a meeting of the Consistory he presented the facts and demanded an honest explanation in front of all the delegates from the communities. They befuddled him with holy water, promising him a letter expressing confidence in him, at which point he stopped insisting on a public explanation. . . . As a result, it was said the next day that he had taken the road to Canossa, and he received a letter more hypocritical than anything one could have hoped for. After thinking it over for a few weeks, he resigned from the Consistory two days ago. All this is nothing but an insignificant squabble, since the

1. This refers to RRL's response to Vallat's telephone call concerning the dissolution of the charitable organizations.

various jurisdictions are well defined by the laws of 1905 and 1942:[2] on one side there's the religion, that's "them"—on the other, the agencies, that's us.

But there is a deeper reason for the agitation and the hateful resentment. They are dubious about me in the same way they doubted the Popular Front when it was in power. The very wealthy Jews, who are the majority of the Consistory, are afraid the *Union* will make them pay too much for the poor. So we are seeing the scandal, instigated by two or three young Turks, that they prefer to give their money to "Amitiés chrétiennes"[3] rather than leave it with our agencies that are being incorporated into the *Union*. What a sad, confused mentality!

I read *Messieurs les Ronds-de-Cuir* [*The Penpushers*] by Courteline, in a fine edition of his complete works that I bought myself to celebrate the birth of my daughter. It brings up all the despicable actions we are seeing. Also *The French Republic, 1870–1935* by Jacques Bainville, an excellent work.

When I talk about the *Statut* with officials, they often reply: "All that is not aimed at you." It's cowardly and hypocritical for them to say that, but it also has its truth. In the history of French Jewry the law of heredity has been mitigated by the law of adaptation, given our national culture's assimilating powers. So it is not surprising that the boundaries of "Israel" in France are less

2. The December 9, 1905, French law on the separation of church and state had significant ramifications for the Central Consistory. The act effectively limited the organization's activities to a purely religious role. The November 29, 1941, law establishing the UGIF stipulated that all Jewish charitable organizations except the UGIF were to be dissolved, and specified that religious associations were to remain outside this category.

3. A Protestant and Catholic aid organization that assisted Jews during the war. At the end of 1941, in reaction to the establishment of the UGIF, Consistory members proposed to this organization to widen its distribution of aid with help from the Consistory, in order to avoid using the UGIF resources. The Administrative Council of French Rabbis, fearing that the "Amitié chrétienne" might engage in proselytism, asked (and received) assurance that this would not happen. In accordance with this agreement, the Consistory provided funding to the "Amitié chrétienne." See Schwarzfuchs, *Aux prises avec Vichy*, pp. 180–181, 207–208; Zosa Szajkowski, "The French Central Jewish Consistory During the Second World War," *Yad Vashem Studies*, III (1959), pp. 194–196.

clearly defined and tend to blend into this multifaceted nation with its many ethnic types, more than anywhere else.

I rediscovered among my notes these lines from Ernest Renan (in his *Histoire du peuple d'Israël* [*History of the People of Israel*], Vol. I, pp. 396–397), the most profound words I know: "Israel aspires to two things that contradict one another; it wants to be like everyone else and yet be apart; it claims to pursue a destiny that is both real and supportable and an impossible, ideal dream. From the beginning, prophecy and royalty have been placed in absolute opposition to one another. A secular state, conforming to all the requirements of a secular state, and a theocratic democracy, perpetually undermining the basis of the civil order; this is the struggle that permeates the history of Israel and gives it such originality." I can see how enduring these tendencies are, and this conflict, in my everyday activities.

April 10, 1942

I spent a week in Nice with Simone and the two older boys for the Passover holidays. It was only partly restful since the children are demanding young rascals. We lunched in royal style in Monaco, where the restrictions are not so severe, but at what a price! (twelve hundred francs for four). The seven days at the Plaza Hotel were also expensive: twelve thousand francs. The economic organization of our world is falling apart. . . . It reminds me of the inflation in Germany in 1923–1924. I had a glimpse of André Gide, very thin under his hood, in the public garden, and Bucard[4] came and threw his arms around me on the Promenade des Anglais. . . . Now I take up my yoke again.

4. Marcel Bucard, a decorated veteran (French Croix de Guerre), was active in fascist political activity in the 1930s and led the Franciste movement, the first to apply methods used by Mussolini's Black Shirts. During the war his militants took part in various collaborationist operations. Bucard was executed in 1946 after being tried for treason. RRL knew Bucard from their stay together in Bonn in the early 1920s as members of the French delegation, but was not associated with him politically. He mentions him again in the diary on September 6, 1942. On Bucard, see Halls, *Youth of Vichy Fance*, pp. 331–333; in 1984, Frédéric Empaytaz clarified for me Lambert's contact with Bucard.

I read Simenon's *Poisoned Relations*, an excellent novel; Courteline's *La Vie de Ménage* [*Keeping House*], fairly good, and a little book by Argenton on *Les grandes religions* [*The Great Religions*], a lively synthesis and very well composed.

April 18, 1942

The appointment of Laval to head the government[5] seems to me as grave a matter as the signing of the armistice. The Marshal has given in to the Germans' threats. He, together with Darlan, is retaining control of the army, navy, and air force. But from now on there will be collaboration with Germany at the political, diplomatic, and economic levels. . . . Poor France! Laval is neither strong enough nor popular enough to bring about a Peace of Amiens.[6] I fear there will be unrest. . . . Where are we going? What will tomorrow be like? In the face of this danger to my country I can forget about the persecutions of the Jews, which will certainly be redoubled. . . . We shall see. . . . I leave for Vichy tomorrow with Simone, without knowing whether Vallat will stay and be more demanding or has been replaced by a commissioner who will be even more cruel.

What effect will these events have on my political and social actions? I shall soon know, and am on my way to find out without feeling fearful. . . . Admiral Leahy[7] is leaving for New York. . . . The radio is sounding more German than ever as we wait for

5. Laval was appointed prime minister on April 18, 1942, and also took over the Foreign Affairs and Interior Ministry portfolios. He was to continue in these offices until August 17, 1944.

6. The Treaty of Amiens (March 27, 1802) gained Napoleon a truce with England, paving the way for him to be elected consul for life by an overwhelming majority.

7. Admiral William D. Leahy was United States ambassador to France from January 1941 to May 1942. Recalled to Washington for consultation after the Laval cabinet was formed in April 1942, he resigned there as of July 18 while recommending that diplomatic relations be maintained with France. His advice was followed, and it was not until American troops landed in North Africa on November 8, 1942, that France took the initiative to break off relations with the United States. See Leahy, *I Was There*, pp. 110–117.

"prodigious events" to take place. No freethinking person can fail to be worried.

The campaign within the Jewish community against the *Union* and against myself is growing less intense. People are starting to understand that I am concerned only with social work. But André Weil—the "young Turk" of French Jewry (since his henchman, Pierre Dreyfus, is emigrating to the United States)—alone keeps on telling everyone that I am a bit like Quisling in my relationship with Vallat.[8] I heard echoes of his propaganda in Nice, when Pierre Paraf[9] introduced me to Jérome Levy, the former head secretary of Painlevé, who now, after having heard me out, understands and appreciates me. I also had a visit from Seligman,[1] the state councillor, who made a point of congratulating me on my work and of making himself available to me. I did not know him. I am sorry he is not on my Council. He would have made a perfect president.

I must keep on my guard against intrigues. A friend as lacking in intelligence as Millner could prove dangerous. . . . The group around Olmer—André Weil had someone ask me unofficially to get in touch with him. I refused. I don't have to take orders from anyone any more, only from my own conscience and my own good counsel. That works very well. . . . I have succeeded in taking several steps through telephone calls to the Interior Ministry and to the Commissariat. Colonel de Jarnieu insists that I come to Vichy very soon, which is why I am going now.

8. For extensive comments on Weil's activity during the war, see Schwarzfuchs, *Aux prises avec Vichy*, passim.

9. Born in Paris, Paraf was the author of, among other works, *Israël: Histoire d'un peuple* (Paris, 1931) and *Israël dans le monde* (Paris, 1947). Paraf was involved in Jewish community affairs during the 1930s and active in UGIF-south in professional training.

1. Pierre Seligman joined the UGIF Council several weeks later. In a letter to RRL he expressed his feelings about this appointment: "Although I could accept being appointed by Mr. X.V. [Vallat], it did not please me to be named by a note signed by his successor [Darquier]. I am afraid it will be impossible to work with the latter." May 6, 1942, CDJC: CDX-86.

My cousin Marcel Dreyfus, just back from Paris, has given me heartrending details about the life our people must live in the capital.

I forgot to mention—and it could be useful later on—that on March 20 I had a visit from Mrs. Vienot, who came to congratulate me on having accepted this heavy responsibility, and to tell me how happy she is to hear that, to save our agencies, we succeeded in spite of the *Statut* in choosing the technical people who have the confidence of the authorities and of the unfortunates whom we serve.

We are amazed that this *Statut* could have been accepted in France. But do we know that the untouchables in India are persecuted worse than we are? At a recent congress—now, in the twentieth century, but admittedly by covering themselves with the authority of religion—the Brahmins confirmed the distance they are supposed to observe between themselves and these "impure" individuals, contact with whom would contaminate them. This soiling takes place even from a certain distance—less than seven meters for leather workers and blacksmiths, but eleven meters for street sweepers and twenty meters for pariahs who eat meat and beef. Thus the racist terminology here hasn't invented anything new.

May 5, 1942

My readings: *1900* by Paul Morand, a witty evocation of the Paris of my childhood: bus rides and newspapers that cost one sou, big hats, corsets and frills (some day a *1914* and a *1939* should be written); Francis Carco's *Nostalgie de Paris* [*Nostalgia for Paris*], sometimes moving, too often fluffed up with literary critique, nothing new about Villon and Verlaine; Marcel Aymé's *The Miraculous Barber*, which excellently portrays the licentious snobbery before the war, particularly leftist snobbery.

From April 19 to 25 I had a long stay in Vichy with Simone. We stayed first at the Ambassadors Hotel, where I felt ill at ease, then at the Albert I, where I feel at home. We had dinner with my Colonel Pascot, the general commissioner for sports, which means he is a minister in the "collaborating" government. In normal times, without the *Statut*, I would have been his head secretary. But he is still my friend. I told him in all sincerity that he should have had scruples about being part of a ministry that is so suspect in the eyes of the public, and I was right to do so. His wife, with her good sense as a French patriot, was furious.

On Sunday the 19th we had a train from Marseilles by way of Lyon, nonstop. For the trip back to Marseilles on Saturday the 25th we had to wait two hours in Lyon. The time in Vichy was very full. I had several conversations with Vallat, including one together with our president who wanted to meet him. We appreciate the fact that the Germans are demanding that he be dismissed, and that he has resigned himself to dispatching current business. They are talking of that fool called Darquier de Pellepoix as his replacement (wouldn't that be great!) and of attaching the aid work to the Ministry of Justice. . . . We shall see. . . . Vallat's head secretary in the Occupied Zone, Cabanis,[2] has been arrested in Paris and, despite all interventions, even from Laval, is being held secretly in the Cherche-Midi {prison in Paris}. As for Colonel Jarnieu, he is not allowed to return to the Occupied Zone. . . . If these people had known the Germans the way we do, they wouldn't have had to endure such a setback!

Notes on my stay in the administrative capital: negotiations with the technical services of the High Commission, where the lower-ranking staff are showing a deplorable insubordination toward the departing minister. Made contact, with a few sparks flying, with the Treasury accounts agent appointed for the *Union*. Very pleasant visit at the Quai d'Orsay as the administrator for

2. Cabany (Vallat's head secretary) and Jarnieu had made the German authorities furious by the way they carried out their orders for equipping UGIF-north in March 1942. Consequently both of them were dismissed from the Commissariat. See Billig, *Le Commissariat général*, vol. I, pp. 93–96.

the *Alliance*. Visit to the *Alliance* itself, where I am now—justly—the boss.

On Friday the 24th I went to Clermont-Ferrand to visit Chief Rabbi Liber.[3] He wants to make peace. I agreed to meet with our adversaries, with the chief rabbi of France chairing the meeting, at Marseilles the following Wednesday, April 29. But on Tuesday evening they telephoned to say the meeting was postponed *sine die* [indefinitely] at the request of Chief Rabbi Schwartz. Poor old dodderer! At least I can't be accused of trying to avoid the negotiations.

Yesterday there was a meeting of the UGIF Council.[4] An excellent session. I received approval and congratulations. Everything is going the way I want it. Millner, who had to resign (because he lost his citizenship) will be replaced. I have just sent a telegram to Vallat to propose Pierre Seligman, a member of the Council of State. He has accepted—an excellent recruit for my efforts, for the *Union* and for French Jewry.

May 25, 1942

I read Simenon's *The Green Thermos*, a good novel. And I really enjoyed—because I am the right age for history—the first volume of Emile Bourgeois' *Manuel de la politique étranger* [*Foreign Policy Manual*] (1610–1789). What power it grants one to compare our ordeals with those of the tragic years that peoples and nations have already known! I'm feeling the need to read some books on the philosophy of history.

3. Rabbi Maurice Liber had been engaged in organizing aid societies for immigrants before World War I and was one of the founders of CAR. Liber made several attempts at reconciliation between the Consistory leaders and those of the UGIF. His contacts with Lambert and Lévy through CAR made him a most suitable intermediary. See the interesting correspondence in CDJC: CCCLXVI-48; also Richard Cohen, "French Jewry's Dilemma on the Orientation of Its Leadership," *Yad Vashem Studies*, XIV (1982), pp. 173–174; Schwarzfuchs, *Aux prises avec Vichy*, passim.

4. The first meeting of the UGIF Council was held on May 4. From RRL's diary it would appear that before that date UGIF-south had hardly begun its work.

I took a trip to Vichy at the beginning of the month. Vallat had been replaced by Darquier de Pellepoix, but before he left I had to get him to sign the minutes of our Council meeting. This was important because the president's speech[5]—in which I had been particularly careful with all the terms used, and in which, I was told, my "touch" was recognizable—had established our doctrine: we do not assume any responsibilities outside the Free Zone; we do not consider ourselves representatives of our Jewish compatriots; we are nothing more than social workers who have assumed the administration of our agencies for the well-being of the needy, in liaison with the authorities. Vallat countersigned it to please me; thus he has kept his word to us right to the end.

Memo of the trip: Thursday the 7th, left for Lyon. At the station I saw Lazard, who had been asked to submit to the Consistory a conciliating motion adopted by the Council; he had failed in his attempt. Arrived in Vichy 10 P.M. Friday the 8th: visit with Vallat, who was charming; he was emptying his drawers. He told me that Darquier had been appointed especially for Paris, that the Commissariat is particularly concerned about the presidency of the Council, and that Laval has placed an official of the Council of State close to him, to restrain him in judicial matters regarding the Free Zone, a man named Monier[6] who knows Seligman.

Visit to the Commission executives Grateau and Giron, who received me with infinitely more openness than the first time. Through a new decree, since the treasurer no longer has a job and neither does the acting administrator as the result of the appointment of a treasury agent for us, Wormser and I have now become

5. Lévy's remarks, probably written entirely or in part by Lambert, can be found in YIVO: RG 210, XCII-10; some extracts were published by Szajkowski, *Gazetteer,* p. 133.

6. RRL's information was correct. Darquier had been chosen by the Germans and forced upon the French. Laval had tried to avoid German control of the Commissariat by placing it under the jurisdiction of the president of the Council and appointing a general secretary (Monier) to moderate Darquier's activities. But Monier did practically nothing in this capacity, and on June 20, 1942, he submitted his resignation, which was accepted by Laval on September 4, 1942. See Billig, *Le Commissariat général*, vol. I, pp. 130–131.

administrators, and our colleagues are merely "members" of the Council. I have also been given the title of general director. I visited the *Alliance* and did my business quickly at the Quai d'Orsay. Returned to Marseilles on Sunday the 10th.

Since the 18th I have had a lot to do in Marseilles; have put in place and started up my administrative service, at premises that I was finally able to obtain, and conducted negotiations with Couturier,[7] the treasury agent, on the dissolution of our agencies. I hope to be able to save the *Alliance* funds that the former leaders lost in Paris. We are a public corporation, which means there will be lots of paperwork and strict financial control. But I think we will be able to preserve the working methods of all our agencies. Those who are attacking us should be applauding us instead, because it is we who are carrying on the struggle! The day when Gaston Kahn and I had to turn over to Couturier the funds of our committee, now incorporated into the *Union*, we felt like weeping! That evening I understood that the *Statut* really was diminishing us, and that we are the ones who are showing courage in working under such conditions.

Pascot, general commissioner for sports, came to Marseilles yesterday. He telephoned, and I went to the Colonial Medical School to hear him give a lecture on physical education. It didn't amount to anything! I can't believe he is a minister. This is worse than in the Third Republic! With third-rate figures, nothing constructive can be done, and I truly believe that nothing will be preserved in our history of the Pétain interlude.

June 17, 1942

I have been neglecting this diary because I am very busy organizing my ministry of providing for Jewish social welfare. Everything is going as I would wish. I have an excellent system for managing the money of which the treasury man, Couturier, is

7. Maurice Couturier was the official from the French Finance Ministry who was in charge of the UGIF accounts. He was named to this position at the end of April 1942.

keeping the accounts, and the president is letting me take any initiative I want. I give orders calmly and clearly, knowing where I am going and where I want to go. My heavy responsibilities leave me little time for my personal life and family life, but from the point of view of the future this is not lost time, quite the contrary.

I have forgotten to record the events of my last trip to Vichy. Memo: Wednesday the 3rd, left Marseilles at 11:15 A.M., arrived in Vichy at 10 P.M. Turned down a room, fit for sorting mail, at the Albert I, and stayed at the Princes Hotel, where I had a restful view of the trees in the park. Sitting half-naked in the sun in my room, I felt like twenty again and remembered my escapades long ago in Wiesbaden. . . .

Thursday and Friday were business days. At Colonel Jarnieu's office I spoke with Monier, who is in charge of petitions to the Council of State; at first he received me coldly but later became cordial. We were colleagues in the Rhineland and used to dine together in Bonn. How melancholy for us now! I was his superior there, and, from having seen me at work, he knows what I can accomplish. This will facilitate things, and I bless chance, what I call my lucky star. I made an appointment for Albert Lévy and Seligman for the 15th. The next day, more business and receiving visitors at the *Union* office, in particular Pierre Geismar of the Consistory, who came "off the record," despite the anathema that hangs over us, to hear about what I had done to rescue the Jews, both French and foreign, who are being expelled from Le Puy-de-Dôme.[8] The Consistory had not been able to make itself heard there. I explained my intervention to him at the technical level of the agencies.

Since last Sunday the Jews in the Occupied Zone have had to wear a yellow and black star, a sort of round patch, by decree of the occupying authorities and enforced by the French police.

8. On June 3, 1942, the Vichy government ordered the expulsion from Clermont-Ferrand of all Jews who were not living there before January 1, 1938, or who were there as students or officials. It is not clear what action was taken by RRL. A certain reaction from church circles to this Vichy order is worthy of note. See the protest of Vicar Kolb, dated June 13, 1942 (CDJC: CCXIV-6).

There are no words for such infamy. Albert Lévy came back from Vichy and told me that Monier won't be able to stick with a fool like Darquier. It seems the latter has put a garage owner from Levallois in charge of his office in Paris.[9] The Commissariat on Jewish Affairs is turning into a zoo, and I don't think it can go on like this.

I read an excellent collection of new pieces by Charles Braibant, *Resplendine*; *Agnes Grey* by Anne Brontë (a whiny English novel); and Gilbert Maire's *Bergson mon maître* [*Bergson, My Master*]. This one is pushing me to reread Bergson more closely, because I can see that I will find there something for which I have been waiting many years, not a certainty but some fresh light on my thoughts. . . .

I especially want to note these reflections of Bergson's, in 1907, on the Jewish problem: "Here we come to the Jewish question, and you may be sure I don't mind speaking of it either. I am very happy that you asked me the question frankly, and it doesn't embarrass me at all to reply. No need to tell you that I condemn anti-Semitism, first because I am a Jew and have always said so, and then because this doctrine seems to me even more crude than it is barbaric, based on a strangely arbitrary and superficial theory of race and incapable of grasping the nuances in a question where it is especially important to see nuances and distinctions.

"I do not deny that Jews have ethnic characteristics that set them apart, but do these ethnic characteristics form a monolith, as their adversaries claim? As a Jew myself, I must say that my observations point to the contrary. There is Jewish materialism, but also Jewish idealism; there is a revolutionary messianic spirit, and also a conservative spiritualism. Christianity emerged from Judaism, at least in part, and I find this descent extremely natural. In short, in trying to speak of Jews in general, one is exposed to the same difficulties and the same errors as in generalizing

9. This garage owner from Levallois seems to have played only a minor role on the Commissariat.

about English or French people. And it is especially here that I see anti-Semitism either as a mass of prejudices or as a false method, and ordinarily as the justification of the former by the latter.

"Anti-Semitism is a bad way of putting the Jewish question, but here I part company with many of my co-religionists; the Jewish question does exist, and I think it ought to receive consideration. In the end it comes back to a question of naturalization. Not all foreigners are worthy of it, whether or not they are Jews, and this is where I don't want to follow certain people in speaking of Jewish solidarity. Such solidarity, which I am the first to recognize and to practice, should stop short of becoming contrary to the national interest, which all naturalized Jews have an obligation to respect and to serve like everyone else. But they do not always respect it, and this is where they seem to provide reasons for anti-Semitism. As for me, I would never want my Jewishness to be opposed to my being French, nor to my being a Christian, moreover."

July 1, 1942

Written in Vichy at the Albert I on June 21: Women form exclusive attachments. Simone is wrong to resent my going away. But a man has a need to be alone from time to time to get himself together, to gather his energies again and concentrate them, to regain mastery of his will. This getting oneself together is not unfaithfulness; to the contrary, it is a way of restoring one's health as husband and father as well, and regaining one's strength for the daily struggle and one's conscience for the decisions involved in social welfare strategy.

I left Marseilles yesterday at 11:45, as usual, and spent my day on the train reading *Thaïs*. Anatole France has not become old hat for me, and I am still sensitive to his formal perfection and the musical swing of his thoughts. It is a pleasure to rediscover sentences that I used to read aloud when my best friend, Empaytaz, and I were getting to know the beauty of literature (Barrès,

Bourget, Loti, France) around 1910. Then, with Emile Bourgeois as guide, I am continuing to relive nineteenth-century history. He offers an excellent "bible" for action, which takes the place of Stendhal. His masterful pages on Napoleon's dreams of the East can shed light on the German saga of today.

But then, most of all, I am going back to Bergson, beginning with *With Laughter*. I think this time I've found the method for which I have been waiting for a long time, which I suspected would be the true way of enriching my inner life and, who knows?, would formulate wise commandments for me, since I am neither a believer nor an unbeliever. For the first time among all my enthusiasms—Barrès, Romain Rolland, Henri Franck, Goethe, Heine, Gide, and others whom I've forgotten—I am finding, after reading certain pages, that I need to go back and reread them before going on to the next. Bergson is exactly right for me at my age. . . .

At the point where I am now, every morning when I feel the need to remember my mother—and for me this is like a religion, making contact with a memory that remains alive in me and appears before me—I take this sentence, so beautifully profound: "Who knows whether, when we reach a certain age, we may become impervious to fresh, new happiness, and whether the sweetest satisfactions of a mature person can be anything but the reliving of childhood feelings, a scented breeze sent to us in gentle gusts, more and more rarely, by a past receding ever further away?" Isn't my determination to keep this diary a protest against the awareness that the details of my past life will necessarily fade, and the expression of my will to preserve its traces to guide my inner life? With Bergson as my guide, I think I shall soon be able to put my wisdom into words, without formulating my propositions, as I have tended to do under the influence of Barrès' way, the effect of which was an aesthetic desire to worry more about superficial ordering than about respect for time and for life.

"Life," I read just this morning [in Bergson], to my joy, "presents itself to us as evolving in a certain way in time, and as complicating itself in a certain way in space. Considered in time, it is *the continuous progress* (my emphasis) of a being who is constantly growing older: that is to say that life never goes backward and never repeats itself." I can already sense that affirmations like this will enable me to establish a morality that has, rather than the haughty renunciation of Goethe, the conscious acceptance of a universal gestation.

July 8, 1942

Some notes for the sake of the history of the UGIF, showing the bad faith of the Jewish leaders. The Consistory seems to have understood and to want to make peace. At the same time it gives evidence that this whole story is one of personal pique, jealousy and desire for glory. It makes a mockery of Judaism, of our agencies and the unfortunates whom they serve, in spite of the persecutions threatening all of us. While we are arguing in Rome, Sagonte has fallen![1]

On June 26 I had a personal and private visit with Oualid, who told me about the Consistory meeting the previous Sunday. After hearing from Liber, René Mayer, and even Helbronner, they decided to renew contact with the *Union*. The day before, Mr. Couturier, the treasury agent, had come *proprio motu*[2] to see Helbronner (André Weil and Oualid arranged him an appointment) to tell him how much the schism in the Jewish community was hampering our agencies, and that the funds raised by the rabbis and the Consistory should be given to the *Union*, to avoid our having to resort to membership fees and taxes. . . . These gentlemen then admitted that it was all to do with personal issues. So jealousy must be given its due. They would accept the *Union*, but

1. RRL is alluding to the Roman request of Carthage to refrain from attacking Sagonte, a city founded by the Greeks, south of the Ebro River. Hannibal devastated the city in 219 B.C.E., and Carthage refused to disown the accomplishment of its famous general. This was the origin of the Second Punic War.

2. Of his own volition.

without Albert Lévy and Lambert. What pettiness! What contempt I now have for the spiritual leaders of French Jewry! and how wrong I was to account to them for my actions, because I have an infinitely better conscience than they do. . . .

We discussed these conditions with Albert Lévy and Seligman on June 26. There can be no question of accepting them. . . . But to throw a sop to those demanding them, we decided to say, and in fact to consider it, that I am prepared to give up my job as administrator and to remain as general director only. . . . In the future it will perhaps be said, in view of this decision, that I "had" them there. If the Council in the Free Zone must go, for political reasons, I shall in fact, in any case, still be head of the team doing the technical work. To prove as well that I'm not proud and had no intention of "stealing" the *Alliance*, I shall ask the next Council meeting to appoint Seligman in my place as acting administrator; he is Leven's cousin and the nephew of Jacques Bigard.[3] . . . As general director, I'll still be giving the orders. And in this way we will be good losers.

The next day, June 27, I was at Olmer's house with Seligman. We shared with him our decisions, which in no way signified a split within the team; to the contrary. He recognized that he himself, and all those of good faith, could not do otherwise, after seeing Vallat's signature on my Council minutes, than to acknowledge the success of my diplomacy. . . . He admitted that these personal worries were "ridiculous" and "laughable," and he thanked me warmly for having sacrificed my own pride in order to make peace. So that is where things are, and we are waiting for the reaction from the gentlemen of this farce in Lyon.

From June 21 to 23 I was in Vichy for the Finance Commission. I had dinner with Pascot, and we listened to Laval's infamous speech: to say "I believe Germany will be victorious" would have been enough, but he said "I hope Germany will be victori-

3. Jacques Bigart, who died in 1934, had been one of the pillars of the Alliance since becoming its secretary in 1881.

ous."[4] "He's writing his own death sentence," I told Pascot, but unfortunately he didn't know what I meant.

I've finished reading *With Laughter*, in which I found moving passages on joy and cheerfulness. I'm going to continue with my study of Bergson. I also finished the Bourgeois and *Les gaietés de l'escadron* [*Living It Up with Our Company*].

July 21, 1942

I'm thinking about the vanity of the attacks on me by these gentlemen in the Consistory, and about writing a book that would get back at them and be enjoyed by my children and nephews. . . . In conclusion I note this crude reflection on "peace" by Leonardo da Vinci: "It is said that a beaver when being hunted, knowing that it is because of the medicinal properties of his testicles, and unable to get away, stops and tries to gain a peace with his attackers by biting off his testicles with his sharp teeth and leaving them there for his enemies."

In Russia things are not going well; in Egypt they are going pretty badly, but not so badly as a few weeks ago. . . . Before winter comes we shall go through months in which the pressure from the Germans will be difficult to overcome. . . . Moreover the persecutions against Jews in the Occupied Zone are being redoubled. They are now arresting women and children, and deporting men *en masse*.[5] . . . Where is France now if it is letting innocent citizens be tortured without a protest? Barrès wrote on August 9,

4. Laval's famous June 22, 1942, radio broadcast was the subject of commentary for a long time. He claimed it was necessary to send French workers to Germany in the hope that in return a large number of prisoners of war would be released. RRL does not quote the rest of Laval's famous sentence, which stated that the alternative to a German victory would be worldwide bolshevism. This speech was to become one of the main charges brought against Laval at his trial after the war.

5. On July 16 and 17, 1942, 12,884 Jews were arrested in Paris and interned at Drancy. RRL could hardly imagine the scope of this major operation. On the mass arrests in July 1942, see Susan Zuccotti, *The Holocaust, the French, and the Jews* (New York, 1993), pp. 103–117.

1914: "The unity of France is sealed for us, all the way to our grandchildren." He would turn over in his grave now if he could hear the speeches from Vichy about sending workers to Germany.

On the 14th of July I saw, in the streets of Marseilles, the first mass demonstration against Laval and Hitler. The reality of the country is not its legal reality. I saw 100,000 people in the street cheering de Gaulle and singing the "Marseillaise." . . . This war will end with chaos in the streets and, when the Boche leave, France will rehabilitate itself by executing the traitors. I still have hope for my country. I read again in Péguy,[6] "A single injustice, a single crime, a single case of inequality, if it is accepted universally, legally, nationally, and comfortably, is enough to dishonor a people. It is the beginning of a gangrene that will corrupt the whole body. What we defend is just this combination of past, present, and future that occurs only one time. It is not just our honor, the honor of our whole people, in the present; it is the historical honor of our people, the honor of our ancestors and of our children. The greater the past that lies behind us, the greater our obligation to preserve its purity. A single blot is the flaw of a whole family, and the flaw of a whole people."

I reread *Au Service de l'Allemagne* [*Serving Germany*]. I compared myself to someone in Alsace under the heel of Germany. We must not emigrate nor give up; we must submit and wait, hold on and endure.

September 6, 1942

I have just lived through the most tragic hours of my life since the first war. My country has dishonored itself with these inhuman persecutions. They are deporting the foreign Jews, even those who voluntarily served our country in the war. France is disowning its past and violating the right to asylum. . . . Where are we going? Because I was involved, before the deportations, in the

6. This passage comes from Charles Péguy's discussion of the Dreyfus Affair in his *Notre jeunesse* (Paris, 1910).

efforts to stop them, and because I don't think I have shown any lack of courage, I shall quickly note here what I have done and seen for over a month.

On July 27 I leave for Vichy accompanied by Lionel. We spend the night at the Hotel Rivoli. On the 28th in the morning, Spanien[7] joins me for a visit to the National Security office. The news we can't believe is confirmed: ten thousand foreign Jews are to be deported to Germany, people who have been refugees in France since 1936 and the majority of whom have been promised asylum. I have lunch with Colonel Pascot and share my anguish with him. He claims to know nothing about it.

On the 29th at the General Commission I make the acquaintance of Mr. Puech and Mr. Letourneur, and settle some administrative business; at the National Security office, Fourcade tells Spanien and me that this matter is so serious that it is no longer in his hands. It is up to President [of the Council of Ministers] Laval and his general secretary, Mr. Guérard.[8] We request a meeting with the latter. Since it will take a while to get an answer, and they're asking for me in Marseilles where Joseph Schwartz,[9] the representative of the American charities, has just turned up,

7. Raphaël Spanien was a prominent figure in HICEM, the emigration organization. During the revision of the list of candidates for UGIF-south council, RRL proposed his name, and Spanien was appointed to the council. He was French-born and had worked in the Marseilles offices of HICEM. He thought he would be able to put the brakes on RRL, as he wrote to I. Dijour on April 2, 1942: ". . . you know the influence that I have on Lambert, and the very fact of my being a member of the Administrative Council of this Union, living abroad [in Portugal] at least for the time being, and having telephone contacts with the United States, can help me to calm down Lambert's impetuousness" (YIVO: RG 245.4, Portugal B 47). After the summer deportations in France, Spanien returned to his job at HICEM as the organization's representative in Lisbon.

8. Jacques Guérard was in charge of Paul Baudouin's office during the short time Baudouin served as minister for foreign affairs in 1940. When Laval returned to power in April 1942, Guérard was made general secretary of his staff. See Jacques Guérard, *Criminel de paix* (Paris, 1953).

9. At the beginning of 1942, Schwartz was appointed European director of the American Jewish Joint Distribution Committee, a post he had in fact already held for more than a year. Working from Lisbon from 1940 on, Schwartz had an active role in aid to the Jewish communities in Europe during the Nazi period. On his widespread activity during the war, see Yehuda Bauer, *American Jewry and the Holocaust* (Detroit, 1981), passim.

I decide to go, leaving a secretary there to call me back again if need be.

I leave Vichy on July 30 at dawn. On the platform at Lyon-Perrache Station I encounter Mr. Jacques Helbronner and tell him of my anxiety. "That's not correct," he replies. "I sent my secretary, Mr. Kiefe [Robert Kiefé], to Vichy yesterday. Laval has not given in." I contradict him, tell him the opposite is true, and implore him to let Mr. Seligman of our Council come to see him so they can take joint action. We cannot allow such a crime. It is Thursday the 30th; I ask for a meeting the next day, but Mr. Helbronner will not agree to meet before Sunday. He is expecting Mr. Schwartz the same day. The president of the Consistory seems more deaf to me, more pretentious and older than ever. The fate of the foreigners doesn't move him in the least.

On the 30th at 6:30 P.M. I'm back in Marseilles. A meeting is held at my home at seven. During the afternoon I had a telephone call that Guérard was expecting me the next day, so I leave for Vichy again at midnight with Spanien and Schwartz in a jam-packed train. We plan in detail the action we shall take. We have to prevent this crime from taking place.

On July 31, back in Vichy, I shave at the office because my room at the Hotel Rivoli will not be available until evening. After lunch with Spanien and his secretary, Lautman, who is liaison agent for immigration issues, we go to the Park Hotel. We plan on a purely technical step to ask that people who have visas for the United States not be deported. It is up to our chief leaders to register the protests!

We get there at three o'clock. At four, surprised at this long wait, I step outside the waiting room to ask the porter if we are going to be received. "Yes," he says, "but it's the president who wants to see you!" I scarcely have time to recover from my surprise and to tell my colleagues this news when the porter comes to fetch us and, announcing our names loudly, ushers us into Pierre Laval's office. The president offers us his hand and gestures toward armchairs. "Please sit down, gentlemen!"

I stop two steps inside the door and, without taking his extended hand or looking at the armchairs, I reply somewhat emotionally, "Mr. President, please excuse us, but it wasn't you whom we came to see. . . . We asked for a meeting with Mr. Guérard, about a technical question.[1] Your time is valuable, and we are not qualified to meet with you."

"Oh, it's Guérard you want to see," answers Pierre Laval nervously. "Then he will receive you. . . . That's good, because I have a lot of people to see today."

He rings a buzzer, and Mr. Guérard comes in, quite surprised, and takes us into his office, where he tells us the truth. At lunch Laval and Guérard discussed the issue of concern to us, and the president wanted to see us. . . . He would have told us that the rumors are true. But we must understand that the negotiations taking place in Paris are very hard, very difficult. The Germans are the victors, and their anti-Semitic demands come in a torrent that cannot be stopped; one can seek only to channel them. So let us not ask for the impossible. . . . Mr. Guérard, with crocodile tears in his voice, puts forward some German arguments: the anti-collaboration propaganda being conducted by Jewish immigrants in the United States, and a pseudo-plot hatched in Spain. . . . But the President reserves the right to grant exit visas. We shall hear from him.

With regard to my refusal to meet with the president, I explain that I would like to keep my request at the technical level, that I didn't want to go above the general secretary. If the president would like to speak with Jewish leaders, I would bring him the president of the Consistory and the president of the UGIF.

1. RRL's behavior here is puzzling. He chooses at this moment to stick to a strict definition of his "technical" position rather than seize the opportunity to make a vigorous protest to Laval against the deportations. His response bears the mark of the feelings of rivalry that dominated the community. Possibly he believed that a delegation consisting of the presidents of the Consistory and the Union would have a greater impact on Laval, nonetheless his deferring to protocol at this moment is not completely in character.

Mr. Guérard asks me to telephone him from Marseilles about this the next Monday, August 3.

Schwartz meanwhile has been at Tuck's office,[2] the American *chargé d'affaires*. This diplomat was amazed that civilized countries would still have relations with such a government. To him, Vichy is nothing more than an observation post.

On August 1, I go to see Guichard at the Red Cross and Fourcade at the Interior Ministry who, unfortunately, only confirm the news. In front of the Park Hotel I encounter Marcel Bucard with two armed guards; he has aged and is still not of the stuff of which dictators are made. He declares to me that he is struggling against Doriot. These struggles among factions are a sign of troubled times. That evening Spanien and I leave for Lyon, have dinner with Lazard, and stay at the Hotel Russia.

We spend Sunday, August 2, in Lyon,[3] where we have conversations with Lazard, Jarblum, and Schwartz. At five o'clock I go with Spanien and Lautman to the Consistory, where we are received by Mr. Helbronner; Mr. Seligman and Albert Manuel are also present.[4] We give them an account of the information we have and of the meeting with Mr. Laval, which we turned down. To everything we tell him, Mr. Helbronner replies haughtily, "I know," speaking only for himself. When we insist that, to-

2. S. Pinkney Tuck was first secretary at the American embassy in Vichy from December 1941. After the departure of Ambassador Leahy in May 1942, Tuck served as *chargé d'affaires* at the embassy until it was closed in November 1942. He strongly opposed the deportations and played an active part in the abortive plan to send a large number of Jewish children to the United States, for which negotiations went on between September and November 1942. On Tuck's activities in this area, see Bauer, *American Jewry*, pp. 175–176, 260–264; Michael R. Marrus, "Vichy et les enfants juifs," *L'Histoire*, no. 22 (1980), pp. 11–15.

3. The following is a summary of an extraordinary meeting between Consistory and UGIF leaders. The statements made by RRL and Helbronner seem entirely authentic, though no other reports have corroborated their veracity.

4. Albert Manuel, son-in-law of Emmanuel Weill, the former chief rabbi of France, was general secretary of the Central Consistory. He was related by marriage to André Baur of UGIF-north and stayed in constant communication with him during the war.

gether with Mr. Albert Lévy or Mr. Seligman, he agree to go and see the president [of the Council of Ministers], the president of the Central Consistory has the nerve to deliver this criminal statement: "If Mr. Laval wants to see me, he has only to summon me, but be sure and tell him that I am going on holiday from August 8 until September, and nothing in the world can persuade me to come back."[5]

We all look at one another upon hearing these words. Is it possible that a leader of French Jewry would dare to have so little heart and conscience? We deserve these ordeals for having accepted such leadership. . . . Then I tell Helbronner about my visit to the Park Hotel and my refusal to speak with Pierre Laval. He claims he already knows all about it. I ask him very earnestly to go and see Laval, and to accept a joint meeting with a representative of the UGIF. The pride of this dotard of French Jewry is then displayed in all its cruel frankness. "Tell Mr. Guérard that if he wishes to discuss something of interest to the charities, he should summon Mr. Albert Lévy. If there is a question of interest to general policy with regard to Judaism, I shall go to see him *alone*, and in no circumstances together with Mr. Albert Lévy. You heard me: I shall go to see him *alone*." At this point the arrival of Mr. Schwartz, the representative of the American Jews, is announced, and Mr. Helbronner refuses to listen to anything more. . . . Poor Jews of France!

Vichy, September 21, 1942

I am continuing with the story of the past days. Things are happening so fast that I am afraid of forgetting. I have been acting and thinking. I am satisfied with my actions, and my reward will come in the future. But hours and days go by in which I find no time to record my thoughts. Taking action remains the urgent

5. Helbronner was in fact not present at the special meeting of the Consistory on August 23, 1942. See Schwarzfuchs, *Aux prises avec Vichy*, pp. 253.

imperative, so it requires a strong will to stay in touch with oneself. Still, I will keep trying, whenever I can.

My reading in the last two months: Marguerite Audoux, *Marie-Claire*, a good book though with a somewhat childish realism; Maurice Barrès, *Les Saints de la France* [*France's Saints*] (which made me relive the Great War, and my youth), excellent curative; Anatole France, *Sur la pierre blanche* [*On the White Rock*], healing in another way; Simenon, *Talatala*, entertaining colonial setting; Dr. Martial, *Race, hérédité, folie* [*Race, Heredity and Madness*], useful documentation; Carmen Sylva, *Par la loi* [*By Law*], almost worthless; Simenon, *Ticket of Leave*, a good novel; Arthur Meyer, *Ce que mes yeux ont vu* [*What My Eyes Have Seen*]: I'm getting old, because I'm enjoying books that were all the rage when I was fifteen; Sinclair Lewis, *It Can't Happen Here*, a profound and prophetic book; Paul Morand, *Feu M. le Duc* [*The Late Mr. Duke*], amusing, but a bit facile and the technique stinks; Giraudoux, *Amica America*, richly instructive in 1942; Louis Piérard, *Les Réfugiés* [*The Refugees*], true to life and sad, to read again later; René Benjamin, *Le soliloque de Maurice Barrès* [*Maurice Barrès' Soliloquy*], very good; Henri Michaux, *A Barbarian in Asia*, excellent; Léon Bloy, *Le sang du pauvre* [*A Poor Man's Blood*], fairly good but outmodish and a little rancid; Roland Dorgelès, *Sous le casque bleu* [*Blue Helmet*], fair but no awareness at all of the idea of "empire."

My son Tony, three years old, on seeing the first-quarter moon in the sky at noon: "Papa, look, the moon is broken!"

Marseilles, October 4, 1942

Yesterday and today there has been a great commotion in the streets of Marseilles for the anniversary of SOL, the *Service d'ordre légionnaire*, the police and superpolice who are marginally part of the LFC. Yesterday evening they had a torchlight procession. People are keeping aloof, and in private conversations they don't hide their disgust. . . . It stinks to high heaven of Nazism. There will be a bloody revolution the moment the Germans even pull out of

Saint-Jean-de-Luz.[6] I think more than ever that I shall be back in uniform by September 1943.

The news from Paris is atrocious. French Jews have been deported. All these victims are to serve as slaves to build the Siegfried Line (behind the Russian front from Gernovich to the Baltic Sea).[7] Very few of them will return from that hell.

To continue my notes on these past weeks: Returned to Marseilles on Monday, August 3. I told my president and colleagues about the mission I carried out. On Tuesday, August 4, I had lunch with Schwartz of the Joint Distribution Committee, who left that evening for Lisbon. I trained a team of UGIF social workers to go up to Milles Camp[8] to record the "last will and testament" of the deportees who will be leaving in two or three days. While sending written protests against the deportations, I also resigned myself to responding to the Prefecture's request that we put camping equipment and food aboard the railway cars to mitigate, if ever so slightly, the hardships of the trip.

On Wednesday, August 5, we had a visit from Chief Rabbis Hirschler and Berman,[9] who were scandalized that the official Jewish community was refusing to intervene. The chief rabbi of France, Isaïe Schwartz, received an urgent telephone call from Hirschler summoning him to intervene, to which he replied that

6. In the Département des Basses-Pyrenées (Pyrenees Mountains, southern border of France).

7. Lambert's placement of the Siegfried Line is mistaken: it was constructed along Germany's western border.

8. Aix-les-Milles was an internment camp, near Aix-en-Provence, where candidates for emigration were detained until their visas were ratified. In any case, at various times this camp contained more than fifteen hundred Jews. In August 1942, when the deportations from the south occurred, those Jews who were left stranded at Aix-les-Milles were deported to Drancy. See Lucien Lazare, *Rescue in Resistance: How Jewish Organizations Fought the Holocaust in France,* trans. Jeffrey M. Green (New York, 1996), pp. 83–84, 185–188.

9. Born in Paris in 1892, Léon Berman finished his rabbinical studies in 1919. He was chosen chief rabbi of Lille in 1934. In the 1930s he was involved in granting aid to Jewish refugees from Germany. Berman and his family were arrested on October 15, 1943, and deported on October 28 to Auschwitz, where he perished.

"it would be a sword thrust against water." I tried in vain to telephone Vichy in hopes of saving something, or a few people. They told me no one is there.

Thursday, August 6: The Prefecture asked me for slop pails for the transports. I'm determined to find some in spite of all the restrictions. I tried again to call Vichy, but in vain. They didn't want to see me there or even to talk to me here by telephone.

Friday, August 7: A day of struggle for Spanien and me. My teams of social workers had been slaving away and gathered a thousand files on individuals threatened with deportation. We were working at night in the office.

Saturday, August 8: I brought the files to the Prefecture. They will save certain families. I asked that at least the children be left in our care. At 6:30 P.M. I was told that we could save sixty-six of them. Shortly before that I had a visit from McClelland,[1] of the Quakers, who told me of a visit to the Marshal in Vichy on August 5, which he had undertaken along with Mr. Lowrie of the YMCA and R.P. Arnoux,[2] Cardinal Gerlier's[3] representative. Dr. Ménétrel[4] had been present at their interview. They strongly

1. Roswell D. McClelland was an American Quaker who was active during the war years in supporting charitable organizations in Switzerland, Italy, and France. He had been on the American embassy staff in Berne and returned to Switzerland later, in 1944, as representative of the War Refugee Board set up by President Roosevelt. See Bauer, *American Jewry*, passim.

2. Reverend Arnoux had represented Cardinal Gerlier of Lyon on the Nîmes Committee since 1941. In this capacity he joined Lowrie in late August to intervene with Pétain. See the minutes of the meeting of the Nîmes Committee of September 9, 1942 (Leo Baeck Institute, New York: Ar-C1584/B987, 1).

3. Cardinal Pierre Gerlier, Archbishop of Lyon, oscillated between unreserved support for Pétain's New Order and timid and hesitant criticism of some of his actions against the Jews beginning in 1941. His most candid protest followed the deportations of the summer of 1942 but did not go as far as the intransigent moral condemnation expressed by Monsignor Jules-Gérard Saliège. Gerlier's position on the "Jewish question" has been the source of continued historical debate. See the article by Jean-Marie Mayeur, "Les Eglises devant la persécution des Juifs en France," in Wellers, Kaspi, and Klarsfeld, eds., *La France et la question juive*, pp. 147–170; an apologetic view appears in Henri de Lubac, *Résistance chrétienne à l'antisémitisme: Souvenirs 1940–1944* (Paris, 1988), pp. 179–203.

4. Dr. Bernard Ménétrel was Pétain's personal physician and private secretary. For a commentary on this intervention, see Marrus and Paxton, *Vichy France and the Jews*, p. 262.

protested the deportations of foreign Jews to Germany and insisted that at least the children and foreigners who were about to emigrate be saved. The Marshal declared that he was not informed about this measure, and sent the delegation to President Laval, accompanied by Dr. Ménétrel. On August 6 the delegation was received by Mr. Laval. This interview was of the least courteous sort. Mr. Laval told them that he himself had formulated and decided upon the measures taken, in conformity with the policy of French-German collaboration. The situation of French Jews is decided by the *Statut*. It is legitimate for France to send foreigners to Germany; it can do anything it likes with them. Mr. Laval did not respond to humanitarian and legal arguments put forward by the representatives of the charities, and he was severe in his judgment of the attitude of American leaders who have been making speeches about this problem for years but have not offered a solution. In such circumstances he could not be expected to take into account public opinion abroad.

October 11, 1942

Notes on the past weeks (continued): Sunday, August 9, I go back up to the Milles Camp with Spanien. My team records the "last will and testament" of people who are to be deported. In the courtyard of the oil filling station, which has been turned into an embarkation camp, anxieties are rising. The eyes of those about to depart question me in their anguish—am I going to save them? I stiffen to ward off the emotion. I take the files to the Prefecture. Children aged two to fifteen will be saved. Is this humane? Their parents will entrust them to us so that they may escape this hell. During the afternoon, in the office, we prepare the equipment to be placed in the railroad cars—makeshift equipment, as if for a life raft: metal bowls, bottles, drinking cups, pails . . . here in the desperate and barren peace of the Provençal countryside, a few steps away from the burnt forest, in the tile factory with its clock and its windows with holes painstakingly stuffed, in front of the little Milles railroad station, guarded by armed police. We must identify ourselves to them in order to step across the level crossing. All such deportations are organized far away from the cities, so that the criminal event will not attract notice.

Monday, August 10 is a terrible day, a heartrending spectacle. Buses are taking away seventy children from parents who are to depart that evening. I have arranged for the children to leave first so they will not see their parents subjected to the roll call. . . . But what a scene, under a blazing sun! We have to hold the fathers and mothers back as the buses leave the courtyard. What wailing and tears, what gestures as each poor father, faced with the moment of deportation, caresses the face of a son or daughter as if to imprint it on his fingertips! Mothers are screaming in despair, and the rest of us cannot hold back our own tears. . . .

Then the deportees' roll call begins in the courtyard under the cruel sun. Many are felled by sunstroke, and stretchers are brought out. . . . The disorder intensifies the cruelty of the measures being taken. . . . Sitting on their suitcases, women weep and men simply wait, stupefied. All these unfortunate people have such dignity; I am astonished not to see more of them rebel, more gestures of despair. I am told later that they were given chloral hydrate in their coffee—the [calming] "mickey" before being sent into battle. Some of the policemen do not hide their distaste at having to perform such a mission. In the crowd, all sorts of reactions mingle. Some of the women have preserved a remarkably refined bearing. Some men remain impassive. Others plead with me, as if I could do anything. . . . I have seen and lived through two wars, but the two cataclysms have not left me with memories less worthy of humanity than these days spent in the courtyard at Milles.

The departure takes place the next morning at dawn. We can see the camp station with the railroad cars, black like hearses, waiting on the siding. The meager rations are distributed in the courtyard, where the deportees are already grouped by carloads. They are surrounded by brutal policemen who do not speak their language. They have to carry by themselves everything they are entitled to take with them. At the gate, on leaving the camp, there is a final roll call [for each carload] before they go to the station; surrounded by armed guards, forty human beings who have committed no crime are being delivered up because they are Jews, by my country which had promised them asylum, and handed over to those who will be their executioners. There are children, old people, war veterans, women, disabled people, old men. . . . I cannot watch each group leave the camp, I hide where I can weep. . . . I see people I know pass by: a lawyer from Vienna, the father of a soldier who was killed in the war, a Polish woman schoolteacher, a doctor from Antwerp, an artist who has a commission in Basel, a family with a visa for the United States. . . . What has become of the time when the French authorities were grateful to our agencies for helping them show the world that France was a land of asylum? I am ashamed of our powerlessness. I still hope against all hope. . . . Two of the refugees have just cut their wrists to escape their tragic fate. They have been bandaged and will be sent off nevertheless. Others have had nervous breakdowns and are being put aboard on stretchers. We lose count of those who fall and must be carried.

I have spent the night in the camp and managed to obtain grace for a few from the police inspector: certain war veterans, old people, political refugees. . . . But I have the feeling that their fate has only been deferred.

Tuesday, August 11, the first train leaves at dawn. My team and the rabbi witness its departure. It was infinitely sad and full of dignity. There has been a suicide in the camp.

Wednesday, August 12, I go back up to Milles to try for more rescues. The condemned people are now glad to see me coming. They know that through my intervention some people were spared even after they were already on the train. This time I plead with more energy, because the scene in the courtyard has become even more tragic. Acts of despair have become more frequent, and the police reaction is so brutal that I must intervene, along with a Protestant pastor who is here. At my request, the police chief reminds his stewards that these are deportees, not detainees. To think that none of these unfortunates has committed any crime except to be born non-Aryan!

Thursday, August 13, departure of the second transport at dawn, in two trains at 5:40 A.M. and 8 A.M. The women and men have been shut up in the cars during the night and forbidden to come out even to relieve themselves. Frida Rosenbaum, age sixty-seven, is being deported. Some groups had only five minutes to pack their bags, and the guards have ransacked their barracks. The mobile [. . .] dealt brutally with those who did not walk fast enough. . . . I would need a book to write it all down.

From August 23 to 29 I must go to Vichy for the liaison that has been arranged with the Commission. I leave Gaston Kahn at Milles to witness, in my stead, the departure on August 24 of the third train, in which foreign laborers are being deported.

In Vichy, business as usual at the ministries through useful and confident conversations. On Monday the 24th I see Puech and Ramband[5] Darquier's co-workers, at the Commissariat; neither one amounts to anything. On Tuesday the 25th I see Louis Marin,[6] whose optimistic idealism is a comfort to me. He knows about the persecutions and declares that the Marshal is a "Jesuit" who knows everything and is covering for Laval, intoxicated by the power he holds. In the afternoon, instead of Bousquet[7] and

5. The names of these two officials at the Commissariat appear in the correspondence with the UGIF from time to time, but no particulars have been found as to their roles in this ministry. Puech was mentioned earlier in the diary, on September 6, 1942.

6. A right-wing Catholic politician, Louis Marin headed the Republican Federation party between the two world wars. A conservative, he was known for his Germanophobia, which went well with his constant concern for the security of France. He was part of the disastrous Reynaud government of May 10, 1940, and a staunch opponent of the armistice with Germany.

7. A former socialist and prefect, René Bousquet became general secretary of the French police in late April 1942. He had a front-line role in the French-German negotiations and in preparations for the deportations of the summer of 1942, and figured prominently in the decision to reject the plan to send Jewish children to the United States in the autumn of 1942. During the German campaign to speed up the solution of the "Jewish question" in the summer of 1943, Bousquet was the butt of Brunner's raging against the "weak" French. Due to German and Milice pressure, Bousquet was finally removed from office in December 1943. Tried for collaboration in the late 1940s, he was found guilty but quickly amnestied, and he gradually moved back into French politics. For Bousquet's role in the summer deportations and other biographical information, see Zuccotti, *The Holocaust, the French, and the Jews*, pp. 97–99, 126–131; Henry Rousso, *The Vichy Syndrome: History and Memory in France Since 1994*, trans. Arthur Goldhammer (Cambridge, Mass., and London, 1991), pp. 61–62, 149–150.

Cado,[8] the secretaries in the police office, I speak with Dangelzer, head of the office, who knew me in Paris when he was a small-time editor. I make three requests, with an energy that surprises even me: on behalf of my staff (I demand the same protection as those in Paris), on behalf of war veterans, and on behalf of those who have visas. That evening I have dinner with Pascot. He is moved by what I tell him, but is drunk from the power he holds.

On Wednesday the 26th I write up my notes addressed to Laval, summarizing my negotiations of the day before. I do not mince words. I bring them to Villar, in the president's office, who promises his support (he was purser aboard the *Normandie*). I introduce myself to Darquier de Pellepoix, who receives me with a haughty benevolence. He makes no effort to conceal his pique at being sidelined with regard to the deportation measures, which have been decided upon by the president and carried out by the police. . . . This is a strange regime, whose victims are called upon to witness to its administrative disorder! I go to see Xavier Vallat in a domestic staff office in the Park Hotel. He confides in me that now "the Boche are going a bit too far." Curiouser and curiouser!

On Thursday the 27th I renew my negotiations with Dangelzer and Villar. Spanien thinks I put things too strongly. . . . I think, to the contrary, that sounding sincere in what I say can only support what I have written. I shall not stay as general director unless all my staff is protected—and I declare this forcefully. On Friday the 28th I am back again, and I am promised a solution in my favor and that the police chiefs will be notified. I visit the Red Cross, but they have no information about the deportees. On the morning of the 29th I return to Marseilles.

On August 31 the Prefecture asks me to send a team to the Blancarde station to resupply a train filled with deportees when it stops there on its way from Nice, especially with drinking

8. Henri Cado was police chief in Marseilles until October 1940 and later served as Bousquet's assistant. For his handling of certain issues in this capacity, see Klarsfeld, *Vichy-Auschwitz*, pp. 316–317, 338–339, 499–500; Billig, *Le Commissariat général*, vol. I, pp. 300–301; vol. II, pp. 217–219.

water. I send Marcel Dreyfus with a detachment. At noon he reports to me on the distress he has seen: thirty-two cars, of which twenty-nine are freight cars with rudimentary furnishings and three are third-class passenger cars, with thirty deportees each, men and women separated, guarded by armed police. A medical unit in an ordinary freight car has three desperate Red Cross nurses. On arriving in the station they say they have a patient at death's door, sustained only by injections of camphorated oil, but their request that he be taken to the hospital is not authorized by the Prefecture. He will die before they get there. . . . In the station, the doors and windows of the cars are opened. . . . The faces are painful to look at, and the odor is horrible. The unfortunate people fall upon our water and provisions . . . but without a cry or complaint. Only their faces, tense and ravaged, their eyes full of tears, testify to the suffering they have endured. . . . A woman tries to throw her child out the window, to entrust it to us.

This last detail pushes me to telephone to Villar, in Vichy, in place of Guérard who is not there. In emotional and occasionally violent terms, I declare to him that Mr. Laval "will have blood on his hands" if he doesn't allow parents being deported to leave their children with us, as was done for the first transports. . . . But my plea is in vain, since Hitler is in command!

On September 1 and 2 I go back up to Milles, where another transport is scheduled to leave on the 3rd, and try, together with Spanien, to rescue a few more. But the police are growing irritated, and they haven't filled their quota. . . . During the night of the 1st, roll call is held and the cars are filled in a chaotic way unfit for human beings. Babies are carried aboard without any milk. There are increasing scenes of desperation. I am ashamed to be so powerless, but I must stay there to see what happens. People I have saved from the first two transports are now being taken without any questions raised. . . . It is the most inhuman chaos. And the director of the camp is incompetent, he hasn't made his quota. . . .

At seven o'clock in the morning the police inspector, de Rodellec du Porzie, and his chief secretary Auzanneau[9] turn up in white suits to inventory the cattle to be delivered. . . . Catastrophe and fury. There are two empty cars because the disorderly roll call in the night produced nothing. As if he were dealing with mutinous sailors, the commandant orders everyone off the train and back to the courtyard, where the bell is rung—women to the left, men to the right. Many are in pajamas or are only half-dressed. Two lots of thirty are chosen, surrounded immediately by armed guards, and are off to the train without being given time to get dressed or to get their baggage. . . . It's too much! After all, we aren't in Dachau here. The Quaker representatives are protesting, and I'm thinking of leaving. But I have to stay. Policemen are weeping. . . . I go toward the first group to be taken aboard; a man half-shaven, with a towel around his neck, is making signs to his wife at the back of the courtyard while a fifteen-year-old child looks at me numbly. . . . This must be the way they choose hostages to be shot during a civil war! . . . In the first row of the victims who have been selected is a Knight of the Legion of Honor, Fischer, the Viennese publisher. I can't stand it any more! I rush across the courtyard like a madman. "You can't deport a Knight of the Legion of Honor!" I tell the commandant.

"Go and get him!" I push the guards apart, grab Fischer by the arm, and put him behind me in the middle of the courtyard.[1]

9. Both of them worked in the Prefecture of Marseilles. For background material on Rodellec, see Donna F. Ryan, *The Holocaust and the Jews of Marseille: The Enforcement of Anti-Semitic Policies in Vichy France* (Urbana, Ill., 1996), p. 61 and passim. Ryan has brief comments on Robert Auzanneau. See below, entry for February 1, 1943.

1. The description of his action offers a window into its profound psychological and existential meaning for RRL. All through the month of August he had stoically carried out his "professional tasks," facing great cruelty and repeatedly expressing his grave thoughts on the demise of French humanitarian values. The diary entries describing the events of August are both highly personal and objective, and reveal RRL's inner agitation, which finally reached a boiling point when he saw a Knight of the Legion of Honor among the deportees being sent to Drancy. It is as if suddenly the balance between his professionalism and his innermost feelings was shattered, and he reacted "like a madman." Perhaps this was a moment of clairvoyance in which he sensed that as a Knight of the Legion of Honor himself, he too could be deported from his beloved France.

Numb with fear, he must have stayed there for an hour, without the courage even to think of moving away. . . .

Such scenes as this are the mark of a shameful regime. It's a dry run of the St. Bartholomew massacre.[2] Since everything gets out in spite of the censors, public opinion is becoming concerned. They have now handed over sixteen thousand Jewish refugees, regardless of the asylum law.[3] The police have conducted manhunts and are still doing so, but people feel sorry for these unfortunates who are being so hounded. The clergy have lodged an offical protest.[4] Convents are hiding those who are fleeing, seminaries are keeping children. . . . Some day these raids must be written up in full detail. The saddest part is the contemptible cowardice of officials who, when told to carry out such inhuman measures, don't have the courage to resign or at least to admit to finding them abhorrent.

October 15, 1942

To continue my notes on recent weeks: September 20 to 28, another trip to Vichy. Since I have taken only four days' vacation, I took Simone and the two older boys with me to the Albert I. I was criticized by the wagging tongues, but I'm strong enough to thumb my nose at them. But for normal business trips it's better for me to go alone.

2. Once again RRL's metaphors evoke historical associations. This massacre of French Huguenots began on August 24, 1572, St. Bartholomew's night, and continued for several months, during which thousands (perhaps tens of thousands) of Huguenots were killed by Catholic elements in France. But RRL is overly optimistic here—alas, it was not to be a dry run. See his diary entry for June 15, 1941.

3. The figure provided by RRL seems high for early September 1942. According to a variety of other sources, it would seem that the number of deportees by that time was about nine thousand.

4. Protests and open condemnation of Vichy's collaboration in these arrests were being led by eminent churchmen. For the first time since the institution of the racial laws against the Jews, indignation was expressed publicly. In recent years researchers have been giving more and more attention to this issue. *Inter alia*, see Marrus and Paxton, *Vichy France and the Jews,* pp. 270–279; Zuccotti, *The Holocaust, the French, and the Jews*, pp. 228–251. A satisfying explanation for the short-lived nature of this outburst of public indignation has yet to be offered.

On Sunday, September 20, we left Marseilles at 11:45 A.M. The train stopped in Lyon, where we changed. From the gate of Perrache Station I saw a demonstration against the larger police presence. I could see that the streets were blocked off. It's an unstable regime that must use force to maintain itself in power. . . . They'll be thinking less about the Jews now that they must organize manhunts here. Arrived at the Albert I at 10:40 P.M. The hotel form had a space to fill in one's religion. Did anyone ask me that at the Chemin des Dames?

Monday the 21st: I worked in the UGIF office and did business with the National Security office (Bernard—Camboulève—Duhamel).

Tuesday the 22nd: I did business at the Foreign Affairs office (Cheviette), had lunch with Colonel Pascot, worked in the office, and received some visitors.

Wednesday 23rd, business at the Council president's office (Villar) and the Interior Ministry (Dangelzer) on behalf of the UGIF staff, dinner with Camboulève.

Thursday the 24th, new attempts at the president's office (Villar) and the Interior Ministry (Dangelzer). Also visited the Commissariat (Rousel and Huguenin) and the National Security (Verdier). They can't get me any answer. . . . It's a sign of the regime and of the times that no official wants to take responsibility even for carrying out decisions.

Friday the 25th, business with the Red Cross (with Guichard and General Verdier, who were happy to see me again: "Vive la Coloniale!"). Visited Dangelzer. The United States is offering asylum for a thousand children.[5] We must have exit visas for them—and nothing is assured.

5. It was the American *chargé d'affaires* in Vichy, Pinkney Tuck, who proposed to his government in mid-September that he be authorized to negotiate with Laval to allow for as many Jewish children to emigrate to the United States as it was ready to receive. This proposal by Tuck followed the request by Joseph Schwartz, cabled to the Jewish Joint Distribution Committee in New York, for the United States to grant one thousand visas to Jewish children who had been abandoned in the Free Zone. The UGIF participated at various stages in these negotiations, but the project did not materialize. See Bauer, *American Jewry*, pp. 259–263; Irving Abella and Harold Trooper, *None Is Too Many: Canada and the Jews of Europe, 1933–1948* (Toronto, 1983), pp. 105–119.

Saturday the 26th, visited Dangelzer and Villar again. I cannot have the protection of my staff confirmed, but from now on none of my employees will be deported.

Sunday the 27th: Left at 6:30 A.M., spent the day in Lyon with the children, went to a fair; we traveled overnight by sleeping car and were back in Marseilles at dawn on Monday.

Here is an appalling document to be preserved for later, an extract from a letter written by a young social worker to her father. This young woman had been assigned on July 18 to the social services for the *Velodrome d'hiver* [Winter Cycle Racing Stadium in Paris]. There, Jews who had been "rounded up" from their homes during the night of July 15 and the following days had been interned.

"Fifteen thousand Jews have been 'parked' in the Vel d'Hiv. It is horrible, demonic, something that grabs you around the throat so that you can't cry out. I'll try to describe what it looks like, but if you multiply whatever you understand of it by one thousand, it will still be only part of the reality.

"When you come in, you can hardly breathe at first on account of the stench. Then you come into the big velodrome, which is black with people piled up against one another, some with bundles already dirty and grey, others with nothing at all. Each person has a bit more than a square yard of space on which to lie down, and those who manage to get to the upper levels are few. The handful of toilets (you know how few there are in the Vel d'Hiv) are stopped up, and there is no one to fix them. Everyone is forced to go to the toilet along the walls. The sick are on the ground floor, and their basins simply sit next to them, because no one knows where to empty them. As for water, since I have been there I have seen only two outlets, like the ones in the sidewalk, to which someone has fitted rubber hoses; the crush around them is beyond description. The result is that people can't wash themselves or even drink.

"Rations consist of half a ladle of milk per child under nine years old (and they don't all get any), half a ladle of noodles or mashed potatoes for meals, two slices of coarse bread less than an inch thick for the whole day (and again, not everyone manages to get any). It may be all right for those who still have their own provisions (they're a minority), but I can't answer for what it will be like in a few days.

"The state of mind of these people, these men and women, is indescribable: hysterical screaming, cries of 'Let us out!,' suicide attempts. Some women try to jump from the top of the bleachers. People throw themselves at us: 'Kill us!'—'Don't leave us here!'—'An injection so we can die!' . . . And much more, so much more!

"We see people with tuberculosis, disabled people, children with measles or chicken pox. The sick are on the ground floor. The Red Cross tent is in the middle but has no running water or gas. Instruments, milk, gruel for babies (some are only thirteen months old), all have to be heated on alcohol or methanol burners. It takes three-quarters of an hour to give one injection. Water is carried in milk cans that may be more or less clean, and distributed with ladles.

"There are three doctors for fifteen thousand people, and not enough nurses. The majority of the internees are sick. (They went into hospitals and took even people who had had operations the day before, so some are disemboweled, hemorrhaging, etc.) I have even seen a blind man and some pregnant women.

"Our medical unit doesn't know which way to turn. Even worse, we are totally immobilized by the lack of water and forced to neglect hygiene completely. We are afraid of epidemics.

"Not a single German here—they're right, they would be torn to pieces. What cowards they are to make French people do their dirty work. Policing is done by mobile guard units and teenagers from youth workshops. You can imagine what they think of all this.

"We social workers and nurses have had impressed on us by our instructors, 'Be sure you don't tell anyone outside what's happening here.' That's just vile; they want silence kept about this appalling crime, but we won't let them. Everyone should hear about what is happening here; people have to know."

I have read other testimonies about the transports to Drancy and Pithiviers, and the deportations to Poland. It's enough to make one's hair stand on end! Mothers have been deported with their breasts heavy with milk, after their babies have been taken from them. . . . If those who are guilty of these things don't pay for them one day, there is no justice.

Vichy, October 22, 1942

I am again in Vichy, to submit to the Commissariat the minutes of our Council's meeting on the 15th.[6] Arrived the evening of the 20th after a good trip. Yesterday, the 21st, paid my usual visit to the Commissariat, where I found chaos and incompetence. Made contact with the Sûreté [National Security], and worked in the office. In these autumn mists one can better understand how, in Vichy, people can forget about everything that goes on elsewhere in France.

During a previous trip I read a serialized novel by Pierre Véry, *Goupi mains rouges* [*Red-Handed*]. It's like second-rate Simenon, and in that genre only the first-rate is acceptable. André Gide is right. . . . On the train this time I read Saint-Aulaire's *Talleyrand*. A good book and good meditations. By thinking about how great events began, and by digging for the motives of those who constructed them, one is truly enriched and learns to know oneself better. Talleyrand, I find, was a good leader. He was more lucid and practical than Napoleon. He can serve as a model . . . for me in my work with the Jewish groups. Thinking back without

6. This was the first meeting of the Council of UGIF-south after the deportations. See the minutes in YIVO: RG 210, XCII-10. An excerpt from Lévy's speech at the meeting: "Amid the painful ordeals through which our country is going, the Jewish community is the most harshly affected. We are conscious that we have not deserved such a fate and, as our faith teaches us, while working with a stronger will than ever, we pray for the healing peace that will soothe passions and repair the injustices."

modesty to my actions last year, I find them to be analogous to those preceding the birth of the Restoration. On this point, Saint-Aulaire puts forward judgments that I can relate to my past conduct, if only to emphasize my own satisfaction with it: "The force of events is often only a flattering pseudonym for human weakness. There is no evidence that it would have been equal to the prudent audacity and the supple energy of Talleyrand. . . . He did not confine himself to endorsing the dictates of fate but rather inspired them. Thanks to him, there was not a single day of that anarchy which, in the presence of the enemy, might have had tragic consequences. . . . If, as his detractors claim, Talleyrand was just a practitioner without a doctrine, he would in that case at least have made an amazing bonesetter."

I read, contritely, Barrès' *L'amitié des tranchées* [*Friendship in the Trenches*]. The doctrine of the people of Alsace and Lorraine between 1870 and 1914, the doctrine of the Jews of France in 1942: "All these young boys and girls have compelled the world's admiration for that which is the sign of a superior human being: the will not to accept anything that does not accord with their inner sentiments, the will not to submit to an inferior way of life" (p. 305). These are distinguished words, and I shall remember them.

Marseilles, November 3, 1942

For the record. Notes on the end of my last stay in Vichy. On Thursday [October] 22nd in the morning, at the Interior Ministry, I finally had good news! My staff will be covered by the security provision I had hoped for. The decision is signed and sealed. I have won. I had lunch with Canon Müller, the senator from Strasbourg, a pure patriot who does not lay down his arms! This old man gives me courage. We must not have doubts about the future. The people of Alsace are going through a Calvary as painful as that of the Jews, and the government will not allow anyone to say so. Our defeat in 1870 did not reduce us to this point! What a blot on the history of France is this regime under which we are now bowed down! In the afternoon I did business at the Sûreté, and had dinner with Fouques-Duparc who has aged greatly. Have I changed that much? I don't think so.

On Friday the 23rd I worked in the office and had business at the Refugee Service with a heartless little anti-Semite, a Mr. Fraisse, a name I won't forget. It was he who had the idea of depriving the Jews who were evacuated [during the fighting] of their official relief benefits.[7] Fortunately we acted on this. I am demanding a text that would amount to a "law" on refugees. . . . Had lunch at the office, spent the afternoon at the Commissariat, and went for a walk after dinner with Pascot. I am trying to understand his psychology when I tell him about the crimes committed by Laval against the Jews. . . . He finds comfort in saying that the Marshal is playing both sides and that it would be worse without Laval. . . . That amounts to accepting servitude through selfishness and cowardice! With sentiments like that, our nation is being lost and a culture is being allowed to die.

On Saturday I returned to Marseilles, with a brief stopover in Lyon as usual. The buffet carts on the platform were pretty poor, couldn't find anything to drink or to eat. That sentence I heard at the Interior Ministry came back to me, characterizing the cowardice of the regime that takes orders from Berlin: "You know very well that the decisions are made elsewhere, we are only the secular arm striking you." Words to remember on the day judgment is passed against Cado, the assistant secretary at the police office; under Blum he was the ministry's representative in Narbonne.

7. In October several prefects in the Free Zone decided to stop paying regular benefits to which Jewish refugees were entitled within their *départements*. They demanded that the UGIF take charge of them, thus freeing the *départements* of all responsibility for them. UGIF-south opposed these measures strongly, affirming that it was not permitted under UGIF statutes, nor did it have the power to furnish basic assistance to the Jewish refugees. Lambert asserted that the UGIF had been created to aid the needy and for no other purpose. The UGIF was able to defer this measure until May 1943. For correspondence on this issue, see YIVO: RG 210, XCII-57; YVA: 09/19; CDJC: CDX-10, CDXV-64, CDXVI-209.

Yet, to me, all orthodoxies are suspect

André Gide
Journal (1933), p. 1175

To know what one wants
To want what one thinks
To think what one knows

20.8.43[8]

Marseilles, November 29, 1942

Notes on the last three weeks: The feverish emotions of the people around me make me even calmer and more composed. I am still as determined as I was in my lookout post at the Chemin des Dames; I feel like twenty again.

Sunday, November 8: Found out from conversations in the street that Anglo-American forces have landed on the North African coast. General Giraud[9] has taken over command of French troops there. Noguès and Esteva[1] are supposed to have rallied round. . . . This news was confirmed by the French TSF and foreign broadcasts. In the evening we had an air-raid warning.

Monday the 9th: Admiral Darlan has joined up with the Anglo-American troops. What will the German reaction be?

8. Written on the inside front cover of the second notebook. Lambert obviously added the quotation from Gide's diary and his own personal reflection that appeared on two other occasions in the diary (see entries for December 11, 1941, and January 3, 1943) on August 20, 1943, the day before his arrest. Following his intervention with Laval on August 14, 1943, RRL realized that the die had been cast, as can be seen in his note to the Consistory vice president, Léon Meiss: "It is an extremely tense situation, a very deceptive atmosphere, a relative indifference toward problems that affect us, when the demands made are becoming harder for all." (August 14, 1943, Joint Archives, Saly Meyer Collection, France, General, 1941–1943).

9. General Henri Giraud was in command of the Ninth Army when he was taken prisoner by the Germans in May 1940. He escaped prison on April 17, 1940, and later took part in the November 1942 landing of Allied forces in North Africa.

1. General Auguste Noguès and Admiral Jean-Pierre Esteva were, respectively, governors of Morocco and Tunisia. At the time of the Allied invasion of North Africa, Noguès was Pétain's sole representative, replacing Darlan.

They have announced massive demonstrations in the Free Zone for the anniversary of the armistice. Anxieties are rising everywhere, waiting for the German reaction.

Tuesday the 10th: The Anglo-American operation is a success. This truly is the second front we had been expecting for the beginning of winter. The Russian offensive at Stalingrad is going well. I really think the end will come in the autumn of '43.

Wednesday, November 11: Since daybreak, the most disturbing news has been circulating. It is Radio Paris that clarifies the facts: German troops have entered the Free Zone. What to do? Families are anxious, and easily frightened people are nervous. It's a bit like June '40 all over again, but in people's apartments instead of on the highways. I go to the Prefecture for news, but no one there knows anything. Lack of authority is *de rigueur* for them. All demonstrations have been called off via TSF radio. At 5 P.M. white posters appear in the streets of Marseilles, from the regional prefect, announcing that this evening the Germans will be here. We are under curfew and in mourning, the mass of people numb with indifference, but in our circles is a particular anxiety. I am becoming more and more calm. My parents-in-law come to spend the night. From now on we shall be living more like our friends in Paris. At night we hear the trucks rolling in and the noise of motorcycles.

Thursday, November 12: The city of Marseilles is under occupation, a depressing sight. The German military has taken over the largest hotels: the Noailles, Grand Hotel, Splendide, and Astoria. Pierre Ruget Boulevard has been turned into parking lots. There's not a single flag. The French military are rubbing elbows with the German greys, and the French police are still functioning. One wouldn't call this enmity, but we are all constricted with anxiety. . . . What will the Marshal do? This time he has definitely lost the opportunity to rehabilitate himself in the eyes of history. The capitulation of June '40 was all for nothing.

Friday the 13th: The Germans are getting set up all over the place, and their number is increasing. It's said there are 75,000 of them, but Toulon[2] has been spared entirely from their control. They're telling me at the Prefecture that the Jewish organizations must be prepared for evacuation, but without giving me either precise orders or a particular location. I am drawing up a rational plan for all my departments but am not thinking at all of leaving Marseilles, despite certain people's impatience. My instinct is to have absolute faith in the future, and duty compels me to be the last to leave the ship. My wife and children are not to be separated from me. They're saying that Marseilles will be a no-go zone. We shall see. I am not afraid of the bombing raids. The children who were assembled in Marseilles to emigrate to America I am sending back to their institutions in central France.[3] The borders are closed and occupied. We must keep our minds as clear as possible, for the hours to come will confront us in particular with tragic problems. I am ready to face any responsibility.

Most of the newspapers are no longer in circulation. We are not under "occupation" but simply under "control." Strictly speaking, this nuance may preserve us from the worst consequences. I have my team well in hand. All our agencies now recognize me as their boss, and my office is turning into a military HQ in full swing.

Before all this happened I had the greatest reward of my social work career, which allows me to envisage a future of maximum security for my wife, my children, and myself. My straightforward and self-motivated actions, despite all envy and criticism, have been magnificently rewarded. The Joint [Distribution Committee], that brings together all the Jewish aid organizations in the United States, has asked me to be their director for France. I accepted in principle, but I refused to resign as general director of the UGIF at this time of greatest danger. I was right, since America is now practically at war with the official French government.

2. The French navy base.

3. The occupation of the Free Zone by the Germans put an end to the project on behalf of these children.

But when peace comes I shall be able to accomplish an enormous amount of humanitarian and constructive work. *Labor improbus omnia vincit.*[4]

From November 15 to 20 I continued preparing for evacuation, telephoning in vain to Vichy for orders or authorizations. The leaders aren't making their intentions known. More and more it is local initiative and responsibility that is worth anything. German troop strength in the city appears to be on the wane, but services are settling in better. There is little artillery equipment in evidence. The cars are old models, the soldiers either very young or older. Some well-decorated ones have come back from Russia. They are very correct and refrain from any contact with the population. I think back with melancholy to my experiences in the Rhineland.

Friday the 27th: During the night we heard waves of airplanes overhead. On the way to the office I saw armed soldiers, a great bustle in the streets, guards in front of buildings and at intersections. Word is going around that the soldiers are imprisoned in their barracks. The national navy HQ on Cambrezi Street is occupied and guarded by the Germans. By the end of the morning we learned that at dawn German troops attempted to occupy Toulon and to take over the French fleet, which proceeded to scuttle itself.[5] The Arsenal is on fire, and there is said to be fighting in the streets. . . . Emotions are running high. How can anyone speak of collaboration anymore? French radio is silent.

As of Saturday the 28th we now know the truth. The army and navy have been "demobilized." Pétain is nothing but a fig-

4. By relentless work, everything can be overcome (Virgil, *Georgics*).

5. The takeover of the French fleet and of Toulon was the objective of the famous Operation Lilac of November 27, 1942. Following the German invasion, the French ordered that the fleet be scuttled. See Henri Noguères, *Le suicide de la flotte française à Toulon* (Paris, 1963). On the effects of the affair at Toulon on relations between France and Germany, see Geoffrey Warner, *Pierre Laval and the Eclipse of France, 1931–1945* (New York, 1969), pp. 351–357.

urehead any longer. The entire empire has removed itself from his command, and Hitler has just reunited France. . . . Will military events go quickly enough to keep the "control" of the Free Zone from becoming total occupation? The entire fate of our families depends on the answer to this question. They are reassuring me at the Prefecture, which has now changed its attitude toward us. When the Germans are here, we are considered less as Jews than as French. . . . I am sending our president to Annecy {in the Alps} for a rest. When faced with the most serious responsibilities, I prefer to be alone here with all my technical staff. News from the Russian front is excellent.

December 2, 1942

The hours go by, the news is good. The Russian offensives are expanding. There is progress in North Africa. Is this 1918 already, as people are chalking on walls? I do believe it, since my hopes are so high.

On November 11 Pétain allowed the Germans to arrest Weygand and deport him. Thus the old Marshal has dishonored himself for good in the eyes of history. He ought to have refused and made himself a prisoner like the Belgian king. A few days ago he handed over Paul Reynaud and Mandel. . . . It's unbelievable! What bloodshed, in days to come, is being prepared for us by such cowardice! And how much smaller the Jewish problem seems in the face of this generalized inhumanity! But, when we are in mourning, all of us always think of our own pain.

December 7, 1942

In our families the fever of anxiety is rising. What will the future be like for us? The Prefecture has asked me to evacuate my foreign staff members to Gap while the Interior Ministry in Vichy could not give me precise instructions. The Germans have arrested the Czechoslovakian Committee and demanded lists of nationals of the Greater [German] Reich. One of these days, inevitably, they will take over the administration and police here as well. Since there have been some attacks, curfew at 9:30 P.M. is now obligatory. My responsibilities are increasing, and I often wake up in the middle of the night to weigh them silently. . . . Shall I ever see the peace that brings healing? I'd rather be in my artilleryman's lookout tower, in danger of being shelled, than to be in this uncertainty about the future of my wife and children. . . . How petty our personal rivalries and everyday worries of normal life seem in the midst of this torment! Oh, when shall I ever have time again to write and to think?

I am leaving for Vichy this evening with Maurice Brener,[6] since the Commissariat is taking advantage of this total occupation to treat us like bad soldiers. I'll have to negotiate again, firmly and with dignity. I am confident.

Italy is being subjected to a fury of air raids. It's from this direction that liberation could be on its way.

I have made two visits, yesterday and the day before, to Mgr. Delay,[7] Bishop of Marseilles. Our chief rabbis don't come up to the ankles of these churchmen, who are men in the full sense of the word.

6. Maurice Brener, a first cousin of Simone Lambert, was both RRL's personal secretary and his confidant. Associated with the American Joint Distribution Committee, Brener played a decisive role in the distribution of funds among the various resistance groups with whom he had contacts and connections. The implications of Brener's close relationship with RRL are still shrouded in conjecture. RRL had officially registered Brener on the UGIF staff so that he could benefit from "UGIF immunity." This enabled Brener to make several trips to the occupied North, about which RRL was informed. Whether RRL was fully aware of Brener's liaisons with resistance groups, and whether RRL was associated with them, is unclear. Was Lambert engaged in a dual role—maintaining an official façade while supporting illicit actions? Whatever the case, the continuous contact between these two men, to November 1943, must be considered in discussing RRL's attitude toward clandestine activities. See Introduction.

7. Monsignor Delay, Bishop of Marseilles, openly protested the deportations of August 1942 while affirming that "the Jewish question presents us with difficult problems both nationally and internationally." Like other church dignitaries, Delay had trouble distinguishing between "Christian conscience" and "the great words of the Marshal." See Ryan, *The Holocaust and Jews of Marseille*, pp. 169–171, 176.

December 18, 1942

So much is happening that it has kept me from writing down my hopes and anxieties. . . . I am in the battlefield and shall have the right to speak after the war is over. There have been many people, since November 11, coming to ask for advice. It's odd to realize that quite a few people want others to make personal decisions for them.

On the day after the German occupation I had the most disagreeable of business to do in Vichy, accompanied by Maurice Brener because I never go to the ministries anymore without a witness. The day before I left Marseilles, the evening of the 7th, Darquier de Pellepoix put out on TSF radio a racist bulletin that made me dubious about the future. For a moment I was hesitant about leaving. . . . But we have to keep fighting and not desert the fort of the agencies the moment they are in danger. I cannot become now what I have never been, someone who runs away. So Darquier, with all the eloquence of an excited street vendor, announced new measures against the Jews who have not yet been neutralized by the *Statut*. . . . So should we now come out powerfully, or be so assimilated as to escape notice? . . . 1. Stamping of the word "Jew" on our identity cards; 2. Measures to be taken against Christian accomplices; 3. Dissolution of the youth organizations in the UGIF. . . . In the future we are promised further threats: wearing a badge, as in the occupied zone,[8] administrative and political measures, legal action against mixed marriages. . . . Anxiety swells in our circles. Will this war last long enough for all of us to be deported to Poland? I hope it won't. From now on no one can hold a grudge against the Jews of France since we must live as if we were suspects during the Terror.

8. Darquier did not succeed in forcing Jews in the southern zone to wear the yellow star. In general his attempts at intensifying anti-Jewish legislation failed, and he did not make his mark in this area. Yet, in conformity with the law of December 11, identity papers had to have the word "Jew" stamped on them, and the fourth department [youth division] of UGIF-south was effectively closed in January 1943.

In Vichy on December 9 I saw M. Antignac,[9] head of the Investigation and Monitoring Service, who is supposed to be the liaison person with the UGIF; a cavalry captain, impassioned and unjust. I acted and spoke with "directness" toward him, and I think my frankness and dignity did not displease him. I dealt with certain technical questions and am satisfied enough. He's trying to force me to fire all the foreigners on the UGIF staff[1] (a quarter of our entire team), declaring that this is the price at which he can "save the rest of us from deportation"! I'm wondering whether Vichy is still part of France!

After a month of military control of the Free Zone, I have noticed that the Laval-Pétain fiction is still being maintained. . . . So much the better for us, for the people of Alsace and for the prisoners! But what are we to expect for the future? This uncertainty weighs heavily upon us, and I am overcome with emotion when I kiss my children. . . . American radio is undoubtedly announcing that yesterday, in London, Washington, and Moscow, a resolution, signed by all free states, condemned the savage extermination of the Jews of Europe and promised punishment for those guilty of it. . . . But can we hold on? I still believe in my lucky star, as I used to during air raids, because my mother suffered too much on my behalf when she was living. . . . The war will last another year at least. There will be other disturbances, political and social, be-

9. Joseph Antignac was appointed head of the Investigation and Monitoring Service of the Commissariat, for the southern region, in August 1942. He soon rose in the organization. In November 1942 he was already Darquier's chief secretary and in January 1943 became his head of personnel. In these various functions he was often in contact with the UGIF leaders, always displaying his total contempt for them. In June 1944 he replaced Charles du Paty de Clam as head of the Commissariat, and at that late date was still expressing his unshakable loyalty to the principles of the "national revolution." For a biographical portrait of Antignac, see Billig, *Le Commissariat général*, vol. I, pp. 120–125.

1. This encounter with Antignac preceded the Commissariat's official initiative to "purge" the UGIF of its foreign employees. The Commissariat originally intended to dismiss them all at the end of February and then to "offer" these Jews to the Germans for deportation. Prolonged negotiations followed between the two UGIF Councils and the French and German authorities, resulting in a minor dispensation for the UGIF. RRL returns to this issue several times. See Richard I. Cohen, *The Burden of Conscience: French Jewish Leadership During the Holocaust* (Bloomington and Indianapolis, 1985), pp. 166–171.

fore regeneration comes. In great ages there is great suffering. We shall have learned at least, once and for all, no longer to care about goods and furniture, and—what is more serious—to have doubts about putting down roots as families. . . .

Is this possible? When I am suffering under these humiliations by law, I dream of spending my old age in a house on a hill—somewhere other than in France. . . . But I know very well that it wouldn't be possible!

1943

Nice, January 3, 1943

When I am old, I shall retire to the Côte d'Azur. There, between eleven in the morning and dusk, the pure blue sky and the sun's vigor, in the middle of winter, dispel one's bodily woes and moral anxieties. . . . That's a trite observation but remains a valuable one, even when Italian uniforms are blotting out the English Promenade [in Nice].

I have come here with Simone, without the children (the older ones are in the Alps, and the little ones stayed in Marseilles with their grandparents), to forget the fever of action for three days—in which I have succeeded.

I rather thought we wouldn't get away, since on the 31st the Germans arrested a chaplain in the camps, Rabbi Kapel, and Geiger,[1] our director at Carcassonne, for going to our center at

1. Shmuel René Kapel served as a rabbi in several communities in France. Drafted into the army as a chaplain at the beginning of the war, Kapel later served in this capacity in the internment camps in southern France. While fulfilling this responsibility he was also active in resistance activity. He later published a memoir of his wartime activity and described his arrest. See Shmuel René Kapel, *Jewish Struggle in Occupied France* (Jerusalem, 1981), pp. 87–88 (Hebrew); see also Lucien Lazare, *Rescue as Resistance,*

Aulus, less than twenty miles from the Spanish border, without a special safe-conduct. It caused a great shock among the charities. The police chief in Toulouse, who knew about this trip, intervened at our request and got them released.

It has been a busy week. On Sunday, December 28, I left Marseilles at 6:30 A.M. with Lionel and Marc, to drive them to Gap. It's a pleasant *département* capital in the Alps, quiet and muddy. The surroundings are certainly picturesque. On Monday the 29th at 4:40 A.M., in darkness and the north wind, I got back to Marseilles after a long, tough trip. On Tuesday the 30th at 7:30 A.M. I left again for Lyon, arriving there at one o'clock with Maurice Brener, to savor the joy of being received at the Consistory, which has made its peace with the UGIF.[2] On Wednesday the 31st at 7:30 A.M. I returned again to Marseilles. And on January 1st at 10:30 A.M. I was finally able to get away to Nice with Simone. We leave here tomorrow at 2 A.M. . . . and the trains are packed, but our anxious minds needed a change of scene.

No one must find out, but our president[3] has left Annecy for Switzerland. It was a well-guarded, elegant act that leaves me alone with heavy responsibilities, but that doesn't frighten me. On December 22 our Council met without him to review the budget. After the meeting, delegates from the Consistory came to see us.[4] The time of personal rivalries is over. My enemies have

---

trans. Jeffrey M. Green (New York, 1996), passim. David Geiger was in charge of the UGIF offices in the *départements* of Aude, Ariège, and Pyrenées orientales [eastern Pyrenées Mountains]. He lived in Carcassonne where the UGIF maintained its regional office until January 1944. In an interview Kapel confirmed that the intervention by the police chief of Toulouse contributed to their release.

2. RRL's enthusiasm was rather premature. The Consistory had indeed taken a big step toward resolving the differences between them, but it was not yet "peace." That was to come only after the mass arrests in Marseilles at the end of January 1943. See the Introduction and below.

3. Lévy's departure for Switzerland was, of course, illicit. The "secret" was kept for a while and then, at the February meeting of the Administrative Council, it was suggested, in his name, that RRL take his place. I would risk the supposition that RRL was the author of "Lévy's speech." For the text of the speech, see YVA: 09/12-1.

4. For a brief discussion of what took place, see YIVO: RG 210, CDX-10, XCII-12.

laid down their arms. The year ended with a fine victory. I congratulate myself on my straightforward energy and the tenacity of my will. . . . I must not rest on these pseudo-laurels being handed to me by those who were attacking me not long ago. . . . I've come to know human beings better than that. Those who know what they want, and who want what they know, are very rare. Clear-minded judgment is the most precious of qualities for a man of action. Stendhal did not think enough about that during his life. But his dreams were of romantic conquests while I am concerned above all with social action and collective leadership.

Marseilles, February 1, 1943

We have been through a time of fear such as I shall never forget. Through energy and willpower, and the awareness of my immense responsibilities, I have kept calm and well oriented. I have stayed strong and been useful. As I used to do at the front, I've been thinking a great deal of my mother, and memories of her have comforted me during the uncertainty about what to do when one man's determination often doesn't seem to be enough.

A quick report on what has happened—just for myself, since I am not entitled to comment on it.[5] On Friday, January 22, beginning in the early morning hours, there were massive raids and arrests all over Marseilles, to be expected due to the arrival during the preceding days of mobile guard units, coming by bus or train from Toulouse, Lyon, Nancy, and even from Paris. Reliable sources told us that a conference was held on the 21st at the railroad station to consider the use of eighteen trains prepared to leave for an unknown destination. We didn't know whether these were for [German] redeployments or for sending off suspects arrested following the measures being planned.

5. This entire report was submitted, in a slightly different version, to the Central Consistory. See YIVO: RG 116, file 25. On the events in Marseilles, see Ryan, *The Holocaust and the Jews of Marseille*, pp. 1–9, 163–165, 181–186, 196–199.

Shortly before noon both the German and French police assigned to the railroad station began making arrests, entirely indiscriminately, and transporting the arrested persons by truck to the Sûreté and then to Baumettes Prison for identity checks. Jews were being arrested merely on sight of their stamped identity cards. In the evening the arrests continued, and there were also raids in certain neighborhoods during the night. We tried urgently to speak with the police at their administrative offices but got no results. We were told that these were general measures being taken by the police, by agreement with the German authorities, toward the definitive cleansing of the city of Marseilles.

On Saturday, January 23, buses moving through the streets after curfew caused people to suspect that unusual operations were being organized. In the morning we were told there had been police raids in many downtown neighborhoods. All Jews, French or foreign, were systematically arrested. This police operation had been prepared meticulously and with the utmost rigor by the authorities. Locksmiths were requisitioned to open the doors of houses whose occupants were presumed to be pretending to be away. These operations were in full swing between 11 P.M. and 5 A.M. Women were taken away in the police vans without having had time to dress; the sick were forced out of their beds; old people were taken away forcibly, and parents separated from their children. All the next day we tried to meet with a responsible official at the Prefecture. They promised to call us back the next day in the afternoon.

Sunday, January 24: We find out that overnight the raids and arrests were even more numerous and rigorous, spreading especially into the business neighborhoods downtown where the Jewish families native to Marseilles live (Sénac Street, Academy Street, Pisançon Street, etc.). At ten o'clock they tell us that three UGIF officials, including Mr. Leiba, the director of CAR, have been taken away by force. I go to the Prefecture but find no one there, because at this same time orders are being carried out to evacuate the Old Port (shades of June 1940!). These have drawn an unusual deployment of military forces into the city, and the civil authorities are in a perpetual meeting with the German generals at the Town Hall, in the midst of the areas being evacuated. The number of relatives and friends coming to tell us of arrests during the night is increasing by the hour.

In the afternoon we call a meeting of UGIF leaders, with Chief Rabbis Salzer[6] and Hirschler and Professor Olmer, to agree on the steps to be taken. There we discover that during the morning a train left the station headed for Compiègne, containing about fifteen hundred persons, taken especially from among the Jews who were arrested and are now still at the bishop's palace or were taken the same night to Baumettes Prison, without being allowed to communicate with their families or with anyone else. I go again to the Prefecture where, despite the absolute orders not to let anyone in, I manage to get to the inspector's office and insist on seeing his assistant, Mr. Boule. I tell him that I am outraged by the events taking place in Marseilles, and I protest vehemently against not being allowed to see the least among the responsible officials. Mr. Boule tells me that "the immediate evacuation of the Old Port on the orders of the German authorities prevents the officials from being present at the Prefecture." Mr. Bousquet, general secretary of the police, has come from Vichy and is directing the operations. I demand to see him to protest the arrests and deportations this morning. Since I can't wait later than 7 P.M. because of the curfew, I ask Mr. Boule to arrange an appointment for me with Mr. de Rodellec as early as possible on Monday. He is willing to allow me this intervention and asks me to telephone him during the evening.

Monday, January 25: At 9 A.M. I am admitted to the office of Mr. de Rodellec du Porzic after a brief conversation with his chief secretary the night before. I express to him once again our outrage and our most vehement protest. The police inspector replies that unfortunately it is no longer in his power to grant me either the

6. Israël Salzer was chief rabbi of Marseilles.

guarantee of protection I am seeking for UGIF officials or the least assurance regarding the fate of our fellow Jews. I ask him then, since he refuses to give me any other details, if he will allow me to request an appointment directly with General Mylo, commander of the German troops, or if he would himself request a hearing for me. "I myself have an appointment with the general at the police chief's office at ten o'clock," he tells me, "and I shall ask him for either an interview for you, or a guarantee for your public institution, or assurances about what has happened to your people."

That afternoon I meet with my department heads at the UGIF again, and the Council members who are in Marseilles, to ask for their suggestions and instructions. We find at that time that arrests are increasing around the railroad station, and we decide that no one will leave Marseilles until I have obtained from the authorities a guarantee that no more arrests will be made.

Tuesday, January 26: In the morning we learn that the raids are continuing and arrests are increasing in number. It is extremely difficult to get around in the city since entire neighborhoods have been blocked off by both the French and the German police. I myself cannot go home for lunch since I learn by telephone that my street is barricaded. I go back immediately to the Prefecture where, despite the refusal of the porter to take my card inside, I insist on being seen by Mr. Auzanneau, the chief secretary of the police inspector. He comes out into the hallway for a few minutes and confirms to me in emotional terms what the inspector himself told me the previous evening: "The French police no longer have any power over matters concerning you. All Jews are to be arrested."

Returning to the office, I decide during the afternoon, with the agreement of Chief Rabbis Hirschler and Salzer, to send telegrams of protest to Vichy. Toward evening, having received no answer to my request for a hearing and for a guarantee for my staff, at 6 P.M. I send two forceful letters to de Rodellec. To the porter who brings them, Mr. de Rodellec protests my sending telegrams and says he wants to see me immediately. I am admitted at 7 P.M.

The inspector, far from reprimanding me, tells me that a grave danger to us has just been averted. He tells me that they had a dramatic night at the Prefecture, and that the regional authorities, in the presence of the secretary of state for the police, threatened the German authorities that they would "scuttle their ship" if the city administration were not immediately restored to them. Thus he now has the power of the police in his hands again. He assures me that my staff is now protected once more. He tells me that he was forced by the German authorities to allow the train filled with deportees to leave for Compiègne, and that due to his efforts there was only one train instead of six. I protest also against the arrests taking place around the train station, alleging that there is no law yet forbidding French Jews to travel within the Free Zone. He replies that tomorrow during the day he will see that this is cleared up, and he advises me to tell my department heads who are in the city to wait two more days before leaving.

On Wednesday, January 27, there are raids in the morning in cinemas and certain outlying neighborhoods, but the large-scale operations seem to have ended.

On Thursday, January 28, I pay a visit to Mr. Barraud, acting prefect for the city of Marseilles, together with Chief Rabbi Hirschler. The prefect, speaking personally, confides to us that the train that went to Compiègne was a "disaster" for the regional authorities, and that such a crime needs to be put right. Efforts are being made in high places to bring the train back to Marseilles. This decision was made following a report given to the Prefecture during the night, to which our telegrams and the letters I had written were appended. Mr. Bousquet, the prefect tells us, has gone to Paris again to speak with Mr. Laval.

I telephone to Vichy for news of the telegrams I sent, and succeed in having them forwarded by telephone to Darquier, who is currently in Paris. Then I telephone to the Prefecture to protest the fact that the railroad station has been barricaded again and that any Jew who goes there is arrested. During the afternoon I telephone again to Vichy and receive official confirmation from Mr. Jean-Paul Martin, Mr. Bousquet's chief secretary, that there is still no official decree banning French Jews from traveling within the Free Zone.

Armed with this official communication, I go to see Mr. de Rodellec at 6 P.M. He tells me then that he will give instructions at the train station, so that French Jews need have nothing to fear. He declares to me that from now on our agencies' officials cannot be arrested and that French Jews need have nothing to fear in his region. Finally, he gives me the news that in accord with the information we provided, which has been verified through [police] inquiries, he has decided, by agreement with the prefect and with permission from the German authorities, that the train which left Marseilles on Sunday should stay at Compiègne under the authority of the French police. He says he will send officials from Marseilles to Compiègne the next day to do the screening, and gives me hope that all French citizens will return. He declares to me that my department heads from other cities can leave Marseilles without risk, and as an extra precaution he countersigns a letter for Gaston Kahn to carry. Gaston is taking a large amount of money back with him to Gap.

I ask him for authorization to send a team of social workers to the colonial camp at Fréjus, where the people evacuated from the Old Port are interned, in case there are some Jewish families among them. He refuses me this authorization and says it is in our interest because the camp is under strict control by a German commission. He thinks a Jewish agency presence there would be ill-timed and dangerous. He will look into the possibility of having one of our chaplains visit.

Friday, January 29: Our offices are being visited by more and more relatives in search of members of their families who were arrested from the 22nd to the 24th. The Prefecture itself is sending to us people requesting information, and has asked us to make the lists and turn them in for its use. The large-scale raids have ended.

The transport of deportees on Sunday morning the 24th took place under particularly cruel conditions supervised by the German police. One officer replied to a request for food for these unfortunates by saying, "Our soldiers have been dying of hunger for eight days at Stalingrad; these Jews here don't need anything to eat."

Piled into cattle cars, some fifteen hundred persons, the great majority of whom are perfectly law-abiding Jews, were transported together with streetwalkers from the port, people condemned under common law, and black people without civil status. They had no water, no food, not a bench to sit on. Two Germans and two mobile guards were assigned to each car, cars that were sealed at departure. Acts of brutality were observed as the train departed. The deportees included travelers who had come to Marseilles for the day and had no change of clothes or coats with them, war veterans, young girls, sick people, elderly people from nursing homes, a released prisoner with double pneumonia, repatriated French citizens, a blind man's wife who was deported carrying her husband's ration cards, the war widow of an artillery captain, entire families who have been members of Marseilles society for several generations, fathers of seven or eight children. There were no social workers of any kind when the train left, and they had sixty loaves of bread for fifteen hundred people.

My firm hope is that these innocent people, deported for no reason, will be returned to their homes, but also that the officials responsible for such a disaster will be punished. When, on the basis of verbal instructions, they turned a general police action into a *deliberately anti-Semitic* measure, the police chiefs of Marseilles became the purveyors or the instigators, conscious or unconscious, of German policy. And they would not have been able to mitigate it if their very clumsiness, the terrible consequences that followed, and our energetic and immediate protests had not touched the higher authorities present in Marseilles and made them afraid of reactions from Vichy and from public opinion.

This is the text of my first letter to the regional police inspector, no. 4305, dated January 26:

"Sir:

"Further to the interviews that you have kindly granted me, I am taking the liberty of writing to you. Please understand that, in view of this suffering we are experiencing, it is my duty to approach you persistently in order to carry out the task dictated by my conscience.

"Current police operations have resulted in the loss of their liberty, and condemnation to a most uncertain fate, of members of our faith, already including fellow war veterans and relatives, and soon to include our fathers, our wives, and perhaps our children.

"I am appealing once again to your feelings as a Christian to allow me to accomplish the mission imposed on me by the authorities.

"I therefore entreat you not to refuse, for these unfortunate, endangered fellow Jews, what—thanks to you—we were able to accomplish at the time of the deportations in August, to temper with humanity the measures to which the foreigners were subjected. Fathers are being separated from their children, mothers taken away from their homes, and children from their families, and no chaplain or social worker is being admitted to give them the help that is called for, and that no country in the world and no person has ever deliberately refused them.

"As difficult as this social welfare task is, my colleagues and I believe it is our duty to perform it, and I am asking you beforehand, with all my heart, to allow us to ensure that it is done.

"Yours most respectfully,"

Letter no. 4306 of January 26:

"Dear Sir:

"You kindly promised me, yesterday morning, to intervene with the German authorities for the assurance of protection—

which you told me yourself you are no longer in a position to give me—for our UGIF personnel, so that they may carry out their humanitarian and social welfare mission.

"Twenty-four hours have passed, during which I have not been able to obtain any answer. More and more people are being arrested, so that anxiety and terror are spreading among all the Jewish families in Marseilles, French and foreign alike.

"I am taking the liberty of asking you, once again, to obtain for my entire staff the necessary safeguard for the fulfillment of the social welfare tasks assigned to us by law. I venture to hope that it will not be more difficult to obtain, here in Marseilles, the same protection that the occupation authorities themselves have seen fit to guarantee us since the founding of the UGIF in Paris.

"Since hours have passed without my receiving any official response to my anxious plea, and since under these conditions I cannot carry out my responsibility of directing a public institution, all of whose officials are exposed to arrest, along with their families, I am enclosing with this letter copies of the telegrams which, with the full agreement of all the leading members of my Administrative Council, I have sent today to the head of state, the head of the government, and to the General Commission on Jewish Questions.

"Yours," etc.

Text of the telegram to Marshal Pétain:

"Confidential. Stop. Following massive police operations carried out by French administration numerous French citizens perfectly obedient to our country's laws notably war veterans from Alsace and Lorraine repatriated prisoners young girls and minors were arrested because Jewish and some sent right away to unknown destination. Stop. We protest with our last energy against such measures. Stop. Heartfelt request do not refuse us grace to offer in such circumstances help of our religion and charities as authorized in Paris. René Hirschler Chief Rabbi of Strasbourg. General Chaplain. Israel Salzer Chief Rabbi of Marseilles. RRL General Director UGIF."

Similar telegram sent to Pierre Laval, plus two telegrams, one as a report and the other for the security guarantee, to Darquier, signed by me alone.

Finally, my SOS telegraphed to Jacques Helbronner, president of the Central Consistory:

"Following massive police operations carried out night and day by French administration numerous French members of our faith perfectly obedient to our country's laws notably war veterans from Alsace and Lorraine repatriated prisoners young girls and minors were arrested because Jewish and some sent right away to unknown destination. Stop. UGIF officers included in first transport. Stop. Impossible to render religious and social assistance. Stop. Interceded without success with regional authorities and not waiting to intercede with central authorities. Stop. Telegraphed requesting intervention general commissioner. Stop. In these sorrowful hours for our community heartfelt request you intercede as long as you have breath, that security and freedom be assured all our families now in danger. René Hirschler. Israël Salzer. RRL."[7]

February 13, 1943

We are very pleased; the train that went to Compiègne will probably come back.[8] I shall believe it only when I have seen the survivors.

Yesterday was very poignant. Together with André Baur,[9] who had just come from Paris, I made contact with the German authorities, that is, with the SS men who are in charge of the Jew-

7. This time Helbronner responded immediately to the request. He sent a vehement telegram to Laval on January 27, 1943 (Archives of the Jewish Theological Seminary, New York, Box 13). All the appeals were in vain.

8. This was more wishful thinking on the part of Lambert than hard evidence. The train to Compiègne never came back.

9. This was the first time during the war that the two men met. Baur had come to the south to see about reorganizing the UGIF, but this did not take place as long as the two of them were its directors.

ish question in our region, Obersturmführer Moritz[1] and Obersturmführer Schmitz.[2] They asked for instructions from Paris, in particular regarding the safeguard for my staff.

I forgot to write a memo on my trip to Vichy on January 12 and 13. I visited Mr. Antignac, head of Darquier's office, with Maurice Brener, to deal with small administrative and budgetary matters. We had a heated discussion on the order to disband the Jewish Scouts.[3] (I managed to save two of the four sections; only the "scouts" are to be disbanded.) Then there was a violent discussion about the foreign staff members, whom I am required to dismiss. I am still hoping to save them. . . . We also visited Dobler, head of the Refugee Service, and Fourcade at National Security. I left Marseilles the 11th and returned on the 14th without stopping in Lyon.

Now I've seen everything. The Consistory congratulated me on the courage of my interventions at the end of January![4]

I read *Au Carrefour* [*At the Crossroads*] by Achad-ha-Am, very profound and rich. I finally finished Gide's *Journal*, which I started in Nîmes in August '40. It is the most vivid, most complete book I have read in many years. Isn't Gide our Goethe?

March 21, 1943

This intensity of action scarcely allows me any time to myself, even to write down every evening how far I got that day. But I

1. August Moritz held various positions in the Gestapo organization in France before being appointed adjunct commander of the Marseilles secret police. His name appears on several documents relating to deportations to Drancy from Marseilles and Lyon. See Serge Klarsfeld, ed., *Die Endlösung der Judenfrage in Frankreich* (Paris, 1977), pp. 195–199; on his duties in France, see p. 238.

2. This Gestapo figure appears in J. Billig, *L'Institut d'étude des questions juives* (Paris, 1974), p. 140.

3. The Scout movement (EIF) was affiliated with the UGIF's Fourth Department. At this time it was beginning to be reorganized under the illegal "Sixth" Department.

4. This took the form of a letter of February 1, 1943, from Helbronner to RRL (formerly Maurice Brener Collection, Paris); see Cohen, *The Burden of Conscience*, p. 179.

must at least leave a few markers for the day when I write my memoirs. . . . I am struggling for social and humanitarian action, and while both the German and the French authorities are candid with me, it is with my fellow Jews[5] that I have the greatest difficulties. . . . I find myself looking forward to the day when I can leave the Jewish agencies and return to French government work such as I used to do at the Quai d'Orsay, or on the banks of the Rhine. My personal life is a tragedy! The ambience in which I have grown to be a man has been a German one. . . . Meanwhile I grow wiser and more detached. I am more appalled by the ingratitude, the underhandedness, the jealousy of the people around me. But a smile from my daughter makes me forget every ordeal.

February 14 to 17 I spent in Nice with Simone and the children. (Those who are jealous hold it against me that we stayed at the Royal.[6] But that was the sort of life I lived before I was with the agencies.) On the 15th, Council meeting at Lazard's home, with Baur. We clarified all the issues. The president is officially considered to have resigned. Our colleagues in Paris act a bit as though they want to treat us, here in the field of battle as we say nowadays, as if we were minors and needed a guardian.

On returning to Marseilles I had important matters of principle to take care of. Then two days with Baur in Lyon, where the UGIF had to be reorganized (the offices had been closed and the

5. Why does RRL make this comment after he has just ironed out most of his difficulties with the Consistory? Several possibilities exist. The tension between Lambert and the Consistory was so deeply ingrained that even a formal peace could not eliminate the basic differences between them. The lasting hold of this controversy on RRL can be seen in the final entry, and ultimately the final words, of the diary! Another possible explanation for the comment to appear here relates to the tension with UGIF-north over the demands for reorganization, and conflict with its representatives over the orders from the Commissariat to dismiss the organization's foreign staff members. These two issues had reached a climax and caused some very unpleasant correspondence between the leaders of both sections. One can also see RRL's meditations as a common refrain among leaders of movements and organizations who, at times of extreme tension, express their desire to break their ties with members of their movement and be free of the daily pressures.

6. As the diary indicates, RRL maintained his bourgeois style of life that included residing at fine hotels for business and pleasure. He must have been aware of some criticism of this behavior, but I have found no documented complaints.

employees arrested[7]) in liaison with the German authorities. Baur, who had been to see the Germans before me, claimed they were demanding that the services be unified on a regional basis. So when I got there I reorganized them at that level. March 1, 2, and 3 in Vichy to report on the Council. March 5, 6, and 7 in Nice, I took the necessary social welfare measures required by the arrival in the Italian zone (where they were said to be protected) of foreign refugees and even French ones. (I left Simone and the children there for a week and went back on the 13th to fetch them, whatever the envious think of it; I'm thinking of my wife and children.)

March 26, 1943

This was a good day. An SS man, Bauer, was very understanding and I was able to have two old people released, the Crémieux, who had been falsely denounced. I also got permission to set up a center providing lodging in the suburbs of Marseilles for elderly Jews whose apartments are to be requisitioned. In Paris such people would be interned.

Notes on my last trip to Vichy on March 1, 2, and 3. On the 1st I visited Jacques Guérard, general secretary to the head of the government. Mr. Laval, he told us, is having difficulties in his negotiations with the Germans on the Jewish question. He tried in every way to calm us in regard to the situation of French Jews. No new measures against them are being planned. Foreign Jews, on the other hand, are being abandoned.

On the 2nd, conversations with Mr. Antignac. The resignation of our general president is accepted. But one of the administrators in the Free Zone must temporarily take on the duties and the powers of the general president. So I must submit, and now

7. In early February the Germans had arrested some Jews at the UGIF offices in Lyon (5th Department) along with some officials of the organization. Although limited in scale, these arrests made the Consistory leaders aware of the fragile status of French Jewry.

find myself holding this office by decree. I am officially ordered to dismiss all foreign staff members by the 10th of the month, with the exception of 1 percent, twelve persons of my choice for whom I shall be responsible. We also discussed several technical problems.

On the 3rd, conversation with J. P. Martin, Bousquet's chief secretary, a useful and satisfying contact. On the 4th I spoke with de Quirielle, head of the 14th office at the Sûreté (a heartless villain), and Bernard, deputy police director. I was not able to get them to allow our delegates to enter the internment camps. On the 5th I spoke with Estèbe at the Marshal's office, a useful and encouraging conversation. On the 6th a visit to Guichard at the Red Cross.

As I grow older and wiser, I am having to abandon some of my cherished illusions about ordinary human beings. People continue to be jealous and attack me. I am almost the only one who remains honest, loyal, and sincere. I vow that from now on, when I am listening to someone whom I consider my elder, for my own protection I need to keep these three questions in mind: 1. What is the hidden motive of what this person is saying? 2. What decision would he be interested in seeing me make? 3. After our conversation, what will he claim I said? And finally, I'd be wrong to think that everyone else can understand things as quickly as I can.[8]

Vichy, April 16, 1943

At the Albert I as usual, alone this time, doing my business in this city that is too quiet to be a capital. Those who are directors,

8. We have here one of the more striking glimpses of Lambert's arrogance. Presumably tired and frustrated, bearing the heavy responsibilities of the UGIF, RRL shows a scathing contempt for his colleagues in the north. The tone of the diary has shifted since the events in Marseilles. Proud and pushed to the hilt, RRL lacks the composure to maintain the vivid diary entries of earlier days and seems to jot down his notes quickly, less frequently and almost halfheartedly.

conscious of their powerlessness, are leaving matters in the hands of their chief secretaries. Is this apathy the calm before the storm?

Wednesday the 14th was spent traveling, which I find restful. I read a good Simenon *(Le fils Cardinaud* [*Young Cardinaud*]*)* and a historical pamphlet, cowardly and obnoxious, by Pierre Dominique *(Un Etat de quat'sous* [*A State for Sale Cheap*]*)*.

Thursday the 15th negotiations at the Commissariat. I am hoping to recover a certain number of my foreign staff. Made an appointment to return today. Had lunch with co-workers who were there from Grenoble and Lyon.

Friday the 16th: Have been to the Gestapo, Commission on Unemployment, National Security, Refugee Service, and the administrative office of the president of the Council of State. By taking action I am able to see and know more than the central administration. For us there are no new measures that we need fear. Had lunch with Pascot, who remains a loyal friend. He would like to see me definitively named general president, and said he considers me the only one who is qualified, now or in the future.

And tomorrow I shall leave at dawn, traveling toward the sun and my brood at home. Twenty-seven years ago I was taking part in the great attack at the Chemin des Dames. Tomorrow my eldest son will be fourteen years old.

I have read a great deal in the past month, and should note, not in the order read: Caillaux' memoirs, a lively and difficult book; Col. Alerme, *Les causes militaires de notre défaite* [*The Military Causes of Our Defeat*], an excellent if unintentional plea on behalf of Léon Blum; Jean Hennessy, *Diplomatie et fédéralisme* [*Diplomacy and Federalism*](worthless); Anatole France, *Trois comedies* [*Three Comedies*]; Jacques Spitz, *La guerre des mouches* [*War of the Flies*] (cure for forgetfulness), and a perfect essay by Henri Clouard, *Bilan de Barrès* [*An Estimation of Barrès*]. I also read, in the Rieder collection, *Anatole France* by I can't remember whom, not that great, and *Stendhal* by Alain, a poor piece of gossip, the schmaltzy sort of work in which one gives the appearance of splitting hairs, sentence after flowery sentence. . . . Verbosity was the affliction of the years '18–'40 with Alain, Julian Benda, Suarès—a topic for children's compositions. I also read that delicious evocation of my childhood, *1900* by Paul Morand, and Volume I of *Le bergsonisme* by Thibaudet, in small doses, contritely.

I have taken part in a great many activities during these past weeks, working in liaison with the German authorities. The train to Compiègne isn't coming back—and the people from Marseilles have been deported. I have been frequently in contact with Andrieu,[9] the successor of le Rodellec du Porzic, a very humane and refined person, the grandson of Clovis Hugues. And the weeks go by.

May 16, 1943

This has been a month of anxiety, of ordeals and actions difficult to carry out. Like Titus, every evening I've asked myself whether I have done a man's work, and every evening I have not had to blush at my efforts. . . . In the midst of all this action, I have not been able to write down what I've seen, what I've suffered, for myself and for others. . . . The future—I don't dare think of it—though liberation is certain, remains horribly dark. My times as a soldier, looking back, seem like paradise to me. . . . Whatever happens, my sons will not have to be ashamed of their father.

Forgotten travels: From April 19 to 21, with Simone, to drive Lionel, Marc, and Tony to Gap for the holidays. The Alpine air is delicious along Napoleon's highway. From April 29 to May 1, to Grenoble to make contact with friends and discuss future problems, when peace comes.[1] They are thinking of asking me to play

9. Robert Andrieu, born in 1908, served in various prefectures during the 1930s. In 1942 he replaced Rodellec de Porzic as head of the Marseilles police and actively tried to prevent the raids and deportations of Jews from the city. Andrieu was also engaged with a resistance network, which led to his removal from office and eventual arrest in 1944. Decorated after the war with the Croix de Guerre and the Medal of Free France, he returned to service in local administration after the war. See Ryan, *The Holocaust and the Jews of Marseille*, pp. 196–198.

1. RRL was in Grenoble for the founding of the Center for Jewish Documentation (Centre de Documentation juive), an illegal and clandestine organization whose main

a specific role in that future. Events will turn out differently from our predictions now. 1943 will not be an exact second edition of 1918. From May 1st to 3rd we returned by way of Gap to pick up the two older boys, leaving Tony there, away from the dusty north wind which wore out his throat this winter. Since then I have stayed in Marseilles, where I am finding a good companion in the person of Carcassonne, the surgeon.[2]

I've done considerable reading during these day-long journeys. My worries have caused me to prefer history and criticism more and more, and among novels, only the most excellent. To make my language more colorful [. . .] my good poets of twenty years ago. Henri de Régnier, *Poems from the Winged Sandal* (the really wise person is the one who [. . .] on the sand . . .) absolute beauty and grandeur. . . . Jean Richepin, *Les caresses* [*Caresses*]; Paul Bourget, *Recommencements* [*Beginning Again*]; Léon Daudet, *Panorama de la III République*; Simenon, *Le fils Cardinaud* [*Young Cardinaud*]; Alexandre Zévaes, *Jean Jaurès* (a helpful tonic at this time); Paul Stapfer, *Montaigne*; René Millet, *Rabelais*; Robert Delavignette, *La paix nazaréenne* [*Peace of Nazareth*], a colonial novel [. . .] extraordinary light that one almost has to reread it to appreciate all its human beauty. In this book are found the most profound pages on the romantic feelings of young soldiers in '14–'18 [. . .] compared to certain pages than the first pages of *Chartreuse*.

---

purpose was to collect documents on the period of the war. RRL was considered one of the founders of the Center and helped mobilize support for it. See Isaac Schneersohn, "Naissance du CDJC," *Le Monde juif*, no. 7 (1953), pp. 4–5; Henri Hertz, "Le drame juif et le drame de la France," *ibid.*, no. 18 (1963), pp. 34–37.

2. Professor Fernand Carcassonne joined the UGIF Council in 1943. He immediately became an active member and was considered a candidate for its presidency at one point in 1943, a proposition that he declined. After RRL's arrest, Carcassonne went into temporary hiding but later resumed his position on the Council. In one of his last letters as a member of the Council, addressed to George Edinger of UGIF-north, he wrote: "He [SS Bauer, RIC] shared with me his view that without doubt all the Jews would be expelled from the Mediterranean area. . . . For my part, I shall stay faithfully at my post in Marseilles until the day when I receive a new order to leave. I don't know how much longer this will be" (February 16, 1944, YVA: 09/92).

May 18, 1943

Like Titus, I don't count yesterday as lost. Thanks to my vigorous diplomacy, I got three people released from St. Pierre prison.[3] It's a great satisfaction to save human beings from deportation, and without doubt from a slow death, if the war should last another year. But I don't think it will. After their victory in Tunisia, the Allies will attack Italy, and I think there will be news from there before the end of the summer. Mrs. Bloc from Bandol, a widow and the mother of a soldier who died honorably in battle, asked SS Bauer who it was that got her out of prison; his reply was "Mr. Lambert, the general of the Jews."

Notes on events in Marseilles from April 28 to May 9, 1943: Beginning April 19 the German authorities have been carrying out massive arrests of French Jews in the region of Nîmes, Avignon, Carpentras, and Aix-en-Provence.

The only satisfaction at first from daily visits to the German police was information on the families hit by the arrests. They were concentrated in St. Pierre prison in Marseilles and then sent on to Drancy on the average of forty persons a week, in two transports of twenty on Tuesdays and Fridays.[4] After the arrest of the sub-prefect of Arles, Jews were arrested more quickly and were almost immediately deported. In this way the families of Jean Bernheim, Pierre Lévy, and Jacques Valensi, among others, left Marseilles again after being there two days. On April 27 I managed to have Mrs. Blumenfeld released with her three young children after their arrest in Nîmes, on condition that my organization would guarantee them lodgings at the center [. . .].

Between April 28 and 30 police checks and raids began on trains at Avignon, Carpentras, Aix, La Ciotat. In this way Jews

3. St. Pierre prison in Marseilles had been requisitioned by the Germans for the detention of Jews and other prisoners. From St. Pierre the Jews were transported to Drancy. See below.

4. RRL's description is accurate. For examples of these transports, see descriptions in Klarsfeld, *Die Endlösung*, pp. 195–198; see also Marrus and Paxton, *Vichy France and the Jews*, pp. 307–308.

were arrested who were on their way to Nice for the holidays, including Guy Cohen, France Gugenheim and his five-year-old son, Julie Sultan and her fourteen-year-old son, Marcel Ullman and Henry Weill, all sent on to Drancy on May 4.

On May 1 there was a bombing in Marseilles, boulevard [. . .], following which two SS men were seriously wounded.

May 2–3: According to information obtained at the regional prefecture, it appears that severe sanctions are expected. There are many more arrests on trains. The French police are carrying out numerous identity checks and arrests in "extremist" parts of town. No information is available from the German police.

May 4: All Jews found on certain trains coming from or going to Nice are being arrested by the German police, at La Ciotat or at Miramas. Identity papers and tickets are being confiscated, and everyone must submit to a check at Marseilles station. Maurice Brener, Mr. R.-R. Lambert's secretary, is detained like the others on the way back from Nice—but is released after examination of his "mission orders."[5]

I lose no time in reporting these facts to Mr. Andrieu, the regional police inspector, who immediately intervenes in Vichy and Marseilles. The German police tell me that all these measures are the result of the bombing on May 1, and that yet more serious punishments are expected. The chief rabbi of Marseilles is warned immediately.

May 5:[6] I am summoned by Andrieu, who tells me that the German authorities asked him for a list of persons to be arrested in retaliation, and that he refused. At 6 P.M. I am called to the German police who demand, under the threat of arresting me and 10 percent of my staff, a list of two hundred prominent Jews of Marseilles. I refuse, as I must. Their answer is that I will find out in the morning the decision of the German authorities as a result

5. On the developments in Nice, see Daniel Carpi, *Between Mussolini and Hitler: The Jews and the Italian Authorities in France and Tunisia* (Hanover, N.H., 1994).

6. The following resumé of the events of May 5–7 covers the period discussed in Marrus and Paxton, *Vichy France and the Jews*, pp. 307–308.

of my refusal, and that I will be informed of this decision by telephone during the morning. They tell me, moreover, that the French authorities, in response to the same request, have given the same answer.

I obtain some information about people detained at St. Pierre, get the sealed apartment of a deported Frenchman opened to send him clothing and other personal effects at Drancy, and am even granted the immediate release of Mr. Lebel, who has a prostate disease.

On May 6 at 8:45 A.M., German policemen from Section IV J come bursting into the UGIF offices at 58 Joliette Street and, with their guns aimed at the staff, forbid them to use the telephone or to go near the windows and doors, so that the refugees, both French and foreign, coming to collect their benefits, are trapped like mice. As they arrive, the men are placed in one room, the women and children in another. One woman jumps out the window, breaks both legs, and is taken to the hospital. Mr. Gattegno and his secretary are shut up in their office because it has a door to the office where the men are being gathered. At 11:50 A.M. Mr. Blum, the office manager, is finally given permission to telephone to me to report on this police operation. At 12:30 I receive a telephone call, from Joliette Street, from Mr. Bauer inviting me to meet him there immediately. I go there, and Jacques comes with me.[7]

On arriving there I protest vehemently to Bauer against an operation of this kind in a relief office. Bauer tells me that he has received orders to arrest one hundred Jews in Marseilles in retaliation for the attack on May 1, and that he is beginning with this operation. He tells me that he summoned me to prevent disorder, and that if there is the least resistance to the German police officers, if there is even the smallest gesture, infinitely serious penal-

7. Jacques Lambert.

ties will immediately be inflicted on the entire Jewish population of Marseilles.

I agree to calm these unfortunate people, who are encouraged by my presence, in exchange for the following: 1. Bauer's official promise that he will carry out no further operations of this kind on UGIF premises without informing me in advance; 2. that my staff be allowed to record the requests of the persons being arrested; 3. that the German police not be allowed to look at any of the files, nor to confiscate any equipment, funds, or papers; 4. that the police officers put their guns back in their holsters; 5. that Mrs. Fabre-Monteux, age sixty-five, not be arrested and remain in the care of the UGIF; 6. official assurance that none of the men or women arrested at the UGIF will be included in the transport to Drancy tomorrow evening until I have reported this operation to the French police and asked for their protection.

Noticing that one of my staff members is missing, Mr. Jean Oulman, I am told that he has been shut up with the men because he disobeyed orders by opening a window. His colleagues confirm that it was to get fresh air for a woman who felt faint. I then ask that he be released. Bauer refuses, so as not to gainsay an officer under his command, but promises to discuss the issue with me at 5:30 P.M. I reply that I shall respond to this summons only if I have some hope of obtaining further releases, especially of children and women. Bauer assures me he will insist to his bosses that I be given satisfaction.

At 1:30 P.M., after collecting all the identity documents of the persons being arrested, Bauer sends about sixty persons, without violence or other incident, in two military buses to St. Pierre prison. Exceptions are made for five or six Italian and Turkish Jews. With great difficulty I manage to keep a French plainclothes policeman, Mr. Vayssier, who had accompanied a person under his protection to the UGIF office, from being included in the transport. In Joliette Street, armed SS are keeping order, but the operation is barely noticed. The sixty persons include about fifteen men and a few children, 80 percent French, of whom half are Algerian-born.

At 4 P.M. I go to the Prefecture and am about to be admitted to Andrieu's office when Commandant Mühler,[8] the German police chief, comes in. Since I can't wait, I go at 5 P.M. to Paradise Street where Bauer is expecting me. I protest to him anew, indignantly, the fact that the operation was carried out in the very offices of the UGIF. Bauer expresses to me his personal regret but states his obligation to obey official orders. On behalf of his superiors he confirms to me that my presence there prevented worse sanctions, with incalculable consequences for the Jews of Marseilles. He gives me to understand that collective punishments had been prepared, operations at people's homes and even raids in streets with certain concentrations of Jews. These measures have now been discarded. He also assures me that not a single person will be deported tomorrow.

I asked that mothers of large families whose children are left alone at home be released immediately, in particular one mother nursing a four-month-old baby from whom she has been separated since morning, and also Mr. Jean Oulman. Bauer agrees to release Oulman after two days in prison, and promises to contact Paris by telephone for a collective solution to the issue of mothers and children. He will give me an answer the next day at 6 P.M.

At 7:30 P.M. I am admitted to Andrieu's office, the regional police inspector who is serving as regional prefect while Mr. Lemoine is in Vichy. I report to him on what happened in Joliette Street that morning and on my interventions with the German police. I request support from the French authorities. Mr. Andrieu is astonished at having been left in ignorance of all this by his own services until seven in the evening, and expresses quite freely his sympathy and indignation. He promises to take action

8. SS Sturmbahnführer Rolf Mühler headed the *Kommando der Sipo und des SD* at Rouen before being transferred to Marseilles, where he performed similar duties and was Moritz's superior. Mühler took part in Knochen's *Einsatzkommando* and in the negotiations with the Italian authorities on the "Jewish question." See Hilberg, *The Destruction of the European Jews*, p. 693.

on his side most energetically. He says that at 4 P.M. he had a visit from Commandant Mühler, who did not say a word about the morning's operation. And yet, since the attack on May 1, the French police have taken measures (the arrest of a guilty person, discovery of weapons, checks and pursuits of other suspects) that satisfied the German authorities and averted collective punishment of the city: "This is a fool's bargain!" says Andrieu.

He immediately calls Commandant Mühler on the telephone, is not able to reach him, then calls Mr. Cado in Vichy. He demands the authorization to protest vigorously to the German police since, as the one responsible for public order and peace in Marseilles, he can no longer perform his duties if French Jews are subjected to collective punishment without his knowledge, especially in a public institution that it is his job to protect. Mr. Cado will speak immediately to Mr. Bousquet, who is returning to Paris at 8 P.M., and if necessary to President Laval. Instructions will be given to Mr. Andrieu the first thing in the morning.

I thank Mr. Andrieu wholeheartedly, and he asks me to come back to see him tomorrow at the end of the day, after visiting the German authorities again. I am authorized to share with them the reaction of the regional prefect: the measures taken in Joliette Street are contrary to the French-German agreements for the Marseilles region in particular and for the zone of operations in general.

All through the day more and more people have been coming to our offices—relatives, friends, and neighbors asking for news of the people who have disappeared and are presumed arrested.

On May 7, first thing in the morning, instructions are received by my aid workers to avoid gatherings and excessive numbers of visitors in the offices (benefits are to be paid by postal money order and through home visits by social workers). By telephone I obtain the immediate release of Mr. Baze, detained in St. Pierre, who has a serious stomach illness.

At 6 P.M. a new effort at the German police station. I ask to see the general troop commander in order to request that the women and children be released immediately. Bauer replies that there is no use in doing this. My request is already being considered, and instructions from Paris are expected. The answer will probably come on Monday, May 10. But I don't wait—I insist right then on two symbolic releases, those of the mother nursing her four-month-old baby, Mrs. Tordjman, and a sixty-three-year-old woman, Mrs. Osiel. These two releases are granted on condition that they take place before nightfall. Orders are given to my people by telephone, and the two detainees are released at 7:30 P.M.

During the day I am informed that the arrests on the trains are continuing. For example, Mrs. Bloc, the widow whose son was killed in 1940, who lives in Bandol, was arrested at La Ciotat. Our offices are seeing one emotional visit after another. Fear is growing in the Marseilles neighborhoods where the Jews who have been arrested lived (self-employed small craftsmen in the Joliette district).

At 7 P.M., accompanied by Jacques, I am received by Andrieu who insists that his chief secretary and the deputy inspector, Mr. Portal, also attend our meeting. In the name of the French authorities he congratulates me on not having hesitated to respond to Bauer's summons to Joliette Street, because he now knows that my presence averted cruel reprisals, not only against the Jews but also against the people of Marseilles, as the result of incidents that would not have failed to take place if I had not been there. Andrieu allows me to read, very confidentially, the official letter in which he demanded of the German authorities that from now on the French police be present at all operations of this kind in order to "protect every French citizen, whether Jewish or not, who has the right to protection from the country's authorities."

I thank Andrieu most warmly. I am moved to read the words with which he signed the letter, affirming that he was expressing his sentiments "as a man, as an official, and as a Frenchman," and that he could not accept operations of this kind in a public institution without the knowledge of the person responsible for public order and peace of mind in Marseilles. Finally, he requested—with agreement from Vichy—that the French citizens of the region who were arrested in Joliette Street not leave Marseilles until he as regional prefect, with my assistance, had gone into St. Pierre prison to investigate each case and requested through several individuals the release of citizens in good standing, women, and children.[9]

In response to his official letter, Andrieu has been informed by the German authorities that his request, which was quite similar to mine, has been forwarded to Paris for a decision. Finally, Andrieu promises me that, in comparable circumstances, he will be at my side to support me in my actions. I thank him once again and tell him that I was planning to go to Vichy this very night, but now it will no longer be necessary.

Most of the women arrested in Joliette Street were carrying with them the ration tickets for their entire families, a dramatic situation for those left at home. I arrange with the general director for supplies, Mr. Casanova, for the family members who were not arrested to receive temporary ration tickets, for which my offices would be responsible, either until the detainees are released or until the ration cards are returned as requested by the German authorities.

May 8: Arrests on the trains continued, but at a slower rate. During the morning, German nurses appeared at the home of the wife of a man who was deported on the train to Compiègne, to fetch their four-year-old daughter who was fortunately not there.

German police inspectors entered the front hall of the synagogue on Breteuil Street during services. Recognizing one of my officials, Mr. Weissler, they asked him if there were any foreigners in the synagogue. When he said no, they went away again.

Mr. Jean Oulman of the UGIF was released during the morning as promised by Bauer. He reported that the operation had resulted in the arrest of sixteen men, fifty-two women, and six

9. RRL's description of Andrieu's very humane attitude confirms Andrieu's support for resistance activity during the occupation.

children, who had all been placed in one room at St. Pierre prison under deplorable sanitary conditions. He reported that the individual releases obtained since the arrests had enormously raised the hopes of those still detained.

June 20, 1943

Yesterday was a fearful day. Having returned the previous evening from Grenoble, I went to Paradise Street early in the morning. Bauer told me that last week bombs had been thrown into the movie theater reserved for German soldiers. One of the guilty persons arrested was a Jew. He said he would confer with his superiors and come to see me in the office between 3 and 5:30 P.M., since it was Saturday and I was to be out working with one of our teams. A bad omen. . . . I told him I would wait for him calmly and with a good conscience.

Before noon I went to see Andrieu, who told me that he had been asked to deliver one hundred Jews and had refused, saying he was not "the finger of God." So I knew what was in store for me and got ready to refuse in turn, with all the consequences that might ensue. . . . But I received no visit at the office, and today, Sunday, there is dead calm. What should I think and hope for?

Since I have been traveling a lot, I have also read a great deal during May and June. I am continuing to explore history and criticism: Caillaux' *Memoires*, Vol. II, interesting in its lively style and the cold-blooded malice of its judgments. Jules Lemaître, *Les Médaillons*, bad poetry; the beginning of "Le Parnasse [Parnassus]" was really difficult. Martine's *Stendhal*, a good monograph but without originality; Georges Brunet, *Victor Hugo*; René Doumic, *Lamartine*; René Millet, *Rabelais*; Paul Stapfer, *Montaigne*. I am returning to the "great writers collection," which reminds me of my university years and makes me feel young again. Lucas Dubreton, *Rachel* (bad, and poorly written); Emile Faguet, *Balzac*; Firmin Roy, *Washington*, rather lifeless, too much like a compilation; Dr. Leprince, *Les cerveaux cambriolés* [*Burglarized Brains*], Jules Verne for grown-ups; finally, that heartrending book on the suffering of the wounded, by J.-J. Agapit, *Dites-la-leur* [*Tell Them This*], the counterpart of Duhamel's books on the first war.

June 22, 1943

During the past month I took some trips, and these travels together with hectic events in Marseilles have kept me from writing down my daily reflections. My thoughts run through my fingers like water, but they leave their tracks on my life itself. So I am making these notes but promising myself once again not to let so many days go by without getting back to it again.

May 23–24 I was in Nice,[1] with Simone, to make contact with the Italian authorities and attend meetings on technical matters. On May 28 I went to Lyon for the day, since there had been serious incidents. Chief Rabbi Schoenberg[2] had been arrested. But my regional administrator, Raymond Geissmann,[3] has shown

1. This was an important stay in Nice for RRL, which needs further study. During the last several months he mentioned several trips to Nice but never provided any details. On one of these occasions he certainly met the Italian Jew Angelo Donati, who served as intermediary between the Jews and the Italian authorities in the French zone under Italian occupation. In the spring of 1943 Donati was in the midst of preparations for his scheme "to evacuate all refugees concentrated around Nice to the free zone in North Africa." His name rarely appears in RRL's correspondence, but we can assume that he knew about Donati's important proposal. In a letter of July 7, 1943, to André Lazard, Lambert wrote in veiled terms: "P.S. concerning our 'diplomatic' mission to Donati, I prefer not to write and am waiting until I get to Nice to sort this out with him amicably. I trust you will agree" (YIVO: RG 210, XCII-61). For clear evidence of RRL's contacts with Donati, see Léon Poliakov, *La condition des Juifs en France sous l'occupation italienne* (Paris, 1946), p. 121. The above quote is from Léon Poliakov and Jacques Sabille, *Les Juifs sous l'occupation italienne* (Paris, 1955), p. 39; on these issues, see also Susan Zuccotti, *The Italians and the Holocaust: Persecution, Rescue, and Survival* (Lincoln, Nebr., 1996); for another perspective on Donati, see Schwarzfuchs, *Aux prises avec Vichy*, pp. 321–325.

2. Rabbi Bernard Schoenberg, who diligently cared for needy Jews in the internment camps in the south, was released following Geissmann's intervention. He was arrested again in Lyon in August 1943.

3. Raymond David Geissmann was born in Mulhouse in 1913 and worked as a lawyer before the war broke out. He was involved in community affairs before becoming director of the 5th section of the First Department of UGIF-south. Appointed director of the department in April 1943, Geissmann also became UGIF regional director for the regions of Lyon, Vichy, and Clermont-Ferrand. His close family connections with

elegance, a clear mind, and grit. I covered his needs and gave him precise instructions. He is trusted both by the Germans and by the Consistory.

On Sunday, May 30, I left Marseilles again, and dined and spent the night at Toulouse. On May 31 at 7:40 A.M. I left Toulouse (on the train bound for Paris, what nostalgia!), and arrived in Limoges at 12:50. I was received as the boss for a tour of our institutions and a meeting on technical matters. On June 1 I visited the German police (SS Gessler[4]) to introduce my regional administrator, Julien Samuel.[5] Then I visited the nursery of the home for children of Couret and Masgalier, as touching as can be (children of deportees). I was received like a king. On June 2 at 5:45 A.M. (I'm a morning person) I left Limoges for Périgueux. At seven I stopped in Thiviers to visit a home for aged persons evacuated from Strasbourg. Arrived in Périgueux at noon. Went to the Prefecture, then in the evening by car to Bergerac to see a home for orphans from Alsace. I was treated there both as boss and friend. The Jewish community of Alsace remains, in its social welfare achievements, the model for Jewish families in France. On June 3 I left Périgueux at 6:31 A.M. on a small freight train, and caught the Bordeaux-Nice train at 11:13 at Agen, returning to Marseilles at 10:30 P.M. Passing through Moissac and Toulouse I had visits with my department heads. . . . I don't envy men in public life!

---

the Consistory leaders contributed to the improvement of relations between the two organizations, and he was consequently appointed RRL's liaison officer directly with the Consistory. Geissmann later became the head of UGIF-south and moved its head office to Lyon. See Schwarzfuchs, *Aux prises avec Vichy*, passim.

4. The reference may be to SS Obersturmführer Giessler.

5. Julien Samuel was the director of an OSE health-care center in Marseilles from June 1941, before becoming UGIF regional director for the Limoges region. During the discussions on the creation of UGIF, Samuel favored doing everything possible to avoid the dissolution of the welfare agencies. As the war progressed and deportations intensified, he maintained his position as regional director of the Limoges region but also figured prominently in the "Limoges sector" involved in hiding Jewish children. Samuel was arrested in the autumn of 1943 but managed to survive the war.

On Saturday, May 29, I had sent Simone and the two older boys to Cannes, and on June 5 I went to bring them back. The four of us got back only on Monday the 7th, because I needed to have a good sleep on Sunday, far away from the office. The suffering that people there are enduring made it a painful visit.

On June 10 I spent the day in Montpellier to visit my new colleague on the Council, Hémardinquer,[6] and to visit the German police (SS Schubert) to introduce my regional administrator, Dr. Richard Kohn, a doctor from Paris, intelligent and levelheaded.

On June 12 Simone and I drove the two older boys to Gap, where they joined Tony in the green countryside on an isolated farm, sunny and well supplied with animal life. On June 14 I left for Grenoble with Simone, arriving at 6 P.M. On the 15th there was a meeting of the Finance Commission, on the 16th a meeting of my Council. I was satisfied all in all, but the UGIF is going to have difficulties that will loom very large if this war goes on. On the 17th I had meetings and visits. At the hotel they were after me as if I were a government minister. Jews are active people and don't show much respect for a person's need to rest! On the 18th, in the morning, we took a quick tour of the Stendhal Museum (finally! but it was in no way comparable to the Beethoven House [in Bonn], no ambience; cold collections of mementos).[7] Returned to Marseilles at 6 P.M.

June 29, 1943

I read Duff-Cooper's *Talleyrand*. What a great book and what a great person! Despite his petty side, I admire Talleyrand for his

6. A well-known doctor, Jérémie Hémardinquer joined the UGIF Council in June 1943 and remained at his post until the summer of 1944. Because he was elderly (seventy-five in 1943) and a resident of Montpellier, relatively distant from the center of UGIF activity, Hémardinquer had little influence on the Council's orientation and activity.

7. Lambert's intellectual and cultural preoccupation with these two pillars of European culture is clearly expressed in his *Beethoven rhénan* (Paris, 1928).

understanding of human malice and of the futility of things. I am going to read other books about this prince of diplomats, because there is a lot to be learned, not from his betrayals but from his willpower and his awareness of what is real. His patriotism and his distinguished character rose above what were, at times, some rather base infatuations. I do not measure up to his greatness, but I feel close to him when, despite the anxieties that threaten to lay me low, despite my overwhelming responsibilities, I insist on my time alone and on my bath routine each morning when I wake up.

I also read C. F. Ramuz, *Joie dans le ciel* [*Joy in Heaven*], an attempt at a Christian epic, too weepy for my taste in these times when the focus should be on manly action.

After raising the alarm the other day [June 19], the German authorities have not followed up on their threat. Breathing easier, I took a quick trip to Toulouse to make contact with the German authorities, who received me politely. I left with Simone on Friday the 25th and returned by the Sunday train on the 27th, at 4 P.M.

On my return I heard that eighteen Jews had been arrested at Aix, including leading legal and scientific experts. Interceded for them yesterday at the Prefecture and with Bauer.[8] What joy this morning—I obtained eight releases, with the UGIF guaranteeing their care, including the physicist Henri Abraham, professor at the Sorbonne, greatly to my credit.

July 2, 1943

SS Hauptscharführer Bauer is going on leave for some two weeks, and I managed to get three more people released this morning. . . . It's fine weather, even though the wind is changing.

8. Although the German authorities were extending their hold over all areas of southern France and found greater cooperation among Vichy officials, Lambert persisted in presenting his case before various German regional authorities. He continued to believe he could make a dent in their designs by presenting a proud and determined protest, possibly thinking that his good German education would be of some value.

I am also hoping to halt the collective arrests of Jews in Marseilles, on condition that those allowed to remain on the coast be limited to people indispensable to the economic and social life of the region. . . . The German authorities find this an excellent idea. We shall discuss it again when Bauer comes back. I'd be proud to achieve such a result.

But I still have to struggle with jealous and incompetent people. The UGIF in Paris is attacking me and jamming things up for me because, having lived under the German heel for more than three years, they can't stand to see us clinging to the fictions of the "Free Zone"[9] and "French government." After the war I'm going to found a "Jewish Anti-Semitism Society," though, through my actions, I have come to appreciate some friendships: Gaston Kahn, Carcassonne, Rudnansky. I shall speak of them again when I have time to write portraits of them—unless that has to wait for my great postwar book, which I am beginning to carry in my head, "The Drama of the Jews."

But I must watch myself, for in times of discouragement I can see only two parallel solutions to the Jewish problem: Zionism, or baptism in the diaspora . . . Barrès, help!

July 9, 1943

The days go by, and the events we long for haven't yet transpired. . . . Still, everyone thinks the war will be over by winter. I wish for that with all my might, because I doubt I shall be able to escape being enslaved for more than another six months. It's tormenting! But even so, my instinct tells me to be confident. I remember my composure as a soldier in 1916, during that terrible April offensive that was my baptism by fire.

9. This was a source of constant friction between the two UGIF Councils. People in the south continued to enjoy a certain amount of freedom and had the feeling that those in the north, having lived with the Nazi presence for three years, could not truly understand their dissimilar experiences.

Empaytaz wrote to me: "I expect you have a great deal to do and that your present position is particularly heavy for you, but how satisfying it must be morally, even at the cost of enormously hard work, to think one is doing something useful and serving one's entire community." It's by the light of his friendship that he can see this.

I read Vol. III of Emile Bourgeois, which covers the period from 1830 to 1878. Excellent textbook, with very good pages on Bismarck. I also read, in translation from the English, Robert Sencourt's *Life of the Empress Eugénie*. That era is both very close to us and very far away.

July 12, 1943

On Saturday, the day before yesterday, around ten o'clock, we heard that the British and Americans had landed in Sicily. If this operation succeeds, and if there are other actions elsewhere, our hopes may be realized. . . . One day we think we'll be back in Paris for Christmas (some even say for All Saints' Day [November 1]); another day we are dreading being deported to Poland in the spring of '44.[1] . . . It takes a lot of energy to keep oneself composed and clear-minded. I am going back to regular correspondence with Frédéric[2]—it cheers me up, and every morning, in the tepid intimacy of my office, I promise myself to open this notebook.

On Saturday I visited la Clue, our home for the aged, and yesterday, Sunday, our children's home, la Verdière. It was so satisfying for me personally to see a Sorbonne professor and these chubby-cheeked cherubs who know, and say, that they owe their freedom to me.

1. This brief remark captures Lambert's inner flux and his conflicting evaluation of the future. He understandably hoped that the Allied offensive would bring victory and freedom, but he knew deportations to Poland were still possible. Did RRL know that Poland meant Auschwitz? Did he know what Auschwitz meant? It appears that in 1943 Auschwitz was becoming more of a reality for him, and it would seem he knew that Jews had been massacred, but this does not imply that he was fully aware of what Auschwitz signified.

2. Frédéric Empaytaz, Lambert's close friend. See Introduction.

August 17, 1943[3]

This has been a month of action, of expectation, and of fear as well. I am a bundle of nerves and by evening no longer have the energy to take up my pen. As a soldier I was alone and needed the joys of my inner thoughts to fill my solitude. But in this struggle today, in the midst of a world in disarray or in agony, I look at my wife and my admirable children and must weigh my responsibilities in the face of an uncertain future. . . . So I find myself throwing accusations at my country. Have I deserved to be treated as a pariah? Haven't I been a loyal son, proud to breathe the air of France? I have always contributed my building block to the edifice we share, in both happy and perilous times. . . . And yet today I am one of those who can be chain-ganged and deported, at your mercy. When peace and quiet come again, if I get through this torment, I shall revise all my ideas of the morals of society.

I have read or reread quite a few books during the past month: Edouard Rod, *Stendhal*, which took me back to my undergraduate studies, but today in my maturity I can see gaps in this forty-year-old study; Michel Corday, *Anatole France, d'après ses confidences* [*according to his confidential confessions*] fine and relaxing; Georges Bernanos, *Un crime* [*A Crime*], not bad; André Maurois, *Fragments d'histoire en 1992* [*Fragments of History in 1992*], amusing but nothing more; De Monzie, *La saison des juges* [*Judges' Season*], a book that surprised me with its vigor and crudeness. A formal condemnation of the new order. I wonder how the censors allowed it to be published; Charles Maurras, *La contre-révolution spontanée* [*Spontaneous Counter-Revolution*], good writing but poor thinking; by the same author, *Casier judiciaire d'Aristide Briand* [*Aristide Briand's Police Record*], a pamphlet admirably put together. How convincing hate can be when it is handled artistically and, what is more serious, so that it appears justified.

3. Written after RRL's trip to Vichy on August 14, where he protested against the recent measures being taken at Drancy and against the arrest of André Baur. See the Introduction.

I have also done a lot of traveling around throughout the past weeks. Here is my date book: On July 17 the two older boys, Simone, and I went to Cannes just to get away for two days, returning to Marseilles on Tuesday the 20th.

Sunday, July 25: Left for Grenoble with Simone and the children. Rigorous police check on the train at Avignon. They asked me if my wife was entitled to travel. I answered them in German. . . . This is how one gets arrested and deported. . . . On July 26 I played tourist and went on a tour of Grenoble. I was enchanted with the house where Stendhal was born, with its long corridor. What has become of my dreams of yesteryear? The 27th there was a meeting of our Council, hosted by our general president. I was very pleased with our team. At the hotel I was pestered like a government minister. On the 28th I went, with Simone and the children, to see a children's home near Voiron, where the director is an Orthodox rabbi who looks like Rasputin. In such a milieu I feel quite Christian and Latin.[4] On the 29th we returned to Marseilles in tropical weather worthy of Senegal.

On August 13th I went to Lyon.[5] I was received at the Central Consistory in the afternoon, for in hard times one makes peace. In the evening I left for Vichy, where I spent the night at the Admiralty House. On the 14th negotiations at the Council president's office and at the Commissariat. Left that night for Marseilles on the sleeper train.

4. RRL is referring to Rabbi Schneur Zalman Chnéerson, who headed an ultra-Orthodox charitable organization (Kehillath Haharedim—[Association des Israélites Practiquantes] Association of Orthodox Jews of France) affiliated with the UGIF's Third Department (Health), which assisted East European Jews in the interwar period.

5. RRL records these events almost like an automaton, without offering the slightest glimpse into the atmosphere or the importance of the meetings. He had gone to Lyon to discuss the deteriorating situation of French Jewry with the Consistory leaders, and to persuade them to join him the following day in a protest in Vichy. As it turned out, Lambert went there by himself. The same day he sent a note to Léon Meiss informing him of the dire situation (noted above). A German source mentions this intervention on August 15, 1943, see CDJC: XXVII-36, published in Klarsfeld, *Die Endlösung*, p. 212; the Consistory archive is apparently silent on this development; see Schwarzfuchs, *Aux prises avec Vichy*, p. 301.

On Monday, July 26, Jacques came in the morning to our hotel room in Grenoble to tell me that Mussolini had resigned. That is a historic event. A dictator simply takes his leave, like an ordinary government minister in the Third Republic. . . . Huge hopes have been aroused. . . . But Italy has not yet surrendered. . . . However, I believe that these lesions will grow deeper. . . . Messina was captured yesterday. The Russian offensive has become gigantic. . . . I really think we shall be in Paris by Christmas. This hope will give us the strength to hold on, to keep surviving.

August 18, 1943

I was admitted to see Guérard[6] in Vichy, and the impression I had of things there was discouraging. Such heaviness in the air. The government is powerless in the face of German demands, which have become harsher since the events in Italy. He [Guérard] told me that Laval has become nothing more than a shock absorber. He is even wondering whether he should stay. As for the Jewish question, he cannot do anything to make the measures at all humane. We are left to our own devices and have no hope other than through action at the local level based on the fiction of the Free Zone. The policy I have been following is the only rational one. On my desk is a piece of paper that proves it: on August 16 I obtained the release of fifty-one adults and thirty-eight children in Marseilles. I can be proud of that. If only Laval had been acting, across the board, with such a well-calculated method! But he doesn't know German.

Baur[7] has been arrested in Paris and sent to Drancy, because his cousin escaped from the camp. I had to try to intercede on his

6. This refers to his visit on August 14.

7. Baur was arrested on July 21, 1943, after protesting the measures enforced by SS Hauptsturmführer Brunner at Drancy and after trying to intercede with Laval. Baur's attempt to intervene with the German and Commissariat officials was the cause of his arrest, not the fabricated assertion that he was taken hostage because of his cousin's escape from Drancy. RRL intervened on his behalf on August 14.

behalf—but with no hope of success. The government, it seems to me, is nothing more than a fiction. Its executives shrink from taking responsibility. The regional prefects are the rulers.

I had my forty-ninth birthday a week ago, which astonishes me. . . . Soon I shall have to think of beginning to make plans for my retirement. . . . This had to be the moment at which I found out, through Chaplain, that my entire library [in Paris] has been cleared out, my precious books, my precious papers, my precious family mementos, my wartime letters. . . . I am not spared from torment. Have I deserved this, when it affects me to hear that Bonn has suffered in an air raid? Shall I have the strength to preserve my humanity when the time comes to settle scores?

August 20, 1943[8]

I was summoned yesterday to see Tuaillon, the deputy regional prefect who is substituting as regional prefect while Lemoine is away. He himself had had a summons from Laval on Monday, and was given instructions to keep me informed about the situation of the Jews in view of the problem of [German] redeployments. . . . Well, well! so they know me, in Vichy! We had been hearing that Laval's position is no longer very secure, because he had refused to provide the Germans with 500,000 men to work in Germany, and a million to work for them in France. . . . The negotiations have been concluded, and by September 5 Laval must furnish another 50,000 workers for forced labor. . . .

I have just been told officially that: 1. French Jews included in this mobilization of workers will under no circumstances be sent to Germany; 2. foreigners in supervised work units in the Free Zone will not be transferred to Germany either. Very impor-

8. In this final entry, written the day before his arrest, Lambert is both reserved and reflective. He knows that his hour has come, as he intimates in the three paragraphs beginning "Word is going around that . . .". It is as if he were writing his own epitaph, priding himself on his vision and his concept of moral support, distinct from that of the Consistory. Nonetheless he also relates to the current situation as if he is still the one who must deal with it.

tant points that I am pleased to note. In exchange—and I think, on hearing this, that my UGIF is imagined to be more powerful and more official than it really is—I am requested to take measures to keep the Jews who are called up from going off to swell the ranks of those trying to dodge the mobilization (there are currently 150,000 of these). I promised to speak with my friends about this and to look into the issue. I also used the occasion to ask that no cuts be made in my staff, so that my organization would not be disrupted. When Lemoine gets back he will no doubt call me in. I shall be expecting this.

Word is going around that there will be some major events in two or three days. . . .

During my war with the Consistory leaders, I thought about writing a pamphlet entitled *Jewish Princes*. I gave up this plan because I won. But I should copy these notes I have come across from that period: "They preferred their comfort to uncertainty and the heroism of struggle. . . . It was easier to protest and to abstain than to stand fast through action. . . . It is the purpose assigned to an action that justifies one's attitude. . . . We have an awareness of Judaism itself, while they preferred and defended only the garment that covers it. We chose the heroism of uncertainty and of action, the reality of concrete effort."

Also found a note from 1941 on the role I expected the UGIF to play: to spread through the ranks of Judaism and throughout the country, by our influence, the spirit of solidarity and mutual assistance, thus contributing to the creation within our communities of the moral elite that is needed in order to make progress. Material aid is a means of last resort, intended for use in facing unexpected occurrences, or in situations that are beyond the resources of families or individuals. Moral support is more precious and often more effective.

Letters to Maurice Brener, written from Drancy

October 10, 1943–November 5, 1943

October 10, 1943

My dear Ména,[1]

I should very much like you to send us some news of Renée,[2] Denise, and Georges, and also of yourself, even though we've heard about you in person from Drori, Lajeunesse, Feist, and so many others. We are very worried about you. As for us, despite the vexations of hospitalization and the atmosphere in the clinic, we are glowing with optimism.[3]

I shall have learned a lot from our stay here—beginning with a harsh judgment of the patients and the doctors,[4] the patients more than the doctors. Jules, Bernard, and his family have been

1. Maurice Brener, as identified by Brener himself in 1977.

2. The names of Lambert's family members.

3. The "clinic" refers to the Drancy internment camp. The description of their state of mind is, of course, obviously ironic.

4. The patients = the Jews; the doctors = the camp authorities.

evacuated farther on;[5] parting with them was infinitely sad. But we hope that our living conditions and the way things are organized will soon be changed, as the season requires.[6] We hope to be recovered and back home in a month or two.

If you're writing to Chaplain,[7] please tell him that I shall never forget the tangible proofs of his friendship that he has given me by his actions. I cannot say the same for Mr. Council,[8] all told, since after Raoul's[9] departure I was expecting mass resignations or some other collective action, which would have had an effect. Tell Gaston[1] there is no longer any reason to continue Marcel's[2] treatment. And don't trust Dr. Sixteen[3] any more than Dr. Paradise.[4]

You may burn the little slips of paper in the small right-hand drawer of my desk; they are receipts for money orders sent to relatives. Please also make a note for me, because I'm afraid I'll forget, that my friend Twenty-seven[5] owed me 179 francs when I left—and also, on my behalf, that the St. Pierre Clinic[6] has kept 450 francs of mine, and that I gave 100 fr. to Jules and 600 fr. to

5. This means to Auschwitz.

6. RRL's erstwhile optimism that the defeat of Germany was imminent.

7. RRL's war buddy, who appears at different junctures in the diary and who interceded on his behalf.

8. The administrative Council of UGIF-south.

9. Lambert himself. Clearly he was expecting the Council either to resign as a whole or to make a collective intervention on his behalf.

1. Gaston Kahn, who was serving as RRL's temporary replacement.

2. RRL's message was to stop the support for UGIF-north (Marcel is Marcel Stora, who had replaced Baur) which UGIF-south had been providing for about six months. It would seem that the reason for this is the failure of the north to intercede on Lambert's behalf. See below RRL's letter of October 26, 1943. Throughout his letters, RRL was acting as though he could continue to direct UGIF's operations from Drancy.

3. RRL is warning Brener against the activities of the French authorities. "Dr. Sixteen" could be either Darquier de Pellepoix or Couturier, the treasury agent assigned to UGIF affairs. Darquier had succeeded Xavier Vallat, who is designated as XV in certain secret documents. Thus it may be concluded that "Sixteen" was Darquier. In our meeting in 1977, Brener suggested that "Sixteen" referred to Couturier. Whichever it was, the placing of Dr. Sixteen in reference to and opposite "Dr. Paradise" (the Germans: see below) makes it clear that "Sixteen" referred to "the French."

4. The German authorities in Marseilles had their office on Paradise Street.

5. Not identified.

6. The prison in Marseilles.

Bernard before their sad departure for the Kamenès-Pau Clinic.[7] You may inform Alix and Josette that they have been transported.

Julie's daughter[8] is marvelous; she has an exhausting job caring for the four children, but the whole clinic is attentive to our needs. Let Julie and Gustave[9] remain calm and confident, as we are, and equally certain that we shall all be back together again by December 15.

Affectionately,
Trentinian[1]

October 17, 1943

My dear Ména,

We are waiting most impatiently for news from you. Not to know how Julie and Gustave are, nor Renée, Denise,[2] and Jacques,[3] is very hard for us.

I expect that at your end you have reassured them all about what has happened to us. I expect you have also received my letter asking for packages to be sent through official channels, in any case not by way of Belleville.[4] I haven't received them yet but expect to have them this week. In case my previous letter to Gaston has gone astray, I'll repeat the instructions: the official address with my title, and two packages a week. I'll acknowledge them and give you my news as soon as possible.

Nothing new here—what life is like here, you know. Simone is adjusting because she has to, but she gets very tired with the children. They are doing well and are coping with the climate, both physically and morally. The eldest is an orderly for the director, which keeps him busy all the time.

7. Auschwitz.
8. Simone, RRL's wife.
9. Simone's parents.
1. RRL, then aged forty-nine. I do not know why he chose this pseudonym.
2. Denise Eskat, RRL's cousin.
3. Jacques Lambert, RRL's brother.
4. One of UGIF-north's offices was on Belleville Street in Paris. It was in charge of sending packages to people interned at Drancy.

We are expecting a massive shipment for the clinic—which we expect will include the six packages of clothing for the president's family.[5]

And the days go by, all alike and monotonous. It takes an iron will to guard against the mindlessness here. It's almost two months since we left the south coast! I am beginning to think we shall be spending the winter under these same conditions. We shan't complain as long as we are not referred to Dr. Kamenetz.[6] In the end that's the only thing that matters.

In the last few days we have seen quite a number of people arrive from Dyka's[7] and Jules' town. They are unanimous in condemning Gouques[8] for what he agreed to do. I am not expressing an opinion, but do tell Gaston to be very careful in that quarter. Be prudent and keep your distance. Watch out for Dr. Sixteen, and in no case put your trust in Schneider;[9] I'll be responsible for dealing with that situation later. What of Jacques and Marcel?[1]

Robert d'Allei's father, Lucien, has gone to join Claude Crémieux, in an excellent state of mind.

I have asked Chaplain to do several things for me, and he might ask you for some funds.

Please send another one-kilo package, without waiting and without a double wrapping, with "Trentinian" on the inside address, in care of Delion,[2] containing jars of jam, noodles, and if possible a bit of sausage or smoked meat.

Affectionate greetings to both you and Gaston,

Trentinian

5. RRL's family.

6. Kamenetz was another subterfuge. It implied Auschwitz.

7. Dyka was the pseudonym of Jules Jefroykin, the representative in France of the American Jewish Joint Distribution Committee, who played an important role in resistance activity. "Jules" might mean here Julien Samuel of UGIF-OSE, who was active in the efforts of Jewish resistance activists in hiding children (see above). It would appear then that "town" indicated resisters who were arrested in October (probably in Nice) and sent to Drancy. This adds evidence to our hypothesis that RRL was aware of Brener's contacts with elements in the resistance.

8. Not identified.

9. This may be a reference to Germans.

1. Jacques Lambert and Marcel Dreyfus, RRL's cousin.

2. Probably a contact within the camp.

Tuesday, October 26, 1943

Madame Lombardo
(for Mr. Maurice)
22 Avenue de Monfray
Marseilles

My dear Ména,

We were happy to have a visit from Alice,[3] Claude,[4] and all the children. But we didn't understand their having been pressed to make this tiring journey. It was stupid to make them come here, since they could have continued their tour by way of Lorraine.[5] They have not left again, so we have been spared that heartbreak. But the priest has gone without them, the one from the town where Micky[6] was, and many other friends with him.

Alice told us about the consultation before their trip.[7] If what she told me is true, I am of the same mind as you and hope that if a crisis of this sort arises again, the action taken will be bolder and in accordance with Dr. Sabord's prescriptions.[8] These concessions to illness will not postpone the admission to the clinic of

3. Alice Salomon. On October 20, 1943, a children's home (La Verdière) run by the UGIF at La Rose (Bouches-du-Rhône) had been seized by the Gestapo and all the children and staff sent to Drancy. The director of the home, Alice Salomon, "voluntarily joined the transport of the deported children rather than let them face death all alone." Her arrival at Drancy with the children obviously caused RRL much grief. He begins this letter with bitter irony. See Szajkowski, *Gazetteer*, p. 168. Alice Salomon was deported to Auschwitz on November 20, 1943, and perished there.

4. Claude Gutmann (?), a twenty-nine-year-old UGIF official, was active in social work among Jewish youth in the southern zone. He was on the Gestapo's blacklist because of his illegal activities, consisting of providing Jews with false identity cards and other false documents. Gutmann was deported with Alice Salomon to Auschwitz and did not return. Mühler describes his arrest on November 17, 1943, see Rutkowski, *La Lutte des Juifs*, p. 208.

5. As we shall see from the following paragraph, RRL thought the deportation could have been avoided if the children had been sent to Lorraine, and from there over the border to Switzerland. The children were not immediately deported to Auschwitz.

6. Sacha Krinsky was then in Le Puy-de-Dôme. Micky was his son's nickname.

7. See discussion of the roundup of the children's home in Introduction.

8. That is, to disobey and sink the ship! RRL openly supports Brener's position, namely, that the children should have been dispersed.

those who are fainthearted, the most fainthearted . . . I know now what Alice has done for us—and I wonder what the others were thinking, besides you. Thank you again, I am counting on you and only you.

I am writing to the Sylvabelle store[9] about the very important matter that was dropped. . . . Because of this negligence,[1] hundreds of patients will die from the cold this winter. Please pass the word on.

I heard of your visit to Paris, and I hope you mentioned me and my family to Dr. Petrive.[2] It is unacceptable that my family and I should not have a better sort of hospital room, such as others have who are natives of Teheran.[3] It's so hard on Léa.[4] Since you may have seen this with your own eyes, I'm asking you to do something about it, even if you have to make another trip to do so. Winter is coming, and I'm afraid for the children; this public ward is so drafty.

With regard to food supplies, the doctors[5] have not kept their word and have been "spiriting away" the contents of all packages addressed through official channels, except for the clothing. So please don't send any more than *two* food packages a month in care of Delion, marked also for "Trentinian," of about two kilos each, containing foods rich in sugar and/or fats or that keep well. There is an outside possibility of arranging sometimes for things to be cooked. Please take Alice's place in fulfilling this vital task.

With regard to clothing, I am waiting for the big shipment from Marseilles. The administration should be ashamed that a

9. The head office of the UGIF in Marseilles was on Sylvabelle Street.

1. This letter has unfortunately not been found. It means that RRL had written to the UGIF to make a more energetic effort in such cases.

2. It is known from other sources that Brener was in Paris in October. Dr. Petrive was a nickname for the German authorities.

3. RRL is complaining to Brener that leaders of UGIF-north (which had its head office on Teheran Street) interned at Drancy had the right to better treatment than did he and his family.

4. Marie-France Léa Cécilia was RRL's youngest child, born in January 1942.

5. The camp authorities.

formal order from its President who is hospitalized has not been carried out a month later . . . if it had been done immediately, his health could have been restored! Well, too bad! If it has not been done, please act on it right away—for if it is delayed again, the consequences for Marseilles and for Raoul would be disastrous.[6]

Please give this message to Julgus[7] for me, with my affectionate good wishes: we were so happy to read Fernande's letter of the 9th, with a word from Dany senior[8] and one from you. Tell Fernande that I have taken note of the addresses, which will be useful—and Fernande's letter of the 16th (tell her the dark-haired Julie has left, with her husband)—and Alice's letters of the 11th and the 18th, for which we thanked her in person,[9]—[. . .].

When I get back I shall have a liter of paregoric each for Jacques and Marcel, as gifts to thank them for the letters they have written me during the two months I've been away. . . . Without Alice and you, Alfred's family[1] might have died of hunger and of the cold on certain days. . . .

Please tell Claude's father, the little doctor at La Rose, 120 Boulevard de la Madeleine, as soon as possible, that his son has not left here.

Most affectionately,
Trentinian

November 5, 1943

Mr. Maurice Brener
101 Sylvabelle Street[2]
Marseilles

6. It is hard to tell whether this passage has a hidden meaning, or whether it is really about a request for clothing.

7. Not identified.

8. According to Brener, this was the pseudonym of Gaston Kahn.

9. Several words are illegible here.

1. Lambert's own family. His full name was Raymond-Raoul Alfred Lambert.

2. This letter was sent to the UGIF office in Marseilles.

My dear Ména,

I was sorry not to have a chance to see you during your last trip to Paris. We have heard news of you from Alice and Claude, and I think you will have had news of us from Mrs. Lombardo,[3] since I wrote to her on Monday.

We were very glad to have your letters of the 8th and the 18th, and those from Fernande, Alice, and *Dany senior*. Please take good care of Simone's parents, and especially don't let the same thing happen to them that happened to the young Laroses.[4] I still don't understand why Alice and Claude were allowed to come to Paris. If I had been there, I'd have made sure that your point of view was the one acted upon.

I am waiting for news of your conversations with Dr. Petrive and your meetings in Paris. Have you been studying new therapeutic methods[5] and given some thought to the patients who are kept in the clinic by incurable illness? There is a dire need for Alfred's children to have a room as good as that of André's children.[6] Since you have seen that with your own eyes, you can intercede—I'm really afraid, for the children, of the terrible drafts in here in the winter. Your Teheran friends, even Fernand,[7] don't show that they understand team spirit, and I find their conduct toward me despicably selfish. Alfred is being well rewarded for his trip to Vichy,[8] and Dany senior is right to think that the Teheran group,[9]

3. See the address of the preceding letter.

4. RRL refers again to the issue discussed in the preceding letter, also using it as a camouflage. He is imploring Brener to prevent his parents-in-law from being interned, and is again supporting Brener's position on the subject of the La Rose children's home.

5. He is asking whether Brener has found any way of bringing an end to his internment. Brener had been at Drancy for two days in late October.

6. André Baur's family.

7. Fernand Musnik, a UGIF-north Council member who was also active in resistance activity. Musnik was arrested in late October, sent to Drancy, and deported from there to Auschwitz on December 17, 1943. He was gassed in early 1944. When RRL wrote this letter, Musnik was already in the Drancy camp.

8. RRL refers to the fact that he had been arrested after having protested against Baur's arrest, and that now UGIF-north's Council was not doing enough to improve his condition.

9. The UGIF-north Council.

despite all this suffering, is not ready for a truce with the southern team.

So I'm asking you to tell Dany senior that *I am ashamed* in front of the clinic authorities and the people here in Paris, ashamed that so little effort has been made from Marseilles to carry out my order, and that there is such a delay in sending the clothing that was requested *more than a month ago*. If the order had been carried out immediately, Alfred would have been able to go outdoors a little; this slowness really hurts. . . . I can't say any more about it to you all, but why don't you understand? These orders should have been important to you all, since the doctors made an exception in allowing us to correspond as directly as this. . . . Because of this, patients have been going out[1] and leaving here without a change of clothes.

At the same time I am waiting for my *six* suitcases that were authorized, because the children are cold. If Dr. Paradise[2] is not letting through what has been authorized in Paris, please send something of the sort for the family; we *urgently need* coats. Put them in well-labeled suitcases. Alice told me that one such was already packed. And please bear in mind that Fernande's daughter does not have a warm dress. . . . If necessary, buy or ask for secondhand things. Let the family, Jacques and Marcel, do their duty for a bit. If possible, please include a pair of low-cut boots for François-Alix, even used ones, size 25 (twenty-five [= children's 7-1/2 U.S.]), the poor child is almost going barefoot.

But all these troubles will pass, and quickly too, I hope. These patients will be cured by Christmas at the latest. Then we can pay our debts of gratitude and the others as well. I assure you that this treatment has made Alfred more mature. As far as he is concerned, he has been focusing on a precise solution to the medical problem[3] that has been at the forefront of our concern. . . . And I

1. RRL's request was probably made also on behalf of other persons who had recently been imprisoned.

2. The German authorities in Marseilles, as distinct from those in Paris.

3. RRL's allusion is unclear to me.

am proud of you, of your calmness and your grit. I also want to thank the father of Dany and Raymond in Lyon[4] for their loyalty, which doesn't surprise me. Have Davray and Joseph[5] been told about the children's illness?

Don't write in care of Delion any more, things are rather difficult with him. From now on, until I tell you differently, could you tell us your news, and could you give your answer briefly, to Chaplain—he can pass it on.

Affectionately,
Trentinian

4. Raymond Geissmann, who was active in Lyon at the time.

5. Jean Davray (?), son of Albert Lévy, author of *Les complaintes* (Paris, 1945). Joseph may refer to Joseph Fischer, the representative of Keren Kayemet (Jewish National Fund) in Nice. This comment again relates to the arrest of the children. RRL was obviously deeply troubled by this turn of events and was trying to prevent further arrests of this kind.

Index

A NOTE ON THE EDITOR

Richard I. Cohen holds the Paulette and Claude Kelman Chair in French Jewry Studies at the Hebrew University of Jerusalem. He is the author of *The Burden of Conscience: French Jewish Leadership During the Holocaust* and *Jewish Icons: Art and Society in Modern Europe*, and was the editor of the French-language edition of Raymond-Raoul Lambert's *Diary*. He lives in Jerusalem.